Walking with Jason

Walking with Jason

John F. Hunt

authorHOUSE®

AuthorHouse™
1663 Liberty Drive
Bloomington, IN 47403
www.authorhouse.com
Phone: 1-800-839-8640

Published by AuthorHouse 4/22/2013

ISBN: 978-1-4817-3230-7 (sc)
ISBN: 978-1-4817-3228-4 (hc)
ISBN: 978-1-4817-3290-1 (e)

Library of Congress Control Number: 2013905140

Front cover photograph: Jason at the Lakeview Area of Rumbling Bald with
Lake Lure in the background, southeast of Asheville, North Carolina.

This book is printed on acid-free paper.

The wilderness will lead you
To your heart where I will speak
-Hosea (Come Back To Me)
Lyrics by Gregory Norbert

JASON WILLIAM HUNT

FOUNDATION®

I have visited your memorial website a few times and am so glad such good work can be initiated in Jason's name.

—Steve Sutorius, coworker, Wilderness Treatment
Center, Montana, e-mail, March 29, 2004

For details: www.jwhf.org

The foundation's mission is to perpetuate Jason's spirit and love as exemplified by his work with youth with needs in outdoor settings. The foundation supports outdoor experiential education programs in the form of scholarships for at-risk youth and grants for qualified outdoor instructor/leader training programs.

The foundation begins where Jason left off. Although Jason is gone, teens have a way to realize their potential as if Jason himself were by their side, guiding them each step of the way. Through the foundation that bears his name, Jason is more than a man who helped improve lives. He has become hundreds of men and women coming together to benefit countless children through outdoor experiential education.

All proceeds from the sale of this book will go to the foundation's Scholarship and Grant Fund. The foundation awards scholarships to qualified programs for children from thirteen to seventeen years old to attend therapeutic wilderness programs. Secondarily, the foundation awards grants for the training of outdoor educators.

The Jason William Hunt Foundation is an Ohio not-for-profit corporation. We operate under the United States Internal Revenue Code's 501(c)(3) designation as a charitable organization. All donations are tax deductible, and all donations are greatly appreciated.

Let Jason's work continue through you.

(photographer and location unknown)

In loving memory of

Jason William Hunt

Son, Brother, Friend, Wilderness Educator
1977–2001

and

to all who guide and guard our
children and youth needing support in the wilderness

Table of Contents

PART THREE
Epilogue

Foreword

My grandmother told me at the funeral of her daughter that the worst thing that could happen to a parent is to outlive her child. For her, in that shattering moment, such a fate was an unbearable violation of the natural order of living. Parents normally get the opportunity to teach their children how to be in the world—and how to leave it.

When an untimely death takes a young person, its aftermath is often a series of extended and entangled tragedies. Such a loss can leave in its wake significantly diminished living among those loved ones remaining. These realities bear witness that a grief of that magnitude is never "gotten over"; it is survived.

John Hunt is such a survivor. Having lost his twenty-four-year-old son to a rock climbing accident in 2001, John knows the grief of such a parental fate. But his response to that fate, captured by his book *Walking with Jason*, is a lesson in how to achieve human healing in the face of such anguish. *Walking with Jason* leaves behind a trail marked by John and his family that teaches us how to have our hearts broken but listen to them anyway.

As this book unfolds and its premises become synthesized, many voices emerge. You will learn that John has a gift for relationship that is anchored deep in careful listening and watching. For instance, he does some of the best writing when conveying his understanding (gleaned during his travels and research for this book) about the premises of wilderness-challenge approaches to learning. Those parts of the book are based on John's efforts to understand more deeply his son's attraction to the field. One of his responses to the tragedy of his son's death was to become a major witness, able interpreter, and supporter for the field his son struggled with but came to love.

There is another voice that must be listened to with even more care. It speaks less formally, with more quirkiness, and with more intimacy. You will hear this voice speak for the Hunt clan, for other kindred souls, for fathering, for the desire to make an honest effort to share in making helpful markings for others. This other voice is that of an aging, retired salesman who wants both to hit the Appalachian Trail in honor of his son's walk in life and to be present for the generation coming. It's a voice worth taking your time to listen to, for within it John takes the grief of his son's departure and alchemically turns it into the gold of this book.

Howard Thurman wrote that we should not ask what the world needs but what makes us alive and then seek that—because what the world needs is people who are alive. John has demonstrated just that. The spiritual trails marked in *Walking with Jason* follow Thurman's advice and extend it with many examples, especially through the honoring of the wilderness educators John meets. The best example of the embodiment of Thurman's advice is John and the Hunt clan themselves. As you will learn in the pages that follow, they all have a special gift, like Jason did, for being alive—being alive despite the grief that living sometimes offers in return. The primary message of John's walk with Jason is one that any Christian could surely appreciate. The circumstances in life that make love the most difficult to find, such as being faced with a hated enemy or life event, are exactly those circumstances that offer the deepest lessons about what being loving is.

Anthony H. Howard
Kamp Kessa, July 28, 2012

Preface

I never thought I would write a book, but then again I never thought our family would lose Jason, my son. After Jason's death, his friends wrote of Jason the person, the friend, and the inspiration. We received such an outpouring of support from his contemporaries, with the often repeated assurance that each was writing not just for himself or herself but "for all that knew him," that we began to feel that something larger, something more mystical and spiritual was happening. We kept all those letters, cards, handwritten notes, poems, and prayers, thinking that someday we could make sense of it all.

Life goes on, and my wife, Rosemarie; our daughters, Danielle and Amy; and I started the Jason William Hunt Foundation. I naively thought we would raise some money each year and help the State of Connecticut's Department of Children and Families (DCF) Wilderness School, where Jason had worked, and the Warren Wilson College Outing Club, where he began to learn his outdoor instructing skills. Very quickly, we realized that the need was greater—much greater.

I was lamenting to Tom Dyer, retired director of the Wilderness School, that the need to help children grow and develop, the need to support them in their formative years, the need to guard them when life and their environment are crashing around them never goes away. It was then that he told me the parable of the river. It is the story about a man saving babies from a river. It seems that this man spotted a baby floating in a river he was near, so he jumped in to save it. But before he could get out, he spotted another and then spotted more babies to the point that he called for help with rescuing them. Soon, others were standing waist deep and shoulder to shoulder in the river saving babies. But with all that was happening, with all the urgency, with all the anxiety to do right, and with all the success, no one had time to go upriver and figure out how the babies were getting in there in the first place.

Each person has a story to tell. This book is a mosaic drawn from the interviews of many truly dedicated and caring people who were willing to share why they go into the wilderness to support children with needs. Some of these interviews are the visible threads, while others are threads that are not visible but that exist nonetheless, giving body and weight to the weaving. We have very little of Jason's writing to reference; the notebook we have skips not just days but years. What we do know and remember has been greatly augmented by those saved remembrances of his contemporaries. In writing this book, one of my intents was to find out more about Jason the wilderness educator as he so enjoyed doing what he did. One of my biggest concerns was doing justice to the two summer seasons (2000 and 2001) that he worked at the Wilderness School because they represent his greatest challenge and his greatest success.

While I did ask some of his friends who wrote remembrances to add a detail here and there, such as the name of a sailing lake or details about how he got into rock climbing, I did not ask anyone to look back and reconstruct Jason. I did not want the fiction of time to color what was so well defined by the fires of emotions expressed at his passing and what, in reading these ten years later, still tug at a broken heart.

Some whom I asked for help never acknowledged the request. I hope my asking did not reopen a wound, and I hope that this book and time will help in the healing. But, oh, those who did reply helped in completing the picture of a young man wanting to do good, wanting to do his best, and wanting to share his passion for the outdoors while working through his own doubts rooted in feelings of inadequacy. They talked of how he faced the challenges and how he was so successful. It is not that Jason has left us; he appears in a thought, a comment that reminds us of him, and, yes, even in the face of another.

I was participating at Mass as a Eucharistic Minister during Communion and the gentleman I had just served stepped away, revealing his son in a motorized wheelchair. The sudden and unexpected sight of this lad threw me back into the hospital room with Jason when I was facing the prospect of—if only he had lived—what he would have been. It overwhelmed me; what seemed to be an eternity was just a fraction of time. Racing through my body was this urge to cry, to turn, and to flee right then and there. I drew a breath and continued my part, although I was shaken in the process. Somehow, I survived.

Another reason for writing this book was a desire to show how the students and scholarship recipients of the programs that the foundation supports are affected for the better. On Graduation Day, Wilderness School students write, by hand, short and unedited "Funder Thank You" notes. I believe this is such a valuable lesson for youth to learn that it has become the only requirement the foundation has of a scholarship recipient: to write a short follow-up note regarding the experience—nothing long, nothing formal, but from the heart. The foundation, in its young and cash-starved existence, has been humbled by the emotions, experiences, maturity, confidence, and hope expressed by those writers. There have been some truly amazing, touching, and inspiring outpourings. We are honored to share some of them throughout the book.

A recent one gave me a chuckle. Sal P., one of the graduates, took the time to go one step further in his thank you note; he thought a little more deeply about what he wrote and made the connection. Sal realized that I was a funder, so he elected to write his funder letter without using the impersonal, generic "Dear Funder." Rather, he decided to make it personal:

> Dear John,
>   Thank you so much for funding my crew 20-day trip to the Wilderness School. I enjoyed almost every

minute of it. My favorite part of it was the climbing/ hiking the mountains and getting to the top of each mountain and enjoying all the views. I also enjoyed rock climbing and repelling that was so exciting and so much fun. Again thank you very much.

Sincerely,

Sal P

Danielle, Jason's older sister, was the first to expose the family to outdoor experiential education when she went to work at E-Ku-Sumee (an Eckerd Youth Alternatives Camp) in Candor, North Carolina. I believe she and Jason were drawn to it as a blending of their parents' interests. Rosemarie always has been a remarkable educator and, in particular, an elementary special education behavioral specialist. I, while a salesman, always enjoyed the outdoors, whether it was bike riding, sailing, or snow skiing. Our attitude toward life is, to quote an old saying, "There are no bad days, just bad clothing decisions."

And so, together, we tried to instill in our children a sense of togetherness and love and an appreciation of the natural world, with a touch of adventure. The more I learned about outdoor experiential education, the more I thought, *Man, where was this when I was looking for a job out of college?* In 1967 the outdoor choices seemed to be Boy Scout management or park ranger. While they both offered that cool campaign hat (think Smokey the Bear), neither was for me.

However, Rosemarie and I did identify with family and the innate wonder of children, and we hoped this was successfully passed to our own children. Almost every parent thinks his or her child is the best, the brightest, the most handsome, the funniest, and more, and rightly so, as a child should be the best offering one can make to society. It is the blending of two great loves. But it is what that child, what each person, does with his or her innate gifts that make the character real. It's what he becomes as an adult and what he contributes to the common good that defines him and thus gives his life meaning.

Trail Markings

The keepers of the Appalachian Trail, like those of many other trails, mark its path by blazing the trees and rocks with specific colored paints. On the trail, a single vertical and rectangular painted white blaze indicates the way to go. At times, a second blaze is added, stacked on but offset from the first, and this announces a change in direction. Additional colors, like blue, may indicate another path. It is a simple but efficient system for helping people stay on course, stay on track.

Often, a child who is at risk, a child with needs, does not have such directional support in his or her everyday life. Without such guidance, the child cannot follow or understand the proper path, life's trail markings.

This is my journey. You are invited to follow my trail markings.

Author Notes: The terms: Wilderness School, Connecticut Wilderness School, State of Connecticut Department of Children and Families Wilderness School, DCF Wilderness School, as well as the abbreviations: CWS & WS, all refer to the same facility and program which was founded in 1974 in Goshen, CT, and subsequently moved to East Hartland, CT, where it remains today. They are used interchangeably in this book.

In order to protect the individual student's identity the State of Connecticut Department of Children and Families requested each student be identified by first name and last initial. This was also applied to the respective parent if mentioned.

Acknowledgments

You can learn more about a person in an hour of play than in a year of conversation.

—Plato

This book could not have been written without the support and encouragement of Rosemarie, my wife and Jason's mother; and Danielle Hunt Palka and Amy Hunt Pierce, our daughters and Jason's sisters. Without their permission, I could not have looked into the wound that does not heal.

Folks who attempt to thru-hike the Appalachian Trail have support teams back home who ship packages and handle details. My main man was Jerry "The Old Postman" Latham, and true to his trail name, he delivered. He helped pack food boxes, got me to the trail, and dropped some of the early boxes off as he made his way back home. Winton Porter was right when he said I would meet folks whom I would want to include in the book at his store and hostel; all I had to do was spend some time there and clean a bathroom or two, which I did. I also helped Ms. Janet in the kitchen at the hostel, which is an education every hiker should experience. Staying on campus at Warren Wilson College in the president's suite as the guest of President Sandy Pfeiffer is the kind of experience I wish I could have flaunted over a couple of my high school teachers and college professors—"Hey, look at me *now*!"

Two very special ladies helped me start the writing process. DC Stanfa, the author of *The Art of Table Dancing*, asked the simple question, "Can you write?" After showing her a sample, it was her affirmation that I could, in fact, write that got the words flowing.

While at the Wilderness School, I kept fielding questions from Anna L. Boysen, a photographer and artist. It was her lesson in mind mapping, given in the woods on a hot and sunny July day that showed me how I could simplify the organization of the book, and my mind as well which of itself is no small feat, to say the least.

I can truly say that my time at Woodson Wilderness Challenge was too short. A special thanks goes to Tex and his staff for letting me "crowd and corner" them on such a busy and emotional day as Graduation Day.

A special thanks needs to be extended to the State of Connecticut's Department of Children and Families for allowing me access to the staff and to their students. My request to visit was approved by Susan Hamilton, MSW, Superintendent who subsequently retired and support continued with Joette Katz, the current Superintendent. I cannot say enough about the opportunity to stay with, work with, and enjoy the moments with Dave Czaja and his staff at DCF Wilderness School. It was truly my chance to walk with Jason.

To Father Thomas Kreidler, Coach Jim Gossett, Frank Wrobel, and my son-in-law Douglas Palka, thanks for filling in the details as needed.

A special nod to Jed Williamson, who in Dave Czaja's opinion, is "a cool dude." Jed provided a transcript of Willi Unsoeld's "Spiritual Values in Wilderness" presentation. Additionally to Philip Koro of Clermont County Public Library for his help in tracking down and acquiring resources from distant parts of this country.

I learned something in every interview. While their names are listed elsewhere I wanted to comment on how unselfishly, openly, and freely they discussed their lives, their experiences and their belief in the power of the wilderness to affect change.

To Kelly Cahill for getting the publishing process started I can only say *"Pumpkin muffins forever!"* To Amanda Carmichael and the rest of the AuthorHouse staff, some whom I met by name and others who I never met, your support is appreciated.

Finally but ultimately this book was written by this weak and humbled servant for the greater glory of my Lord and Savior, Jesus Christ.

Introduction

July 20, 2010
Excerpt, Director's Opening Remarks·
Graduation Day for Twenty-Day Expeditions Crews: "ATC" and
"Aviators"
State of Connecticut Department of Children and Families Wilderness
School
The Wilderness School
East Hartland, Connecticut

Last, I would like to recognize John Hunt, a private supporter who is here today.

John was born and has lived in Connecticut; he now lives outside of Cincinnati, Ohio. I'm going to tell you a little bit about John, and while I might embarrass him a little bit, I hope I do not…. John got involved with the Wilderness School through his son, Jason, who was an instructor in the 2000 and 2001 summer seasons. Jason had a very rough first year as an instructor, and I think it's fair to say that he went home with his tail between his legs. It was by all accounts a very, very difficult crew, and he was disappointed and unhappy with how he had handled that experience. In fact, the course had culminated with Jason, in effect, transferring from his twenty-day field instructor position to a base camp support position for the second half of his 2000 season with us. Further, he was in doubt as to whether he wanted to return—even whether he was competent enough to return—in 2001.

However, over the next six or eight months in conversations with his supervisor at that time, a very persuasive young lady named Jane, Jason and Jane came to the conclusion that it would be good for him to try again, and he came back with a vengeance. He came back, and what occurred in Jason was truly remarkable, equaling exactly what happens to the kids on the course, in taking a failure or setback and turning it into a positive.

Jason performed very, very well. He had two outstanding courses, and he went out of here sky high. He had gone to "the source"—his previous summer's sense of failure—and taken on the challenge, gone back to that climb again and pushed himself through. In short, he truly benefited from it. What's sad is that Jason's life ended tragically a short time after that in a climbing accident far out west in a distant place in the Canadian province of British Columbia.

It was devastating for us, and I can't imagine how devastating it was for John. Well, how did John respond to that? John started a foundation. John started fund-raising, and John started applying those funds to outdoor programs for troubled adolescents [across the country] and here at the Wilderness School. John has funded numerous kids to go to programs and the Wilderness School.

So what better tribute to his son, his son's legacy, than a foundation? Well, if anybody can figure out a way, it would be John. And a little over a year ago, John had this kind of furball idea that he was to walk the entire Appalachian Trail and make it a fund-raiser for his kids, and that, further, he was to write a book. Well, not all dreams happen right away, right? So John's dream of hiking the Appalachian Trail got a little derailed by something known as his new granddaughter.

So he wasn't able to complete that; but I'm pleased to say that the book is alive and well and flowing profusely. In a dry summer, I think I know where all the rain went; it went into John's book because that river is flowing.

In fact, John, who has been here a little over five and a half weeks, has also visited programs up and down the East Coast, and he's interviewing outdoor leaders in addition to our own. While he gave up his immediate quest to hike the entire Appalachian Trail, he's got his other project well underway, where he is trying to do two things. One,

I believe, is to advance the field of outdoor leadership, his son Jason's career path, through a book exploring wilderness instructors, which in itself is remarkable and is really an example to all of us. Two—this is key—he is doing this so he may, himself, walk in his son Jason's shoes.

What John has done is brought a curiosity to this campus, like the human Discovery Channel, since he's been here. He's interviewed every one of us several times. We have all learned to run when we see John because he's got the tape recorder out and the notepad ready to roll. But with him comes a curiosity, as he has worked and worked and worked to try to understand what it is about this place, this program, and most importantly, about his son in this place that was special, what connected the two. What is interesting John is that I think the answer's been in front of you the whole time. It's one of those things, it's right there, and you just have to learn to see it.

John has had the spirit that learning doesn't stop. If you watch our video, you've got this tall, six-foot-six Wilderness School instructor named Ryan talking about just that. Learning doesn't stop when you complete kindergarten, learning doesn't stop at the end of middle school or high school or college, after a career or in retirement. Learning doesn't stop today at the end of a twenty-day expedition.

So, in spite of all the monetary gifts to kids, this is John's greatest gift to all of us here at the Wilderness School. As his time here ends, John is leaving us with this very special example, and so John, we want to thank you for that very much.

You've been a wonderful example to our staff, to me, to our students, to our audience, and we're very grateful to have you.

Dave Czaja, Director
Alumnus 1975
Student Staff 1976
Summer Staff 1977–1980
Instructor 1980, 1983
Program Coordinator 1985–1987
Assistant Director 1987–2009
Director 2009–present

PART ONE

Starting Out

when the sun rises, you can hear the birds chirping
and at night, you can hear the animals lurking
in the morning kids laughing and kids playing
as some others are saying
the forest is a fabulous place to live
- excerpt from a service project poem by
Dan A, Wilderness School Aviators crew member

How Did I Get Here?

Plans Change

I would have to attribute the origination of my brother's interest in the out-of-doors to my father.... When Jason was old enough, he became a Boy Scout and dad reenlisted.

—Danielle Hunt Palka, Celebration of Life, eulogy, October 20, 2001

"Sal! Sal! It's Sal! Where were you at?"

With those words of surprise, discovery, excitement, and joy, a little four-year-old boy with a crop of wildly curly red hair ran through the crowd, joined Sal on stage, and stole the hearts of all who witnessed it. Little G (Giovanni) had not seen Sal, his older brother, for twenty days, not since his family had dropped Sal off at the Wilderness School to begin his expedition. United once again, they stood together, Little G held tightly in Sal's bear hug, with two big smiles in an image of brotherly love. DCF Wilderness School director Dave Czaja turned to the audience and said, "Crew Two just got a little bigger."

It was graduation day at the State of Connecticut Department of Children and Families Wilderness School in East Hartland, Connecticut, and thirteen young lads were completing an amazing step in their lives. Families, friends, social workers, referring agents, supporters, Wilderness School administrators, and field staff gathered to honor their accomplishment of completing a twenty-day wilderness expedition. Unknown to one another at the start of the experience, unfamiliar with the woods, unskilled in the individual and group skills that the wilderness requires, and, most critically, needing to develop their own life coping skills, these thirteen boys, ranging from twelve to seventeen years old, had literally experienced conflicts, accomplished personal goals, conquered challenges, and learned more about themselves in those twenty days than they thought possible.

Where their previous life experiences may have been lacking in positive values, where they may not have been dealt the best of hands in the past, where their lives may have teetered on that fine line between right and wrong, being safe or in danger, they now have a glimpse at a better way. They do not leave with a checklist of do's and don'ts; rather, they have the experience of having successfully met the challenge. They have experienced success, and in experiencing it have internalized it. They have been guided in this experience by dedicated young adults who have the skills to protect them in their quest and, yet, leave the teaching, the instruction, and the education to the wilderness itself.

Jason, our son, was such a wilderness educator. Following his death in 2001, Rosemarie, his mother; Danielle and Amy, his sisters; and I created a foundation to support such programs. The Jason William Hunt Foundation provides scholarship funds so that youth with needs can attend such programs and grow. The origins of this book lie in a desire to memorialize Jason, to hike the Appalachian Trail in a way that promotes therapeutic wilderness programs, and to create a cash stream for the foundation's scholarship fund.

People ask how the idea to hike the Appalachian Trail, which runs from Georgia to Maine over approximately 2180 miles, as a sixty-four-year-old, married, part-owner of a business ever originated. While my explanation seems perfectly reasonable to me, to most others it seems quite the opposite. I guess that just has to do with the maturity one develops through the years of shared life experiences in a Venus–Mars, Ying–Yang sort of way.

Ideas do not just happen. They develop over time, waiting for a trigger to give them life. And for my trigger, I have Rosemarie to thank. I have been a manufacturer's representative in the hand tool, hardware, and locksmith markets for more than thirty years. Often, a manufacturer will run a mobile display van program at each dealer's place of business as a means of marketing product to their customers. To do that, they outfit a truck by trimming out the back section to display product. We are talking carpeting, lights, store display paneling, video players, and air conditioning—in short, the works. It was during such a van promotion that the generator wasn't working properly, the air conditioner was broken, the shocks were dead, and the power steering wasn't power steering anything that Rosemarie said, "Take a hike" and it all came to be. Actually, she claims to have said, "Retire. You don't need this. Do something else." But to me, *retire* meant "take a hike." It was perfectly clear to me.

Let me explain something about my wife. Rosemarie is an elementary school special education teacher with a master's degree in special education for emotional disturbance. All of our family, friends, and neighbors recognize that after thirty-eight years of marriage to me, she qualifies for a "practical doctorate" in emotional disturbance, if such existed. Besides, everyone knows that a great teacher motivates students to make their own proper decisions. So we all know that she was leading me to the only conclusion I could make. Her saying, "Retire" was really code for "Take a hike."

I have always wanted to hike the Appalachian Trail and especially to do it with my family. But life in general—building a family, job demands—consumed our focus. Even though we were outdoors people who biked, hiked, camped, sailed, and snow skied, sometimes getting outside got tough when faced with the demands of a wife and two daughters who desired the comforts of home to meet their personal needs. Sailing, swimming, and even snow skiing were acceptable because restrooms were close by, but going into the woods? Only now are both girls interested in camping, so the chance to hike with them made this decision even more exciting. And besides, they can better explain it to Rosemarie, who is still trying to understand how "retire" became "take a hike"!

And then there is the inevitable question: Why? The answer starts with the fact that I have always enjoyed walking. On occasion, I would walk home from grammar school and high school, which were each about two miles away. In Boy Scouts, I enjoyed hikes in the woods. The idea of walking the Appalachian Trail always intrigued me, and I often dreamed of hiking as a family. When we lost Jason, it became less important, but as I came to accept his loss, walking the trail became a way to memorialize him and to acknowledge the greatly unselfish efforts of so many young adults who lead children on paths of self-discovery in outdoor settings. I also believed that writing a book such as this, in showing how the woods work so well for children with needs, could have a positive impact on those children and workers both. Also, I wanted to push back against some negative comments recurring in books written by Appalachian Trail thru-hikers that imply that the trail is just for them. It became a mission.

Jason was not quite twenty-five years old when, on a climbing trip to Squamish, British Columbia, Canada, he fell. Ironically, he fell from a route called Neat and Cool. It was the last day of his vacation and was to be that one last climb before packing up and heading home. When he fell, he sustained three contusions on his brain, lapsed into a coma, was air evacuated to Vancouver General Hospital, and never recovered. The family gathered in Vancouver, and for nine days we stayed by his side, prayed, talked, put up signs, hung balloons, worked around-the-clock shifts, whatever we could. Three operations later, there was nothing more that could be done to reduce the spasmodic swelling that kept recurring.

While at Turpin High School in Cincinnati, Ohio, Jason learned to rock climb. At Warren Wilson College in Asheville, North Carolina, that skill turned into a passion, and he looked for ways to feed his hunger. He found that he could help others and climb at the same time. He combined Rosemarie's teaching background and my interest in the outdoors and created his own persona. Over the years, he worked in programs such as after-school mentoring and outdoor programs for youth considered chemically dependent, troubled, and/ or behaviorally at risk, in places as far flung as Montana, North Carolina, and Connecticut.

At times, he doubted that he had what was needed to help his students improve. But he kept at it, and in the process he matured and became a better person. The old saying about it is better to give than to receive is proven every day by those who spend their time working with youth with needs. The power one gets from being outdoors, from being in nature, and from working with nature to help another person takes on its own mystical sense of fulfillment and becomes another acknowledgment of higher truths and presence.

To this end, and in memory of Jason, my journey took form. The route was known, the gear was packed, family and friends were scheduled to join me along the trail, and administrators of selected programs along the Appalachian Trail were ready to meet with me to explain their programs. The excitement built as the start date approached. I even picked a trail name: PowerLock. Thru-hikers have trail names. I am not sure why, but they do. Some are given by other hikers, and some, like mine, come by way of one's own life experiences. Mine is related to the several jobs I have had over the years. In the 1970s, I worked for Stanley Hand Tools, which continues to make a brand of measuring tapes with that name. As the 1970s were the days of CB radio, I used "Powerlock" as my "handle." And just before I retired, I worked as a manufacturer's sales representative for Kaba Ilco, the largest key blank manufacturer in the world. So I reworked my CB name by capitalizing the L, resulting in PowerLock. Out of respect for those I met on the trail and in appreciation of their patience with me for taking up their time by asking questions, I will use their trail names here.

My planned beginning was not without a new development or two. The first was our daughter Amy's announcement that she was pregnant, and this was quickly followed by Danielle's own announcement of the same. There I was facing six months in the woods, and our first grandchildren were on the way. Had I known that my simple decision to hike the Appalachian Trail was all it would take to produce grandchildren, I would have done it years earlier. While my hiking partners grew fewer, my family was now set to expand, and it seemed possible for a time to have the best of all worlds.

I actually started hiking the trail on March 14, 2010. That first day,

I chanced to meet and began hiking with Jerry Horton, a gentleman with thirty-one years of experience as a youth minister and who used the woods in working with youth. Later that morning, we came upon a group of Ole Miss students guided by Riley Kurtz. Riley was majoring in park recreation administration with the intention of earning his doctorate in this field. Jerry and Riley were not on my list of preplanned visits, but they had outdoor experiences that I wanted to find out more about. I knew I needed to talk to them, which meant that I needed to find time somewhere along the trail to sit down with each for a chat. Then, late that first night, I called home and found out that Amy had been hospitalized with kidney pains of undetermined origin. Our youngest daughter, six months pregnant with our first grandchild, was in the hospital and I was four hundred and fifty miles away. The next day, I got off the trail and headed home. But even in the process of getting off the trail, I unexpectedly met *Quartz*, a psychiatric nurse with an amazing story about her work with young adults in the woods.

When Rosemarie told me Amy was in the hospital, we decided that I would hike one more day and call home that evening. This would give the doctors time to diagnose Amy's pains and the severity of the situation. Based on their decision, I could then decide whether to continue on the trail or return home. That was the plan, but I didn't feel right. I hadn't been home when Rosemarie got the call that Jason had fallen. As is often the case with a traveling salesman, when I travel is when something back home breaks, leaks, and or fails. Now I was four hundred fifty miles from home and Amy was hospitalized. Granted, she had a history of kidney aliments and had been on prescription meds for it, but because she was pregnant, the doctors had taken her off of her meds and she claimed the pain wasn't the same. It was different, and that had us worried. So I went to sleep that first night figuring that while I hiked I would at least get to talk to Jerry about his ministry and Riley about his plans after college, and then I could figure out what to do about Amy.

I spent the morning of Day 2 as I had the previous day, hiking with three others: Mike G., who was celebrating his fortieth birthday by hiking the Appalachian Trail after selling all he had and leaving Great

Britain to come here; JayB who wanted to thru-hike; and Jerry, who was buddy-hiking a sixty-mile section just to get his friend, JayB, started. In group dynamics parlance, we were in the forming stage, getting to know one another, sharing general life information, and settling on a trail name for Mike that really seemed to fit his British blood—Sherlock. As we were finishing lunch, Riley and his Ole Miss club showed up. Riley shouted over that he had time to chat, which we did as my three trail mates headed north without me. I thought I would catch up to them later, but as it turned out, it would be six months before I would catch up to Jerry via the Internet and get a chance to talk to him about his ministry and JayB's adventure. Sherlock I never saw again.

I finished chatting with Riley and began to hike as he stayed with his group for lunch. It was a sunny day, and the hiking was great but I just wasn't with it. All day long, I had this gut feeling that I shouldn't be there. It continued through midafternoon as I stood in the middle of a forest service road at Cooper Gap (USFS 42/80) looking at my map and trying to figure what to do. Option one was to hike to a water source two miles away and then hike another 1.3 miles to that night's planned stop at Gooch Mountain Shelter. While at the campsite, I could figure out how to get home if Amy's condition had not improved. Or I could go with option two: try to leave right then and at least be close to transportation if I did have to go home. The underlying question was, would it be easier to get out now than after moving on to Gooch Mountain Shelter? But the real question was: *How do I get out now?*

Hikers call it trail magic—people appear, stop, and help; food appears, left on the side of the trail as an offering for hungry hikers. It happens all the time. And there I was standing in the middle of a dirt road somewhere deep in Georgia on the Appalachian Trail when Joshua Saint from the Hiker Hostel in Dahlonega, Georgia, drove up in his white SUV and stopped. He couldn't get me to a bus stop right then, but he could first thing in the morning. I just needed to wait for Leigh, his wife, who was backing him up as he had lost a transmission line, was leaking fluids, and was trying to make it to a garage.

Less than two minutes later, along came the white van and I was off the trail. During the ride to the hostel, I met *Quartz*. She had been section hiking to test her physical condition and was heading back to check in with her doctor and hopefully get approval to thru-hike. She told me how she spent her life in Tennessee as a psychiatric nurse working in a state-run facility in a program that used the woods to teach independent living to young adult men. But then she asked what a tool salesman was doing writing a book about the woods and children with needs. I explained that my wife was a special education teacher and that I had always loved the outdoors. I told her about Jason and the foundation and then casually mentioned that my oldest daughter was with the Charleston County Park Recreation Commission, in South Carolina. *Quartz* asked me for my daughter's last name, which I told her. "Are you Danielle Palka's father?" she asked. What a shock! There I was in Georgia, talking to a woman from Tennessee who was more my age than Danielle's, and yet she knew my daughter in South Carolina!

She remembered Danielle because they had spent one weekend together two years prior on Cumberland Island, Georgia, having met through their mutual friend, Marlene. Then shock went to fear when *Quartz*, remembering that I had said something in the van earlier about two daughters' being pregnant, asked if Danielle was pregnant. My foot was in my mouth; the pregnancy had not yet been officially announced. It wasn't past the official let-everyone-know date yet, and I could hear Rosemarie and Danielle both screaming, "You weren't supposed to say anything!" I quickly recovered, confirmed that she was pregnant, but begged *Quartz* not to say anything about it to anyone, especially to Marlene, who as of then didn't know. What a small world. At the same time, it was, in what would be made evident time and again, a world of synchronicity, as Carl Jung, the famous psychologist, described it.

I was off the trail and headed home. Alpine, a Mountain Crossings employee whose life story is part of Winton Porter's *Just Passin' Thru*, picked me up at the hostel and got me to another Appalachian Trail personality named Cool Breeze, who shuttled me to the bus stop in Gainesville, Georgia. But the bus timeline was too long, so I rented a car and drove home. I got there in time to bring Amy home from the hospital. Although the doctors had not determined a cause for the pain, it was subsiding. But just as quickly, it came back, and she was readmitted. So I stayed with her until the doctors decided that it was caused by the baby's lying against her kidney—just a natural condition of pregnancy. I almost got the feeling that the doctor wanted to say, *Pregnant lady, live with it.*

Now I had to make sense of my timeline and scheduled visits to the outdoor programs. The problem was that I needed to be in Connecticut at the DCF Wilderness School in July, and Amy's due date was getting bounced around from mid-June, to end of June, and to early June. I was a week off schedule when Duke Cutshall called with a new offer to visit Adventure Links in Virginia for a few days, which would kick the schedule off even further.

In the process of making a second attempt to hike the Appalachian Trail, I was invited by Winton Porter to spend a few days "cleaning the bathrooms" at his Mountain Crossings outfitters store and hostel in Neels Gap, Georgia, which is at Appalachian Trail mile marker 30.7. He thought it would be a good way for me to meet people for my book, especially as his experiences running the shop had fueled his recent book, *Just Passin' Thru*. He was right. I spent four days there repairing furniture, helping Ms. Janet in the kitchen, drying and folding towels for the shower rooms, and yes, cleaning the hostel bathroom a time or two. But more important, I kept meeting people with life experiences that were not Appalachian Trail–related but were youth-in-the-wilderness related.

For those of you, who know the trail and its resident personalities, let me clarify a point before you think I am lost and confused. Winton asked Ms. Janet Hensley to come down from Erwin, Tennessee, to manage the hostel for the start of the 2010 hiking season. Ms. Janet's own place has been well known as a must for hikers to stop and visit in Erwin for some time. We had some great discussions during meal preparations, so I was fortunate that she was at Mountain Crossings. I would have missed her otherwise, as it turned out.

It was amazing. All I had to do was walk up to a group of hikers on the patio or during a meal in the hostel and ask, "Does anyone know anything about outdoor experiential education?" A head would turn and nod or a hand would go up. What would follow was a very interesting discussion about the topic as well as a glimpse into the life of the speaker. In fact, I traveled from Cincinnati to Georgia to meet Slingshot, an experiential education high school student from the Graham School of Columbus, Ohio, who was section hiking the Appalachian Trail as part of his senior project and who gave me a student's take on experiential education.

There was also Gray Wanderer, a retired educator with thirty-five years' experience in public schools who had started as a history teacher and retired as superintendent of his local school district, only to work an additional five years as a consultant for the federal Department of Health, Education and Welfare. He guided me through the works of John Dewey and Maria Montessori. I also met Griz, now a Mountain Crossings employee, who actually worked for Eckerd Youth Alternatives, as did Danielle, my daughter, but in a different program. In short, I was in conflict because of the constraints I had place on myself about what I wanted to do–visiting programs and the time I had to accomplish it - hiking the Appalachian Trail.

I sensed the focus switching from casually meeting outdoor programs to more detailed meetings with such programs so that I could meet the staff, learn more about what they do, and maybe sit in on their programs as they helped children develop by using the wilderness. But already, I felt pressure as I was behind schedule even doing that because I had never gotten to talk to Jerry about his ministry.

From the beginning, I knew that the word *hiking* or *walking* and Jason's name would be in the book's title, but I hadn't settled on the exact phrasing. Dave Czaja, director of the Connecticut Wilderness School, explained that I had to spend time in Connecticut because I could walk the same paths that Jason did when he worked at the Wilderness School. So even though I had intended to hike the Appalachian Trail, the thru-hike plan seemed to be concluding; my focus and time were being redirected, and for the next six months I would be out and about, "walking with Jason."

Shoe Tree
My Time at Mountain Crossings

The decision to hike the Appalachian Trail was made in the woods. The top tube on my road bicycle's frame broke, and while in the process of researching and test riding replacement choices, I hiked nearby park trails to stay active. It was during such a walk that I realized that, if I were ever to attempt to hike the trail, this was the best time. If I waited any longer, my now-married daughters were definitely going to be having babies, and I would then be grandfathered for sure. There was no way I would not be home for the births and to offer help where I could. Even now as I write this book, I babysit for either Ms. Addyson or Master Boone. There is just no way that I could not be there.

When I was in high school and college, Doreen and Marilyn, my twin sisters, were married and starting their families. I would often get the call to babysit, and before I could explain why I couldn't because I had this hot date or there was a game I wanted to see, I would be reminded that when I was a baby, the twins would dress me up and walk the neighborhood, showing me off to one and all. In short, I had these two extra mothers who did *so* much for me. Halfway through the call, I would be the one pleading, begging for them to let me babysit. They had my number. I mean, it wasn't until much later in life that I realized that walking four miles from Court Street in downtown New Haven to the Hogan's on Ridge Road in Hamden wasn't about showing me off but about my sisters' finding Pat and Gene, their future husbands. In the end, bottle feeding, diaper-changing, and baby walking came easy to me. Now I am "housebroken" and fully skilled in the five *Ss*: swaddling, shushing, side rest, swinging, and sucking.

Using the trail name Apostle Paul, Paul Stutzman writes in *Hiking Through* that he knew he would not finish the trail if he chose to return home at any point. While I admired him for remaining focused on hiking the Appalachian Trail, I knew that he wasn't me. He knew that if he stopped, it would be too hard to come back. Even though his daughter was asking him to come home and to be there as she delivered her first child, he knew he needed to continue or he would never finish. That is not me; I knew I had to be there with my daughter. I accepted from the beginning that I would go home and hoped to work around it. Others have had to leave the trail to return another day; why couldn't I? But I kept thinking of his line: "Unless it's the most important thing in your life at the time, you probably won't finish."

Planning for the trek came easy. The amount of information available is incredible. I truly believe that there is no rock, no tree, and no trail-related issue that is not documented in multiple ways. Extensive information about the trail is readily available. All one has to do is some research: get online, buy a trail guide, and study. Let me explain it by answering an age-old philosophical question. If a tree falls on the Appalachian Trail, everybody will know about it, even as it is falling. The Appalachian Trail Conversancy and the various regional trail organizations with their volunteers called the Ridge-runners have done a fabulous job of maintaining the trail and helping all who venture onto it.

Once I committed to hike, I quickly came to the decision to write a book about my time on the trail. Realizing that so many of those who complete the trail these days write a book, the question became what I could do to make mine different. It seemed only natural that I write a book about the use of the trail in supporting youth with needs, youth at-risk. First, supporting therapeutic wilderness programs is the foundation's mission. Second, I have noticed in some thru-hikers' books the inference that the Appalachian Trail is theirs alone. I have read comments saying that if a shelter is full when a thru-hiker arrives, there is an unwritten rule that gives the thru-hiker access and that it is so terrible when, as Benton MacKaye called them, "city dwellers" with their children come out to "recreate." In short, all other users are an inconvenience. Now I realize that after walking and hiking hundreds, even thousands, of miles; burning 4,000 to 6,000 calories daily; suffering through blisters, wet clothes and many cold nights, one might become robotic and myopic. But, in truth, the Appalachian Trail was designed not for thru-hikers but for day hikers; it was designed for folks coming out for a break from city life to enjoy time in the wild. Come out, enjoy, and go back refreshed.

I relate to this fact. It was at Boy Scout camp where I learned to swim, and in doing so a whole other world opened up to me. Maybe my three moms (my actual mom, Rita, and the twins) were overly protective, but at camp I got to do things I hadn't done before, things I probably didn't even know existed before I got there.

With my purpose better defined, I then created a fund-raiser plan for the foundation. The 2178 Club's name was based on the trail's mileage for the year; the mileage does change from time to time as issues such as maintenance and property issues, to name a few, force rerouting. Club levels were established, and membership to each was granted for donating at least a specific amount per mile, from a penny up to a dollar. Additionally, I had a blog and used Google Latitude, location-tracking software, so members could track me live. I just asked that they realize that if my icon was moving slowly, I was hiking; if the icon was moving quickly, I was falling downhill, head over heels.

Next, I wrote to selected vendors for sponsorships. The response was great. Nemo sent their new Meta 1 single-pole tent that was so new the label was marked "SAMPLE." Jetboil sent a stove and a case of fuel, but recent regulations made shipping fuel a major problem so the fuel never made it to the resupply boxes. Enertia Trail Foods provided a full range of foodstuffs, not the least of which was their Coleman-branded trail mix and their own chocolate peanut butter pudding, both worth a hike in and of themselves. Benchmark Outfitters, the local go-to place for really cool stuff provided some great clothing.

Resupply is critical on the Appalachian Trail as you cannot carry everything you will need for the entire five- to six-month hike. Post offices, hostels/motels, outfitters, and YMCAs along the way will accept and hold packages for hikers. With FedEx's offer to handle all my resupply shipping needs, I could prepare myself for the long haul. Since I was this well prepared and invested, it was initially depressing when I realized that my plans were changing.

In the parking lot at Mountain Crossings is a tree with pairs of old, discarded hiking shoes hanging from its branches. Inside the store, the walls are lined with discarded backpacks and more worn-out, beat-up shoes. One pair has a sole hanging from one of the shoes, literally, by a few remaining intact stitches. Mountain Crossings holds the distinction of being the only outfitter/hostel you literally pass through on the trail. By that I mean that the trail passes through a breezeway between the store and the hostel; hikers can't miss it. And they don't. In fact, they stop and use Winton's pack tear-down service. It is a great way to adjust your pack after hiking the initial three or four days from Springer Mountain. Winton ships more than nine thousand pounds of stuff home for hikers each season as well as selling them new, improved, lightweight stuff to keep them going. It's not a bad setup.

It reminds me of what Little Dutch Boy (manager of Enertia Trail Foods) told me about equipment selection after his thru-hike: "If you don't use it twice a day, get rid of it." The wilderness does a good job of forcing the hiker to consider his or her baggage. It forces a hiker to consider what is important, what is necessary. And it is a lesson that carries over to everyday life. We often carry baggage that is unnecessary, loads us down, and hinders our progress. Such are the children with needs, but they don't have the skills or knowledge necessary to rid their lives of that excess baggage. It is one thing the wilderness does best.

It was while looking at that tree, with all its discarded footwear decorations, that I realized that I was breaking one of Loon's tenets. Loon stopped at the hostel while I was there. He was guiding a geezer hike, as he calls them. It's a more relaxed way of hiking the Appalachian Trail—he provides a private shuttle between trail heads and schedules the shopping, restaurants, and hostels, where the hikers stay overnight instead of tenting (for the most part). We chatted, and I remembered him from Robert Rubin's *On the Beaten Path* and his quoted admonition that most hiking failures happen because of something "too far, too heavy, too fast, too soon." I explained what I was doing, and he confirmed what I was beginning to believe. I was doing "too much." Hiking the trail and researching a book about youth in the woods are two different projects—closely related, maybe, but best served when separated and handled each on its own. So I figuratively threw my now abandoned plan onto one of the shoe tree's branches and began to get comfortable with a new and clearer focus. To paraphrase the slogan of Judy Gross's company LightHeart Gear, I lightened up my load and my life, spiritually, metaphorically, and physically.

Thus, my time at Mountain Crossings gave me a chance to restart. Instead of stopping for quick visits, I would now allow myself to spend more time researching and not concern myself with the thru-hikers' main goal of making it to Mount Katahdin before weather forces the mountain to close. The trail would be there for another day. Over the next six months, I accumulated over 200 hours of recorded interviews, read numerous books and articles, visited Tex Teixeira and his staff at the Woodson Wilderness Challenge's adjudicated program for two days that included a graduation ceremony, visited Warren Wilson College, attended two Association of Experiential Educators (AEE) regional conferences, spent time at Adventure Links, and then, following the birth of Addyson in early June, visited the Connecticut Wilderness School for six weeks, including staff training.

In the process, I found some answers to those basic storyteller questions regarding who, what, when, where, why, and how of wilderness experiential education. We talked equipment, adventure therapy, and hard and soft skills, and we hiked, camped, dined, and trained with some really dedicated, enthused, and supportive staff. In a few unplanned moments, I got to witness firsthand how being open and in the moment could really make a difference with a child I didn't know until then.

Being sixty-five years old allows me to call both the students and staff "kids." Relatively speaking, they are. In the truest sense of the word, these kids are all good kids. No children are born bad; life just hands them a bad deal in the form of a nonexistent parent, a dangerous neighborhood environment, other injurious forces, and, for a small few, inhibiting medical conditions. They are twelve- to nineteen-year-old students trying to learn how to act and what to become. Some, like the students Danielle worked with at Eckerd Youth Alternatives, are involved with the court system (adjudicated), and for them, such outdoor experiential educational programs are alternatives to jail. They were told, "Do this or go to jail." Others, like those at the Wilderness School, may be living at home, in foster care, or in a residential program. For all, the woods become part of the training.

For some, the programs are a means of prevention before the situation gets worse and the courts get involved. For others, they are the suggestion of a mentor or a foster parent who says to try this for the added help in finding oneself, the boost needed to turn the light bulb on permanently. This book does not have the space to deal with the matrix of causes that bring a child to the wilderness, but it can give a sense of how any child, once exposed to the wilderness, can grow.

The twenty-year-old-and-up staff members are kids in a different way. Many are college students working for a season to see what this is all about. Some, like Marc, Josh, and Kenny, have "been there and done that," meaning that they themselves are Wilderness School graduates or graduates of other wilderness awakenings and are now paying it forward.

Others like Nate and Micah are looking for ways to stay outdoors to develop their passions, whether rock climbing like Jason, paddling, long-distance hiking, or another hard skill. Thus, they are able to live, work, and challenge themselves outdoors by educating. Still others, like Jeff and Shannon, have this impressive way of reaching and connecting with children that opens their minds to a world of opportunity beyond the end of their block back home. Many wilderness educators seem to have this nomadic, wanderlust life style that just isn't ready to accept "residential mainstream normalcy." It is represented by a photo we have of Jason from a trip to the mountains. He sits on the ground with his back to the camera, which is positioned so that it catches Jason and, off to his left, the back of his Ford Ranger. Its tailgate is dropped, and the cap's window is raised, exposing his cooler, water jug, and bedding. But he isn't looking at the truck. Laid out in front of him and consuming the photo is a forest with two tall peaks. The most distant and tallest peak, unlike the closer peak, is barren of trees and dressed in snow. That is his home.

So maybe normalcy is a low-baggage existence with all of one's possessions in the back of a battered SUV or pickup truck. And maybe, just maybe, the house, the job, and all the material stuff are the fiction we create.

PART TWO

Therapeutic Wilderness

Things That Have Worked

Fair, firm, friendly
Calm, cool, collected
Being straight, telling it like it is
Talk like you're in a conversation with them, not at them.

From Jason's journal
August 19, 2001
Rock Wall
Wilderness School

Painted Toenails

Jason Revealed

Jason is a special and wonderful man. I had the honor of instructing with him on his last twenty-day expedition. Jason was remarkable. Everyone could see how strong and confident and compassionate he was. Jeff and I tended to follow his lead as he held us together and remained steadfast in his leadership. Jason's work was passionate. He truly believed in what he was doing and was totally capable of providing teens with safe, quality of life changing experiences.

Now that Jason has entered a new phase in the cycle of life, his spirit and memory, and the importance of appreciating the present, remains with me. My sincerest thanks and appreciation for bringing Jason into the world, where he has so indelibly touch our lives.

—Marc Sacks, e-mail, October 15, 2001

I feel a great sense of peace knowing that Jason lived life righteously, accomplished his greatest goals, touched many lives with his own, and died with the purest soul. It is sad for me to know that I won't see him again. But I'm at peace knowing that he has touched my life in an important way. I want to thank you, his parents, for having him; nurturing his independent and free spirit; and then sharing him with the rest of the world. I feel lucky to have had the opportunity to share his life and I, like so many people, will always carry Jason's spirit in an enormous part of my heart.

—Liza Wilson Bocchichio, Wilderness School
Logistic Staff, November 6, 2001

In 1992, one of Jason's great high school friends, Brian McCormick, came back from vacation all enthused about his latest experience. The McCormick family had gone to Jackson Hole, Wyoming, for a vacation. While there, Brian took a two-day introductory rock climbing class. He loved it and was hooked. So it was only natural upon his return to Cincinnati that he would try to recruit some of his Turpin High School buddies to go climbing. As hard as he tried talking it up, nobody was interested—nobody, that is, until Jason heard about it. Then they were a team of two.

They started with the local climbing walls located in warehouses, places with walls tall enough to accommodate the various routes, outcroppings, overhangs, and multiple pitches with their various degrees of difficulty. Slowly they progressed. Sometimes they would just boulder, which is clambering over large rocks at the base, much as might be found in a rockslide area, without ascending the wall.

Eventually, they moved outdoors to places like Cincinnati's Eden Park and the stone wall at its Mirror Lake. Once they thought they were ready, it was time for Red River Gorge of Kentucky. Located a little over two hours from Cincinnati, it has over fifteen hundred climbing routes and is a major destination for traditional and sports climbing in the Eastern United States. Jason found his passion as Brian explains.

> Jason and I booked a trip for one day with a couple of guides from the local indoor climbing wall shop. It was a great day that introduced us to the Red River Gorge. I was already hooked on climbing but could see in Jason's face that this was what he wanted to pursue. We climbed all day long that day, and the weather and our spirits were awesome and in tune. As the day came to an end, we started to pack up our gear and headed to our cars. Jason and I had met the guides there, so we said our good-byes and drove away from one of my favorite days of climbing with Jason. You would think that two teenagers would have

been talking about hot girls and beer, but we talked of
nothing but climbing and adventures to come.

Climbing requires a team effort. One leads and one belays. The
leader climbs while the belayer is stationary in support of the climber.
In all instances, the belayer controls the rope. The climber has one
end of the rope tied to his harness while the belayer has the other
end connected by way of a mechanical safety device called a braking
bar or belay mechanism that allows him to feed out or draw in the
rope. Too much rope allows an excessive fall and large pendulum-like
swings off the wall. Not having enough rope prevents the climber
from freely moving about. They are in contact with each other and
become a team based on trust and confidence. The term "on belay" is
used by both to acknowledge that the climber is being supported by
the belayer; should the climber fall, the belayer can hold him safely
by stopping the flow of rope, resulting in the climber hanging from
the last-placed mechanical safety device.

There are two basic types of climbing: lead climbing and top
roping. In the first, the leader climbs with the rope dangling behind
him, and the belayer stays on the ground to feed him slack. Once
the leader reaches the top, he sets the top end anchor point, such as
a tree trunk or large rock, and then belays from the top for the other
climbers. The last climber removes the anchors in passing.

All beginners start by top roping. In this method, the rope is
anchored at the top and dropped to the base so that both ends are at
the base. The belayer watches the climber ascend from the base and
controls the rope's feed. Instead of providing slack to the climber, the
belayer pulls in the slack as the rope travels from the climber, goes up
to the top of the wall, turns through the carabiners (mechanical safety
devices) system installed just for that climb, and then goes back down
to connect with the belayer. There are no anchors on the rock face, so
the climber picks the route on the fly. Again this is where the team
element comes in as the two talk about the best way to make it to the
top. Tyler Stracker, a college buddy of Jason's, wrote of a climbing day
that he and Jason shared on Rumbling Bald (front cover photo).

Jason and I went to Rumbling Bald to climb. I recall this day because he was super excited to try a really hard thin crack called Shredded Wheat; all routes there have cereal names. I gave him some "beta" [slang for instructions] and he took off full-bore. He gets to the crux and works it out after several whips. I lowered him to the belay, and he just looked at me very deadpan and said, "Thanks for the flying lessons." We just smiled as this was the nonsense we lived for and we both knew it. I think we left after that but probably were back the next day.

Instructions could be about the route or the gear. Tyler explained further.

"Beta" is climber slang. It originated back before VHS tapes, when beta was the only home video format. Guys would shout out instructions like, "Grab the crimper with the right hand, pop for the underling, and then grab the jug with your left. Now you are set up to cross through with the right and sink the hand jam." So someone said it was like watching a video, the instructions being so accurate, and hence the term "beta" was born. So if you do a climb "on-sight," that means you had no "beta"; you just read it correctly in the moment, etc.… Of course, there is also the subset of "gear beta." Gear beta involves advice as to the correct type and size of piece to use on a route, for example, "At the crux there is a great red camalot over your head." This would allow a climber to have that piece on the ready and not fumble around, wasting time and calories searching for the right piece. Technically I gave Jay "gear beta" on this route, told him what pieces he needed in the "meat" of the climb. It's like surfing or paddling; it's all jargon.

The route is often set by placing in the cracks of the rock face anchors that hold carabiners, which are metal devices in the loose shape of the letter *D* with one side that slides open, called the gate. Through the gate, the leader places the belaying rope, thus allowing the climber to climb higher. But should the climber fall, the anchor and carabiner act together as a stop to arrest the fall. Think of a climber suspended in the air; it is the carabiner and the anchor holding him there with the belayer preventing any more rope from flowing out.

Modern climbing espouses the Leave No Trace principles and philosophy, which has become the ethics of the entire outdoor world. Everything used to climb the rock is brought in and then carried out when finished. This is different from sport climbing, for which permanent-mounted devices, ropes, ladders, and other aids are left in place on the mountain's routes.

Climbers work hard to keep their bodies in the best physical shape. Jason was forever stretching, bending, and twisting to stay limber. He was very trim as opposed to me, whose stomach bulge kept pushing me off the wall each time I tried to climb—or at least that was my excuse. Jason would just laugh and suggest another move to make.

Jason had always been active. Rosemarie and I believed that in raising our children we should expose them to individual activities they would not necessarily get at school. Team sports are fine, but there comes a point in life when team sports are not readily available and yet the body's demand for conditioning never quits.

Jason strove to do well in school, sports, or whatever he did, but he did not like to draw attention to himself even when doing well. I remember during his eighth-grade graduation ceremony as he was returning to his seat after having been called to the stage to receive an award, his name was called again. He looked up, rolled his eyes, and made a facial expression that just screamed, *What! Again? Why didn't you give it to me when I was just there?* He always seemed to be less interested in the recognition but always looking to be a team player, helping where he could.

Jason loved physical activity, and he became a proficient skier, skateboarder, and snowboarder. At one point, I joined the National Ski Patrol at Perfect North Slopes in Lawrenceburg, Indiana. While I patrolled, the family got to ski on a regular basis. Jason would be the first on the slopes and the last off the hill. He'd find or make a friend and spend the day running the slopes. He eventually switched to snowboarding. It was as a snowboarder that he one-upped me. He became the snowboarder model for the Spicy Run Ski Area brochure. It was a trifold brochure that opened to reveal Jason in great form, snowboarding down one of the trails. Overlaying the picture was all the necessary copy concerning times, prices, trail names and ratings, ski school, food service, and rentals. And here is the thing—while this cropped picture was of Jason only, in the original picture, I am immediately behind him in my patented out-of-control freeform. To make matters worse, I was one of the owners of the slopes, and yet I was the one left on the cutting room floor. When I showed him the brochure, he thought it was cool. In fact, he took a couple of copies to show off back at school. He was okay with helping his old man, but what was really cool was skiing Spicy together.

Rosemarie and I tried to do things with our children as often as we could, like the camping trip we took to Shawnee State Forest in southeastern Ohio with the Smiths, some friends of ours. While the moms, Nancy and Rosemarie, settled into the public campground, Jack, with Cara and Josh, joined Danielle, Jason, Amy, and me for a backpacking foray into the woods. At the time, Josh and Jason were in Boy Scouts together, but Jason thought that working on merit badges was too much like school, too much like homework. He wanted more hands-on, more sweaty-sock time. And he wasn't afraid to try new things.

When he wanted to try something new, he had a way of finding the right friend to help him. The day after Jason graduated from high school, he boarded a bus for Colorado. He had a summer job waiting at the Aspen Lodge just south of Estes Park on Route 7. The job would later get extended to New Year's Day, and he loved every minute of it. During that summer I, along with Jay Seals, one of Jason's neighborhood buddies drove out to see Jason. We spent a week there and got to watch him climb. We were in an area that climbers call Ironclads, where Bunce School Road cuts into the Roosevelt National Forest outside Lyons, Colorado. While climbing that day, Jason noticed a couple whom he had seen previously at another climbing site, this time climbing a different route. Looking for someone who knew the climbing sites around Estes, he walked over and introduced himself to the Kriewalds, Marc and KT. With that began a great friendship, one that was not limited to climbing; they wrapped Jason into their lives. Marc and KT became his Colorado family. Jason learned not only more about climbing but also about house restoration as Marc was busy either remodeling their home or building KT an art studio. Marc got Jason a job producing high precision optics for the lasers and telecommunication industry when Jason moved to Fort Collins for college. And there he learned about babysitting

There is a photo that was taken the following summer, when I visited again, of Jason, me, and Storm, who was Marc and KT's one-year-old son. Jason and I babysat Storm on a day hike in the Rocky Mountain National Park. We laughed at how quickly some of the other hikers on the trail assumed that we were three generations: granddad, father, baby son. It felt good and like a bit of an advance telling of how it would be when, hopefully, Jason had a family. And it all felt very natural to be with my son, to be outdoors, and to be helping friends by babysitting.

I don't know what it is, but for a guy who didn't like to draw attention, Jason sure could ham it up for the camera. I think that was his sense of humor and energy taking over. Who else would wash a truck by donning a wet suit and turning some sort of outrageous yellow straw thing into a wig or bungee jump with the zaniest multicolored, longhair wig? Or drag a friend through the dorm, down a flight of stairs to the bathroom, turn on the shower, and throw her in, street clothes and all?

He was much the prankster but also a friend. Need stuff moved? No problem; the truck was always ready. I can remember him driving from Cincinnati to Idaho to help a friend move into her first house.

And sometimes I couldn't understand what was going on. He came home from his first season at the Wilderness School with painted toenails. For that I wasn't prepared. If anything, I expected him to come home at some point with no toenails. He told me more than once how rock climbers often lose their toenails in an effort to better grip the rock. But he had painted nails, and I missed them at first.

When your son comes home after being away for several months, checking his toenails is not a priority. Usually the concerns are how bushy his hair is and how much fuller his beard is. It wasn't until he stretched out on the floor to do some exercises that I noticed that his toenails were painted, different colors even. And so I had to ask. It turns out that while in Connecticut, he would visit his cousins, Lori Bauchiero in Southington and Rosanne Tiso of Waterbury.

He would stay over or at least get there early enough to walk his second cousins to school and meet their teachers. Or he might show up in time to ride BMX bikes with the Bauchiero boys, Dave (age 10) and Dillon (age 6), in the neighborhood or join another second cousin, Bobby Tiso (age 8), with his dad, Bob, for some dirt quad riding in Massachusetts. One day, second cousin Lauren Bauchiero (age 8) was showing him how she was learning to apply nail polish. What better place to practice than his toenails! She thought he was the coolest, the boys thought it was funny, and they all had a good time bonding with their older cousin—someone they could look up to.

Jason was always aware of the fragility of life, not only his own but also the friends and family that he loved. He always made a point to be where his heart called him to be and to live life to the fullest. We used to stay up late and have conversations about why most people settle and are so afraid to live life. We often joked that most people know how to make a living but don't know how to live their life.
—Liza Wilson Bocchichio, Wilderness School, November 6, 2001

Last night I saw Jason in the dream world.... He had been camping and was still camping and told me that everything was okay and that he really did not need the inside world anymore. I told him I thought he was gone forever and he told me not to be silly and gave me one of those long tight squeezes he was always so good at. I told him I wanted him to meet the little man [author note: Spencer Hunt Michaels, her newborn son] *and he told me he already had.... Last but not least, I said to him that we missed him, and he asked me "Why?"*

And I said, "Because you're not here."

He told me, "You're right. I am everywhere."

—Morning Naughton Michaels,
Warren Wilson College friend, July 2, 2002

At one point, the family had five sailboats, four sailors, and one super crew member, Rosemarie. Some of our ski patrol friends were sailors, so we went for a picnic at Cowen Lake and got hooked. Somehow we accumulated a Flying Scot, a Laser, a Sunfish, and two prams. At first Jason was into sailing, but after a couple of Augusts, he grew tired of it. When August comes to Cowen Lake, the wind disappears. You don't sail; you drift and fry. Drifting wasn't Jason's thing. But he never lost the touch. Years later, he was sailing with Hallie Richards and her brother in New Mexico on Abiquiu Lake. Its 5,200 surface acres, compared to Cowen's 700—well, let's just say there is no comparison. But it all came back for Jason on a day when the wind was up and the sailing was exhilarating, and the "old salt" found that he hadn't lost his touch. The experience he had gained on our small lake served him well on the larger, stronger wind-driven lake even in a different sailboat.

Some folks accept only the biggest, the fastest, the newest, and the most expensive things, when in reality the knowledge learned and the experience gained with something small, old, and slow may actually be the best. The old ways of teaching the basics can serve one well in any condition. Oftentimes, programs change to something new, "exciting," and "different" not for the students' sake but to keep the staff interested. Going down the same mountain trail may become old hat for the staff, but it is new to the child who has neither been there before nor even seen a mountain before. Drifting can be boring,

29

but it sure teaches one about the efficient handling of the boat, the economy of movement of folks in the boat, and maximizing resources to get the most one can achieve.

Jason was one of those people in my life that I looked forward to being friends with forever, to taking an annual trip with even when we're old and gray. Jason and I started mountain biking together in the woods around Anderson, we swam together at Turpin, we skied together, we took numerous trips together ... alone, or with Arizona [author note: Jason's dog], *and we even started really climbing together out in Estes Park (I'll never forget how he wanted to skip graduation just to get out there sooner!). I will NEVER forget him.*

—Steve Scheper, Turpin High School buddy, November 15, 2001

Old, Old Wisdom

Wilderness: Raw Power, Mystery, and Awe

Making your way in the world today takes everything you've got.
Taking a break from all your worries sure would help a lot.
Wouldn't you like to get away?

— "Where Everybody Knows Your Name,"
Gary Portnoy and Judy Hart Angelo

On a cold and snowy day shortly after New Year's, Jason returned from
Colorado. The young man who stepped out of the car was hardly the
youth my family had remembered. Jason had matured and grown up.
There was a steady calm about him, an awareness of self, like he had
come into his own. He had discovered something in the mountains
that he was certain was out there, but had really been within him the
entire time.

—Danielle Hunt Palka, Celebration of Life, eulogy, October 20, 2001

When Benton MacKaye wrote *The Appalachian Trail: A Project*
in Regional Planning, his idea was to create a place for city dwellers
to get away from their normal lives and everyday space and "to walk,
to see, and to see what you see." It was meant to refresh folks from
the "hecticness" and "economic scramble" of a daily life driven by
"competition and mutual fleecing." He wrote, "Wilderness is two
things—fact and feeling. It is a fund of knowledge in the spring of
influence. It is the ultimate source of health." But he was not the first
to promote the outdoors for re-creation.

Aristotle wrote, "Nature does nothing without purpose and uselessly." That is a very interesting quote because nature was believed by many individuals over many years of human existence to be unorganized, unstructured; they considered nature to be wild, eclectic. All of it just happens, and no one knows the why or the how.

In the twelfth century, St. Bernard of Clairvaux wrote,

> You will find more lessons in the woods than in books. Stones and trees will teach you what you cannot learn from masters. Have you forgotten how it is written, "Giving them honey to suck from its rocks and olive oil from its hard, stony ground?" (Deut. 32:13, New American Bible).

I particularly like this quote because metaphorically gathering the honey and the oil from such hardened materials symbolizes the personal developmental change a person goes through when open to the power and, as some say, the "magic" of the wilderness.

Traumatized children are often referred to as hardened; it's one of their defenses, their protective shield. Bonnie Sterpka, Wilderness School enrollment administrator, told me how one young girl protected herself. She had been moved so often within the foster home/institutional system that she had learned to keep a bag packed under her bed with some of her clothes for whenever the social worker came to move her again. It was her defense, her way of holding onto what little she had.

In the sixteenth century, St. Ignatius, in his book *The Spiritual Exercises,* suggested leaving one's familiar surroundings and going into the wilderness to avoid distractions in one's attempts to understand the meaning and purpose of one's life.

In all these writings the wilderness is a place to go to, to experience, and then to leave to go back home. Throughout history, the wilderness has been a venue of change. In fact, Willi Unsoeld, the world-famous American mountaineer, wrote that one has to come back from the wilderness or it is all for naught. "The final test is whether your experience of the sacred in nature enables you to cope more effectively with the problems…. You go there to re-establish your contact with the core of things, where it's really at, in order to enable you to come back to the world of man and operate more effectively."

That also plays to the rites of passage or hero journey concept. In growing up, I had never paid much attention to this body of work as it all seemed to be myths, stories and, well, Greek to me. But in reading about it now, it becomes the wisdom of the ancients and a critical part of what is missing in our culture today. It is a process of self-discovery: the calling forth of the individual (the hero) from the group; leaving society and setting out on the journey (the quest); confronting the trials, the hardships, the challenges, and the eventual conquest or attainment of the goal; and then embarking on the return and reentry to society. Once back, the story doesn't end. Now the hero uses what has been learned and gained to help society move forward, maybe even to save society. It is this responsibility to the group, to the society at large—it is this lifestyle change from man child to an active adult leadership contribution—that defines the hero. As Dave Czaja said, "It validates everybody's spirituality, everybody's culture and unifies the archetypes that are within all cultures and, probably, preprogrammed in us."

Today it is missing. Every culture has myths, traditions, and customs—in essence, the people's spirituality. Joseph Campbell writes,

> For the democratic ideal of the self-determining individual, the invention of the power-driven machines, and the development of the scientific method of research, have so transformed human life that the long-inherited, timeless universe of symbols has collapsed.

It is the powers of the myths that help one "harmonize" his or her life to that of society. As Joseph Campbell writes in *The Hero's*

Journey: "When you are in accord with nature, nature will yield up its bounty.... And every sacred place is the place where eternity shines through time."

Most rites or rituals are religious in nature and mark transitions in life: baptisms, confirmations, bar mitzvahs, weddings. They are intended to remind us of the greater worldview. But they seem to have become, in part, merely excuses for a party and not reflection. There is a detachment from the historic and cultural implications.

To paraphrase Sean Hoyer, Licensed Clinical Social Worker, for one to really change, to really learn from an experience, one has to intentionally do something different the next time. We don't learn just by being exposed to new ways; we have to internalize them by intentionally doing them, using them, and making them part of our everyday living. The key to the hero's journey is the contribution made after the reentry to the home society. In the business world, it answers the question, "What are you going to do for me today?"

Nature and the wilderness have been instruments of personal change, growth, and development throughout history. The Buddha, in his quest for enlightenment, is often shown meditating under the Bodhi Tree. In writing the Psalms, King David used the deer, thunder, and lighting as analogies drawn from nature to reveal God in his entire splendor. The prophets all lived in the wilderness.

Jesus Christ, in preparing to begin his ministry, the work of his Father, fasted for forty days in the wilderness. Then, Jesus and the apostles ministered in the outdoors, slept by lakes, and prayed in gardens. Enlightenment, or belief in the Creator, was gained, encountered, and understood by being in the wilderness.

Many have written that Aristotle and Socrates taught by walking about with their students in open discussions. Why is it so special when a teacher offers to take the class outdoors? I never saw a class refuse the offer to go outside from such a "cool" professor.

Realize that these writers and world leaders came from a time that, compared to today, would be considered "primitive." They came from societies that were agrarian with some pre-Industrial Revolution manual labor skills and yet with sophistication that amazes us today.

Life existed without the technology of instantaneous communications that we have today and lacked, as well, the scientific discoveries that have "improved" life as we know it today. Cities, except for a few, were not big then, if they existed at all, so wilderness was close by, around them constantly. They didn't have to go too far to get lost. So the question that begs to be asked is, what was it that they needed to get away from? They didn't have global warming concerns; they didn't have the atomic bomb; they didn't have the electronic jangle of TVs, radios, portable sound machines, tablets, and mobile phones; nor did they have the Internet or texting. What did they need to get away from? We will try to answer that later.

What do you think of when you think of the wilderness? The word is derived from the Old English meaning "wild beast"—a place of wildness. Is it a land of "lions, tigers, and bears"? Do people live there? Is it barren as a desert or an ocean, or is it full of vegetation, trees, rocks, mountains, streams, and rivers? Do you fear what you cannot see as in the woods, where unseen dangers lurk behind each rock and tree and around the bend? Or do you fear what you *can* see as in the desert and on the ocean, which is *nothing* for miles and miles? Do we fear both the desolation of the empty spaces as well as the enclosing hidden-ness of the woods?

Before we moved to our current home, I used to walk in Nagel Park in Anderson Township until a middle school was built on the hillside. It was a heavily wooded hillside with a mulch pathway that, in part, bordered some houses but gave the sense of being secluded. At the base of the hillside was a picnic area with tables and barbecue grills, while across the parking lot were ball fields that were heavily used and that also backed up to private homes. In all the times I used it, I can remember meeting a few other users but almost never more than one or two during the same walk. Other trail users were few and far between.

Veterans Park by my new home is very heavily used by walkers each day. The park is flat and open, the path is paved, and there is virtually no wooden area to walk through. The trees that do exist are on the back boundary. The park is at an intersection of two major roads in the township, directly across from the fire station and a couple of houses down from police headquarters. Additionally, because of the Vietnam Memorial, it is used for many memorial services. If measured by how many people use it, it is a great park.

What is different? Although the Nagel Park path had residential backyards bordering two sides and thus had plenty of accesses for help, it was wooded, it was on a hillside, the path was mulch instead of pavement, the ball fields were off in another area, and there was no use of the woods outside of walking and running. Folks didn't enjoy the woods; maybe they were afraid of the seclusion or the claustrophobic surroundings.

Or maybe it deals with Richard Louv's belief that we suffer from what he calls nature deficit disorder. In his book *Last Child in the Woods,* he explains that we have reduced our time outdoors. Children don't play in the woods but are indoors and wired. He tracks the growth of obesity, attention disorders, and other problems as having grown in direct proportion to our withdrawal from nature. His book has led to a back-to-nature movement (Leave No Child Inside) that is attempting to reintroduce families to the outdoors, to the woods, to the wilds. It is a grass-roots collaboration of local organizations, such as park district and nature centers, working together to increase awareness and use of the outdoors.

Maybe calling it *wild* is a bad idea. But it always was wild. When America was founded, it was inhabited by "wild savages" who needed to be tamed. The West had to be tamed. (Having grown up in Connecticut, the West was anything beyond New York for me). Thomas Jefferson commissioned the Corps of Discovery to find a way to the Pacific and, oh yes, claim the land before the British or anyone else could. But to claim it, they had to tame it. Drugstore dime novels "exposed" the West for what it was and made heroes of cowboys, mountain men, and cavalry soldiers. It was us versus the red man, the Indian, the savage, and the wild and scary West itself. And then at Promontory Summit on May 10, 1869, the Wild West's end was defined with the striking of the golden spike that connected East and West by means of the railroad, the "iron horse." Slowly we began to realize that the country had limits, and men like John Muir and Ralph Waldo Emerson, who had been writing about nature for years, began to be heard. The transcendentalists came to the forefront. Later, Teddy Roosevelt became our first environmental president. National parks opened, and the world became concerned about our shrinking space, our shrinking wilderness. While we thought we needed to change the wilderness, we needed to change ourselves but never really did. Mothers today keep their children indoors, and technology is happy to oblige with mindless and time-consuming entertainment. A sixth-grader asked during a class at Adventure Links in Virginia, "Where did all the leaves on the ground come from?" The idea of fallen leaves accumulating on the ground didn't register because, back home, leaves were picked up—if there were trees at all. Had the child ever played in a leaf pile? Had the concept of regeneration ever been explained before?

What Is the Wilderness?

Seek ye first the kingdom of nature that the kingdom of man might be realized.

—Willi Unsoeld, "Spiritual Values in Wilderness,"
AEE Conference, 1974

The WILD Foundation, Conservation International, and the World Conservation Society have their own definitions of *wilderness* that require large minimum acreages to qualify as such. Even the US government has several different definitions, depending on the federal agency involved. Some want to preserve the wilderness untouched; others think it can be managed, as evident in the US Forest Service Motto, which is, "To provide the greatest amount of good for the greatest number of people in the long run." It took the Wilderness Act of 1964 to bring some uniformity by way of this definition: "The imprint of humans' work substantially unnoticeable, untrammeled by man, where man is a visitor who does not remain, retains its primeval character and influence without permanent improvements or human habitation." Notice that it did not say *untrampled* but *untrammeled*. You can leave a footprint but cannot restrict or impede the wilderness's existence.

This is good stuff, but as Steve Prysunka of Alaska Crossings, a skills-based wilderness program on Wrangell Island in Alaska, told me, he provides services to a culture that has been there for over six thousand years. It sounds very permanent to me, and his people intend to remain there, so what does that do to the Wilderness Act's definition? It is best explained by Marge, an eighty-something, spry tribal elder. She accompanied Steve to the May 2010 AEE Best Practices Conference in Columbus, Ohio, the first time she had ever been off her island. As they were walking through the Seattle airport, she turned to Steve, grabbed his arm, and said, "I can't breathe this air!"

Wilderness to her was the airport crowds, their hectic hustle, and the rush of machinery around her. It all combined to take her out of her comfort zone and throw her into a panic. Her island was safer; she knew it. Even though the government, years earlier, made her people stop speaking in their native tongue and forced them to speak American English for the sake of social integration, she still wasn't comfortable. She survived the airport ordeal and made an important contribution to the conference by just being herself.

One of the programs that Alaska Crossings offers takes the local youth off the island and to the big cities to teach them how to navigate by means of buses and other modes of transportation in a city environment. But for Steve's people, the key is that they have learned to live with the land, not control it as we so often opt to do. In the best of the native people's traditions, they have become one with the land.

John Muir wrote, "When one tugs at a single thing in nature, he finds it attached to the rest of the world." Every time Jerry Horton takes his church's youth to the woods, at the end of the trip, they always ask when they can come back.

> It seems almost like it pulls them back to being a kid, even all of us. The woods make connections with

them in a multitude of ways using all their senses. They see and hear things that they have never seen or heard before even though it has been going on around them.

After Jerry has had his youth group outdoors for a day or so, he calls them together, pulls out his watch, and then tells them to be very quiet and just listen. After sixty seconds, he asks for what they heard and they volunteer answers. Then he has them listen for another sixty seconds but tells them to note only new sounds. Again he waits and then surveys the group. Sure enough, they have a new set of sounds. He explains that these sounds go on all the time and says, "But we are not still enough in our spirit and our body to hear—not just with our ears but with our heart and mind."

Then Jerry tells them that over the remaining several days, he will ask them, "What did you hear today?" Soon they start volunteering responses. Jerry explains,

> It's because they were in the wilderness and they were in this attitude of listening with their ears and their minds and their eyes and their hearts.... I don't know what it is about being in the woods, but they just see and hear things that they've never seen or heard before even though it goes on around them.

Benton MacKaye would be happy; they are seeing what they see and hearing what they hear.

I saw for myself how engrossing the wilderness can be when, during the Wilderness School's staff training, we camped in what had once been part of the Appalachian Trail. We hiked into Dean's Ravine from the west past a photo-op waterfall and settled into camp on bottomland in a very wooded and secluded area. With the trees in full bloom, the foliage concealed an elevated roadway that rose beyond the path and created a wall and boundary. Occasionally a car would drive by, and we could faintly hear it. We stayed there two days in class. When we left, we continued east, and in less than a quarter mile of easy walking, we reached the trailhead. To the inexperienced, surrounded by the ravine sidewalls and closed in by the foliage, the occasional vehicle's sound lacked direction; it could have come from anywhere. Wilderness was all one saw, heard, and experienced.

Natural Consequences

But what is the benefit? Perhaps what nature does best is to help you, as the DCF Wilderness School's motto says, "Learn to believe in yourself!" For one thing, Mother Nature has her own rules. You may sweet talk your own folks, but with Mother Nature there is no discussion. Consequences are a natural flow; they can be immediate and hard. To paraphrase a 1970s TV margarine commercial, you don't mess with Mother Nature.

The power or magic of the wilderness is in the process that, over time, strips away the fiction. Mother Nature does not buy into a person's condition and makes no exceptions to her rules for that condition. As Danielle, my daughter, explained when recalling her time as an outdoor educator at an Eckerd Youth Alternatives Camp in Candor, North Carolina, "If you wanted to be successful meeting the child in the moment, breaking through to the child, you didn't want to know too much of the kid's history ahead of time, lest you would prejudge."

It's best to let nature takes it course. Obviously, medications have to be attended to, and with an understanding of that particular program's enrollment guidelines, the staff is well aware of the general conditions to be faced.

Take a child into the woods, strip away the comfort zone, strip away the realities of everyday life, strip away the neighborhood bullies and dopers, strip away the overbearing or non-present parents, strip away their normal environment and their delayed development, and what you have is a silence of life. You bring a totally different and foreign experience to bear; change is facilitated.

On a Wilderness School course in 2010 that was not unlike a course Jason might have led, Jon K. was the tarp-and-knots master of his crew, the Aviators. He quickly learned to properly set his tarp so that the rain and the bugs stayed out. The guys who do not take the time to properly set up their tarps can find themselves spending the rainy night moving gear and bedding to avoid the multiple rivulets channeling through their tents. Sleeping bags and clothes stay wet for a long time and are an agonizing reminder of what one failed to do properly. The experience becomes one of frustration but also one of learning.

Johnny S. hated bugs. He would scream the second he saw them. Big, small, crawling over his stuff, or spinning a web in the corner of his tarp, they were all bad. But over time, as he watched how others in the crew handled them, he began to mellow. Then one evening, Jeff Bruno, one of the crew's instructors, showed him a giant spider with a beautiful web.

> Instead of being scared and screaming like he was at Six Flags heading for the big drop. Johnny stepped a little closer, and if you can see a sixteen-year-old guy actually look a little younger, it happened. Heavy years of hard times washed away for a moment, and it was beautiful to see him step a little bit closer to the spider web to watch. And as others came over to help that spider do its job by pushing unsuspecting mosquitoes into the net, that spider, with Swiss-like precision, would do its job in nature. It was one of the greatest educational moments.

Jeff would know. Jeff came to the Wilderness School and worked a twenty-day expedition with Jason in 2001. Over the rest of the decade, he worked as a field instructor and a program coordinator at the DCF Wilderness School before leaving to teach in Croatia. But in 2010 he came back and, in doing so, became the oldest person (at forty-one) to lead a twenty-day Wilderness School expedition. Like many of the other instructors, his urge, desire, and need to be at the Wilderness School to help take children into the wilderness helps drive his plans for the rest of the year.

Jeff is quiet but spontaneous—or rather, passionately explosive. He doesn't just introduce a student; he rolls the name off his tongue with flair and excitement. He can get a crew so involved in playing Zen Numbers, an interactive game, during a hiking break that they plead to continue the game when they resume hiking. Jeff enjoys the challenge of finding "the other way" to teach. He will tell you of his basic, traditional career path and how a girl named Miranda changed that.

After college and before he got his master's in special education, he was teaching physical education part-time and was a classroom assistant in an alternate education program designed to prevent students from dropping out of school. Most of the students were challenging to deal with every day due to their behavioral, social, or emotional issues. He found "their excuses and crazy behaviors sad and entertaining." It made sense to him in a strange way because it showed him that he had traits and skills that he could use to work with them, such as "patience, humor, understanding, and motivation." But he still didn't know for sure.

He was about twenty-six years old and teaching in Watertown, Massachusetts, when he took a group of students to the Outward Bound Program on Thompson Island in Boston Harbor. One of the students was Miranda. Jeff remembers that she was always distant. She would engage and then pull back. She often missed school, but whenever Jeff would go to the projects to wake up Sean, another of his students, Miranda would be waiting on the couch for a ride. He knew she cared, but something wasn't fitting. And then they went climbing on Thompson Island.

> So, we're on the climbing wall, and she climbed, like, amazing, like this thing of beauty. The instructors were asking, "Who is this kid?" [She] just had the gene to climb. The first time she came down, her

whole persona had changed. I think my persona had
changed at that moment. Right then and there, I said,
"There's other ways to reach these kids."

The rest of the year, Miranda came to school, got involved in PE,
and showed up every day for her twenty-hours-a-week job, which was
another required aspect of the school. She became successful, although
academics were still a challenge. It was then that Jeff realized, "It's
not always about academics. It's about finding yourself, being present,
and she became more present."

Aristotle wrote, "All art, all education can be merely a supplement
to Nature." Jerry Horton, in talking about how his youth change in
the woods, said,

> It builds self-confidence but also makes one realize
> that you depend on somebody else at times, and those
> two things are very important for people to learn. If
> they don't, they almost become bitter and don't know
> how to socialize with others.

There is a forced introspection that goes on, to use Jerry's words,
"in the raw existence of living in the wilderness." Forced to find
clean water, to build a fire and shelter, to learn to swim or to paddle,
or to work in a group with other kids whom they may not know that
well, if at all—basically, doing things very foreign to their normal
routines—builds up a confidence that they are able to accomplish
something that is both raw and basic.

The youth today can be very arrogant. Between "helicopter
parents" and pampered lifestyles, they think they can do it on their
own or, worse, have it done for them. In the woods, that attitude can
get them into trouble. It may not happen the first day—it may take a
week—but eventually the realization hits that they can't do it on their
own, that they have to work with others, that there is companionship
in numbers, and that in helping one another, they help themselves.
The weather may be terrible, the pack heavy, and the boots worn, but

the hike has to continue, the tents need care, and the meals need to be cooked.

When I visited the Wilderness School in Connecticut, the rivers were running low because of a lack of rain. The staff was afraid that the paddling days would be a disaster with paddlers frustrated and tired from dragging the canoes through the shallow stretches of the river. Thus, it was a pleasant surprise when we heard the reports. Dan A. explained how much fun it was even with the low water flow. It seems that jumping out of canoes, splashing through the water, cooling off by "falling in," and working together to drag and haul the canoes through the low spots made for an enjoyable paddling experience. The challenge and the fun were in the doing, not in the planning.

Into the Mist

words and chance that have not yet been spoken
for the sticks and stones have been broken
it is very cold, there is no heat
so then you begin to ask yourself, how do I sleep
things that crawl that were here before we began
and it is still something that goes beyond
something that not even man can understand
as we can take the time to reflect
do things really happen as we expect
as things began to change
it ceases to exist
and others are waiting to rise from the abyss
as things began to fade away
their so conscious state of mind begins to drift
so many questions unanswered
this is a curse that cannot lift
as a new dawn has begun
the things that once were have now been undone

—Dan A., Aviators Crew 2010

Children, once reluctant to enter the woods, now ask why they have to leave. Youth who had never been in a river before now don't want to get out. The "new dawn" of Dan's poem is the reconnection of a part of their lives they never knew they had. Being in the woods allows them to be kids again and to enjoy just being in nature.

Willi Unsoeld writes about a feeling of "at oneness." No longer is it the challenge between you and the river, you and the rocks, you and the constant up-and-down hiking with a heavy pack. At some point you cross over to being at home in the wilderness. It is no longer the hardship of working it but of "coming alive." You have joy, an enthusiasm, a vision of being one with the birds, the trees, the rivers, the mountains—a vision you share with the ancients' cultures, "a vision of unity." Another way to see this joy and vision would be to see it as Campbell sees it: "not the agony of the quest, but the rapture of the revelation."

Steve Scheper recounted a hike with Jason in a November 2001 e-mail.

> Jason will remain immortalized in my heart and in my mind for we shared the most beautiful sunset I've ever seen. We were in the Colorado Rockies on the Continental Divide about 12,500 feet up, and *everything* was covered in snow. After hiking for about a day and a half, we set up camp on the divide and hiked up the small peak to watch the sunset. As we sat there in silence, it was Jason who turned around and showed me the true beauty ... behind us. As the sun went down, we watched the mountains to the east change from white to orange, pink, purple, and then fade to gray. I will *never* lose that sunset ... or Jason.

Betta Hanson is the first person I have ever met that I can say truly is a "citizen of the world." I met her the first day of the Wilderness School's staff training, and that is how she introduced herself during the opening circle. Born of American parents, she has spent her life living in other lands—"everywhere in Brazil"—as her parents taught in international schools. It was at these schools that she attended Peer Group Connections and developed her leadership skills. After she got her bachelor's degree, she attended the Outdoor Leadership Program of Greenfield, Massachusetts, which is where she heard Dave Czaja talk about the Wilderness School during a professional panel seminar. While there were many different outdoor programs represented that day, she was drawn to Dave and the Wilderness School. It was the type of work that excited her—working with youth and helping them develop their confidence by going into the wilderness on expeditions. Today, she is a house mom in an international school in Switzerland who spends her summer vacations as a course director at the Wilderness School. Her friends ask her why she works in the summer, but to her it is not work; it is community, and it is love.

Her eyes see more in a minute than mine do in an hour. She can walk into a room or campsite and in a very short time size the group up, determining who needs help, who is trying to be the boss, who is pushing others. Her eyes light up when she discusses the magic of the outdoors; she loves to see the change an expedition in the wilderness works with the students. It's *magic* to her. The word rolls off her tongue in a smile. Ask her to explain it, and she can't. There is mystery, there is fascination, and there is awe. For many, the wilderness is sacred. Mystery is sacred. When you define *sacred,* you include *mysterious.* It's what ties together and answers all your questions.

The Numinous

In his book *The Idea of the Holy,* Rudolf Otto coined the phrase "the numinous," referring to a dimension of human experience. He broke it into three parts: the raw power that Jerry sees with his youth, the magic that Betta speaks of, and the fascination that Jeff witnessed as Johnny viewed the spider web. The children's asking to come back and stopping to look, to inspect, and to try are testaments to the allure of the primordial aspect of our existence. There is a draw from deep inside to find out more, to go a little bit further, to try something new, and then to come back and do it again. And what you find is that each time it is different. The experience changes. The sun sets with different colors, and a different bird sings; it is never the same. It is not chaotic, and it is not boring.

It has meaning. The sacred, the mystery, and the holiness gave meaning to this world long before scientists split the atom. What man didn't know didn't bother him because he was one with the earth, the birds, the trees, and the world. The ancients, the Native Americans, had a "feeling," a gut relationship with everything around them. Read the works of Tony Hillerman about the Native American Navajo culture, and you find a history rich in rituals and answers not founded on the scientific model. For centuries, curing ceremonies, dances, and rituals have provided comfort and self-confidence to its people. Likewise, the ancient Asian cultures—Hinduism, Taoism, Confucianism, and Buddhism (and later-day Christianity)—addressed man as a whole and not the detail-specific reductive orientation of our Western "modern" science.

In his work *The Spiritual Universe,* Dr. Quantum, in studying today's scientific puzzlements, looks for answers in the soul, self, spirit, and conscience—items devoid of time, space, and matter, which are the three governing definitions of physics. He speaks of a realm of nothing, or "nonexistence," out of which our existence comes. Once you begin to posit this realm, you begin to see science's inability to label, classify, and organize individual life. How can science quantify what Dr. Quantum describes as "unformed, unoriginated, and uncreated," all of which lacks time, space, and matter?

And if science cannot quantify, then how can it predict with certainty the complex matrix we call a complete human life? Psychotherapy may have been performed as early as the eighth century in Morocco, but it wasn't until the 1890s that it really became a field of experimental study. While John Dewey was developing his educational theory, Sigmund Freud developed psychoanalysis, which affected the field greatly. As James Hillman writes in *Healing Fiction,* Freud, in writing his case studies, believed he was more a writer of fiction than a medical doctor, saying, "The plots are our theories." He believed the patient developed a fiction around the aliment so as to explain it and handle it. "Patients … keep back part … because they have not got over their feelings of timidity and shame." But, in doing so, they leave out or incorrectly prioritize the symptoms. At the same time, the clinician interprets what is told. "Here fictions are mental constructs, fantasies by means of which we fashion or 'fiction' … a life or a person into a case history."

We have that "other sense" as well, but it's been pushed so far back and covered by reasoning that it takes time in the woods to uncover it. Once recovered, we need to build on it, to bring it into our daily lives. That experience, that awakening, that revelation of our innate abilities is the magic. The magic is the experience. It is the field educators bringing youth to places (both physical locations and experiential ones) where it can happen. It is the good work they do by using the props authentically and correctly, using their skills and training wisely, accessing their experience, and working it until the results "just happen."

Leading from the Heart

Profiles of Wilderness Educators

I am thinking about a symbiotic relationship. A person has experiences, and the events in their life help them identify with their gifts and character. It is inherently satisfying to work with your best abilities, your talents. I think that is where the motivation comes from. If you are a caring person, if you are inherently intuitive, if you have a psychological nature, if you have an adventurous fortitude for being outside, if your social gifts, your gifts as a teacher, your patience all come together and you can work with these abilities and gifts, it is satisfying in itself. If you add on top the notion that it is making a difference, potentially changing somebody's life for the better and turning around a difficult circumstance—this serves your sense of compassion, your sense of caring about how the world is, how individuals feel—then those human qualities are also fulfilled and an exchange has taken place. If you combine these dynamics and qualities in some people with adventurous spirits who need a lack of convention in their lives to fulfill their own adventures and you give them enough income that can satisfy some of their adventurous spirit, then you have a great Wilderness School staff.

—Aaron Wiebe, Program Coordinator, DCF
Wilderness School, Interview, July 2010

Jason's journey developed him into a caring, thoughtful, warm, conscientious, loyal, passionate, and true-of-heart person. He loved life, and he lived to love. He loved his friends and the people he met

along the way. Jason was a traveler … too many miles on his truck, but never too many people to visit or places to see.
—Danielle Hunt Palka, Celebration of Life, eulogy, October 20, 2001

Aaron's description of a highly skilled, highly sensitive wilderness educator who chooses a somewhat transient, romantic lifestyle is what I saw with both Danielle and Jason. Danielle's life was not as nomadic as Jason's because, with Eckerd, she had year-round employment. It was, nevertheless, without the comforts of home. When she was on break and rotated away from her crew, she had an assigned bunk bed in the staff cabin, which held her worldly belongings in a duffel bag. Jason, with the need to find seasonal employment, was more nomadic and carried all of his possessions in the back of his truck.

This difference in lifestyle, from when they grew up to being in the field, first struck me as I waited for Danielle at the airport one day. She was working at an Eckerd Youth Alternatives Camp in Candor, North Carolina, and had been paddling on a river with her group. She pulled off at a resupply point and rode with staff to the airport, for her flight to Cincinnati, where I awaited her arrival. Amy, her sister, was graduating from high school and Danielle had planned to attend. However, high waters forced a rescheduling of an earlier planned paddling and camping trip, and now she was coming straight from the river. Our oldest, our college grad, was coming home for the first time since starting what would turn out to be three years at Camp E-Ku-Sumee. When I saw her walking past security, it wasn't what I was expecting: camouflage cargo pants, fatigue T-shirt, muddy boots and—this is the best part—a carry-on "bag" that was an olive, drab, watertight metal ammunition box. It spoke to what she did and that she was comfortable with it.

Then, as I watched Jason trying to support his love of climbing by finding jobs in the outdoors, I marveled at him and his friends and their nomadic existence. I could look inside their vehicles and see all that they owned there—under and over the makeshift bed and tucked into every corner of the vehicle. They were rich in two things: the freedom to follow their desires and the quality of the gear their skills demanded. Being a nomad didn't allow them to be necessarily rich in the creature comforts that a house or apartment would provide, but it was the life they loved. The red Ford Ranger was always ready for the next adventure.

Because of the seasonal nature of so much of this industry and the instructors' desire to stay outdoors, they are always on the move, always looking for the next job. To help with the downtime, Jason Michaels, director of Warren Wilson College's Outing Club, suggests that they learn construction skills and definitely drive a pickup for the practical implications of being able to move building materials for the next offseason job. It's not a bad idea. In my previous life as a manufacturer's rep in the hand tools trade, we used to joke that anyone with a pickup truck was an instant building pro—painter one day, handyman the next, plumber or electrician the day after that, whatever it takes to stay in the field.

Kenny Riley has been a union carpenter for many years in the greater Boston area. He has seen business slow down or even disappear in winter only to pick back up in spring; he has seen that cycle more than once. So it would seem a bit strange that, come June, when the construction industry is booming, he would leave Boston for the summer. He loads his pickup with a different set of tools and heads southwest. He travels to the Wilderness School, as he has done for ten years—not two or three seasons but ten years of leading twenty-day expeditions.

Kenny had a rough childhood. "I was left to my own devices a lot," he said. His father left before he was born, and his mother stayed busy trying to support Kenny and his older sister. When he was about eight years old, he attended his town's outdoor camp and did the same the following summer. Then he did Project Adventure, which incorporated some summer daytime activities as well as after-school activities during the year, all of which culminated in a solo experience of being alone in the woods for a couple of nights.

> I think I always kind of had an adventurous kind of
> spirit. [But this] was a completely new environment,

a new experience, a place where I could examine myself and examine my life, you know, be an active participant in my own growth instead of a passive participant in my own growth.

He had problems as a child and moved on, and now he helps others find their inner strength. He takes the time and the pay cut to help others make the transition from the gloom and depression to the realization that the hardest thing they will ever do on their twenty-day expeditions, and probably in their lives, will be the best thing they will ever do in their lives—find a belief in themselves. Kenny reasons,

You grew up in a different time and a different place than I did, so your foundation is different than mine. You look at things—I am willing to bet—you process things with a different level of priority on different characteristics. So as long as my students are safe and leave the same or better off than when they came and have been emotionally available or at least in an environment that facilitates their emotional availability to have the experience, then they're better off; they're going to be better off. They will have a wider angle to engage their life.

All of this traveling and nomadic lifestyle keeps drawing me back to an image from the movies and from television in the 1950s. In the genre of Western movies, there exists the roaming or nomadic hero; maybe you've seen him. He rides into a strange town on his horse with saddlebags, a bedroll, and his guns—in short, all his life's possessions. Some would call him a drifter, others an out-of-work cowhand looking for his next cattle drive, but in reality he is the good guy. He comes into town unexpected and almost unseen. Maybe a young boy peeks out from behind his mother's skirt; a merchant might glance out through the mercantile window; or maybe the town bully will stand behind the saloon's swinging doors and make a quick read on the "new meat." In any case, there is no waiting band, there are no outstretched arms to greet him. And that is just fine with him; all he wants is a hot bath, a warm meal, and a soft bed for the night. He isn't looking for attention, and he certainly isn't looking for trouble. The townspeople's behavior is just the opposite—they don't make eye contact, and they seem cold and withdrawn. You see, the town has a secret. It is in trouble and cannot or will not save itself. In a very short time, he will be deeply involved; he will become their hero.

There is tension between the farmers and the cattle ranchers, a widow fighting to save her property from the land-grabbing, water-rights-claiming scoundrel, and a marshal who is drunk and owned by the bad guy. Often there is a local who wants to fight, but the town gave up before it even tried. There are a hundred ways that conflict arises in a town that can't find a way to save itself. Shortly, our hero senses that there is a problem, but it isn't until he bumps into the oppressed people. With a deep-seated sense of right and wrong, he enters the fray. Maybe he bumps into "little Johnny," who tells him of his family struggle to save the farm. But he doesn't really bump into Johnny; Johnny finds him. Johnny noticed him from afar and saw that he was walking the walk and talking the talk. Johnny witnessed his horse, his guns, and his manners, like the tipping of his hat when he met a lady, and his soft-spoken way, which said *Help is here*. It is very much as St. Francis of Assisi said: "Preach the Gospel at all times and, when necessary, use words."

In a classic scene of desperation, one of the town leaders says something to the effect of, "Well, mister, I reckon if you're dumb enough to fight that gang by your fool-hearty self, we can get a few of the town's good people to back you up." Together they form a plan, make a stand, fight the good fight, and reclaim the town and, most important, their lives. But before the town can celebrate its hard-won victory, the hero leaves. He climbs back onto his horse, and with nothing more than the same possessions he had when he arrived, he heads out for destinations unknown along that dusty trail.

And maybe, just maybe, young Johnny runs after him trying to call him back, like the cry from a very old movie—"Shane! Come back!" But the hero keeps on riding. It is only then that the townspeople realize that they never got to know him. They never really learned anything about him: he was always called "stranger." No one can explain why an outsider would stand and help them in their struggle, and they never even got to thank him. But in his leaving, they are left with something. What they have is what they had all along but that needed to be drawn out—a sense of their own abilities when facing adversity, a sense of community in the face of challenge, a silver bullet. They'll put it away and keep it safe, but they know they have it and they know they can use it when needed.

The turmoil that the town experiences in its inability to help itself is much like the turmoil that a child in trouble experiences. For the child in trouble, the villain may be life in general—for example, a broken home, drugs, divorce, bullies, or even too many privileges without appropriate responsibility. Without the maturity and tools to effectively handle and deal with the issues, the child often gives up trying. It is not that he doesn't want to be happy; it's that he just can't find the successful path. And so he becomes withdrawn and angry, doesn't make eye contact, and hides his problems behind a hardened facade because "nobody will understand." Thus, to be out in the woods away from all the problems reignites all of his senses, and being supported by an adult who is willing to help sparks an awakening in the child. Over a very concentrated but extended period of time of being in a totally new environment, the child learns skills that he always had but didn't know existed, let alone how to use them. The kid has the realization that he can face and deal with problems in the future because he has the power inside himself. For the first time, he believes in himself. It is not the end to all of the problems, but he knows there is help when life's questions arise.

Children like to ask questions; multiply that by twenty, thirty, or forty-nine days on an expedition, and you have many questions. The crew's staff answers them but leaves their personal lives aside. The crew sees, works, and lives with the staff on the path but does not really see inside or get too personal. What the crew members get is an awakening of their inner strengths. It is like a tool box that will help them survive and grow when they reuse it back home in other situations. It is their silver bullet.

Just as the townsfolk never really learned much about their cowboy savior, so too the students don't learn much about the instructors' personal sides, but it's not that they don't try. Children don't miss anything; they see everything and are not afraid to ask questions. Students love to ask about the instructor's age, especially if he or she looks young. But that type of information can create a distraction if the student begins to wonder how someone so close in age to his or her own can lead the group. Such information does not help in keeping the student in the moment. It gives the student a chance to doubt the instructor, who is working hard to gain that student's trust in a very short time.

When a man and a woman are paired as an instructor team, the first thing the crew wants to know is if they are married to each other. For some students, this is the first time that they have seen a male and a female work together professionally. They have no examples from home. They don't know how to process it.

At the Wilderness School, it all starts with a forty-eight-hour game plan that includes points like the Big Six—students who break these field related policies risk losing the opportunity to stay on the expedition—the Other Ten, which cover serious participation rules that students need to talk about and work on. All of these need to be covered immediately so that the ground rules are clearly defined right from the start. While the leaders are working to set the tone and hold the center, the students are learning about one another as they form a crew. But much of this is subject to change, as the course and the group function more like an organic being and develop their own spirit, energy, and dynamic. When the group falls into conflict, or "storms," as the staff calls them; when a student rebels; or when an argument breaks out, even the best-laid plans come crashing down. The instructor must become one part seasoned professional and one part master of improvisation.

Too many variables, too many personalities, and too much

baggage make each group different. The opening line from Tolstoy's *Anna Karenina* says, "Happy families are all alike; every unhappy family is unhappy in its own way." So it is with expedition crews. When they "storm," they storm differently. There is no one way to resolve every issue. Training, school policies and guidelines, as well as the instructor's ability to deal in the moment define the success or failure of the intervention. It demands versatility, prudence, and the ability to recognize what has changed, what is happening, and what needs to be done to move the group forward. Outdoor educators hone their individual leadership and group work abilities and skills to an art. It is an eclectic practice that combines a high degree of training and knowledge with powerful yet nuanced, subtle skills and abilities. Each practitioner's art form is based on the therapeutic relationship, the care and concern for his or her unique students, and the ability to process the experience in the moment, all skills in themselves. Each outdoor educator brings his or her own set of skills, abilities, training, and knowledge that, over time, develop into his or her own art craft. Because of that process, the outdoor educators as well as the students realize a therapeutic betterment.

I have had discussions with many on this issue. Of those I think Dave Czaja, director of the DCF Wilderness School, said it best.

> There is a quality, a dynamic, among Wilderness School staff [that] I feel at times can be hard to pin down. It describes an approach to the job as much as anything.
>
> Our former director, Tom Dyer, would often describe something he felt was the "art" of instructing, what made it eclectic, that was developed through experience over time.
>
> He and I also frequently discussed that this reflected an innate ability and that it made our instructors much more than guides or facilitators. In another sense, this quality combines the considerable

training, knowledge, experience, and skill required of our instructors with talent, feeling, and heart. Maybe it also involves wisdom.

I do know [that] this way of leading pairs, with all of the training that staff arrives with, … complements those things much like "soft" skills do with "hard" skills—except that this is much more telling of the actual practice of instructing. It is something that makes these individuals effective as practitioners of this art form, joining the tools of the "profession" with an affinity for the kids, a love of the kids and of the work with them. It may or may not be rare. I just know I am always grateful for the staff that approaches their work here in that way, *in leading from the heart.* [Author's emphasis]

Let me give you an example. Anna Boysen was co-instructing on her rookie 5 day trip when Vicky, one of the students, took issue with one of Anna's cooking suggestions. From the beginning of the trip Vicky had been resistant to Anna, this increased after the occurrence and she would not acknowledge or follow Anna's guidance. Vicky was Spanish speaking, and a few days later, as the crew was climbing an intense uphill she said something in Spanish, and Anna responded to her in Spanish. At this point another shift happened in their relationship, common ground was found in a moment of intense challenge as Vicky realized Anna shared a language with her. The resistance she had showed her melted away. You won't find that specifically listed in any textbook describing what to do when a student pulls back. Another instructor might have done it differently and have been successful as well; there is no one track to follow. The key is that it worked. This prudent decision was made on the fly, from the gut, and in the moment; it was improvisational all the way. But the key to improvisation is training, being comfortable in your abilities, and trusting your instincts.

Wilderness School's The Big Six Field Related Policies

Reasons for Removal from Course

1. Non-Compliance with Program Policies and Procedures - Failure to comply with program policies, procedures, expectations or staff directions or requests in a deliberate, repetitive manner
2. Violent Behavior and Threats of Violence – Violent or threatening behavior
3. Severe Emotional Disturbance – When a student's actions present a reasonably assured risk of harm to self or others.
4. Emotional Safety – Intentional, repetitive actions (verbal or physical) that result in emotional distress or intimidation of a persistent nature
5. Sexual Activity – Engaging in or being suspected of sexual activity
6. Use of Drugs, Alcohol, or Tobacco – Using or being suspected of using

Wilderness School's The Other Ten Rules for Participation

1. Stay with the group at all times
2. Do not attempt to leave the program on your own
3. Personal knives are not allowed on course
4. Everyone must eat three meals every day
5. Prescription medications must be taken in accordance with Doctor's orders.
6. Shoes must be worn at all times, especially when in the water.
7. Listen to and follow all procedures for specific activities, such as canoeing or rock climbing
8. Show respect for all Wilderness School participants and staff
9. Show respect for the environment, public property and private property
10. Show respect for yourself (i.e., appropriate language and hygiene) – always be willing to try.

Wilderness School Instructor Manual Revised 2008

How does one develop a case history for a specific child when that child may not have the language skills to verbalize what is going on? In her book *No-Talk Therapy for Children and Adolescents*, Martha Straus, PhD, points out that the normal therapy practice of holding sessions between the patient and doctor or clinician for talking through issues doesn't work for youth. Many children don't have the language, the skills, or the knowledge of what it is that they feel to adequately communicate their issues; many have delayed cognitive and social skills that do not allow for talk therapy as one expects to use with adults. She had to find ways to reach those who can't verbalize. She relates a case where a girl would come to her office and not talk for the entire session. Dr. Straus made the hour available to her, and she came as scheduled but played in a corner. Dr. Straus was there if she wanted to talk, but she never did. Years later, she called for an appointment. She brought her fiancé to meet Dr. Straus as she wanted to introduce him to the first person who had really listened to her! To paraphrase a song, Dr. Straus's consult was best when she said nothing at all.

In *Home to the Wilderness,* Sally Carrighar writes,

> Creativity has been called a functioning of the subconscious mind, implying that subconscious minds have a store of forgotten observations and experience (and perhaps the archetypal experience of the race, as Jung believed), and that so-called creative people have no more than an unusual knack for gaining access to their subconscious.... The sudden appearance of unexpected ideas comes to workers in all the arts of course, and just as fruitfully to creative scientists. I am sure that it also functions in people who have talent for human relationships.

Another way to look at the staff is through the teachable moment. Something happens with the student that allows a dialogue between the student and the staff member. By asking questions, the staff gets the student to consider what happened, how it affected him or her, and what could be done to prevent it in the future. They call themselves field instructors, but in reality they are field educators.

When you look at the roots or the etymology of the words, you find that *instructor* comes from the Latin *instructile,* meaning "to build," "to pile up." *Educator* comes from the Latin *educare,* meaning "to lead out." Thus, *educator* implies that each person already has the knowledge internalized and just needs help drawing it out. On the TV show *The Mentalist,* the main characters, Patrick Jane and Special Agent Teresa Lisbon, have this dialogue with a college professor about one of her students who was found dead. They ask if the professor had noticed if the victim's behavior had changed recently. Her reply is very telling: "No, but nor do I pay close attention. They're all empty vessels to be filled with knowledge." Have you ever seen an automated bottle-filling machine? It is much the same. A group of students (empty bottles) move into the classroom, the teacher spills forth knowledge, and the students leave. Does that sound like fun to you?

It appears that the professor in the dialogue above subscribes to the instructor approach of "learning," somewhat devoid of empathy or compassion for her class. She doesn't seem to care about helping her students draw out their inner selves. Whereas Aristotle and Socrates taught by questioning, forcing dialogue, and making the student think, this professor just piles it on. As such, there isn't much of a chance for a teachable moment.

While "field staff" and "field instructor" seem to be generic job labels, some programs get more formal. At Eckerd, Danielle and her associates were all called chief, as in, "Hey, Chief Danielle." At Woodson Wilderness Challenge, Black Mountain, in North Carolina, it is "Mr." or "Ms.," as in "Mr. Dave" and "Ms. Janie." At Anasazi Wilderness in Mesa, Arizona, the staff is called Trail Walkers, which is a good name. It implies that the trail is already there and needs to be walked. It implies a sharing of the journey. It gives an image of someone who has been down that trail before, someone who knows the trail, someone who can guide others, someone who knows how to keep the others safe. But at the same time, this is someone who lets the trail do the work, who lets the wilderness be the venue of change, and who lets the student internalize the discovery.

One of the ways Anasazi involves the parents is to have them experience the trail themselves. In the process, each parent picks up a trail name. One mother whose trail name is Singing Dove in the Gentle

Wind writes about her experience walking the trail and watching the interaction between the Trail Walkers and her daughter.

> The Trail Walkers are true teachers in the sense that they watched and waited for a teachable moment to use as a catalyst for an awakening. As they guided her through the forest, they guided her through the walls she had built around her heart. They helped her see her "seeds of greatness" that had lay fallow while she made self-destructive choices.

Sometimes it is necessary to be an instructor. When preparing the crew for a day of paddling on the river or rock climbing, those hard skills need to be "piled on." They need to be built upon. And the transfer of that information, of those skills, can consume a large amount of time. As the students pick up the skills, less time is spent instructing. But the real job is in educating, drawing out something from the student that leads them—and here is a really technical term—to their own "aha moments" of self-discovery.

Seasoned professionals, masters of the improvisational, nomadic heroes, instructors, or educators—who are they? They are a little of each when they need to be and more.

Jeremy Poore, program director at Stone Mountain School in Asheville, calls field educator a lifestyle instead of a job.

> You will do this work and very well … if you're interested in changing yourself, interested in challenging and receiving feedback and giving it to other people and really growing as a person, and if you are willing to think of your work as a lifestyle as opposed to just a job you go to. … The work takes too much of your energy, too much of your emotional world, of basically everything, even your guts, to do it successfully. No one would do it for the paycheck; the money cannot sustain it.

Turning Swords into Plowshares

While sitting in the men's cabin at the Wilderness School, Nate Bliss began to tell me his life story. I kept thinking that I had heard this before: a young man goes off to serve his country and comes home only to answer another call to serve. Add in the fact that his family has ties to the early days of Plymouth Colony in Massachusetts, and you have a young man with roots as deep as our nation's.

Nate grew up in the White Mountains of New Hampshire. From the time he was six years old, he can remember the family camping and hiking throughout the Whites. He actually remembers hating it as a kid—the hikes, even the short ones, were too long; the pack was too heavy; and he really hated being away from his friends. But over time it grew on him, and now the outdoors, the hiking, the paddling, the climbing—all of it—is in his blood. His turning point was the time he hiked the southern thousand miles of the Appalachian Trail in 1998. He began to realize the benefits of the outdoors, the discipline involved, and the physical fitness it engendered. At that point in his life, he believed it was time to serve.

So the following year, he joined the Army. More specifically, he became a paratrooper in the Eighty-second Airborne. While no one will call serving in the Army hiking or a walk in the park, there were similarities: three months without a shower; traveling light, as in having only two pairs of socks; plus all the sand, grime, and heat you'd ever want and then some. What had been "roughing it" on the Appalachian Trail became standard operating procedure for daily life in Kosovo, Iraq, and Kuwait. But that wasn't enough, so he extended his enlistment and requested special operations—just another day for a family that has been involved with this nation since Nate's forefather, Abraham Blush, purchased land in Duxbury, Massachusetts, in 1637.

Once out of the service, it was time to finish what he had started. So in May 1994, he found himself at Harpers Ferry, West Virginia; shouldered his pack; and went "NOBO" (northbound) on the Appalachian Trail all the way to Maine. Along the way, he kept meeting the trail's Ridge-runners, dedicated volunteers and paid staffers who maintain the Appalachian Trail. Thinking about what he wanted to do after finishing the trail, he realized that he wanted to stay outdoors and use his self-taught skills. He had the skills but neither the lingo nor the certificates that formal training would give him, so he hired on with the Appalachian Mountain Club's Berkshire Ridge-runners. Now he was outdoors as a goodwill ambassador, and meeting people helped improve his people skills as much as he helped the hikers. Working maintenance projects gave him first-hand knowledge of the trail and its workings. After a couple of years, he decided it was time to do more—maybe teach, but not in a traditional classroom setting. Remembering his many meetings with the Wilderness School crews on the trail while working as a Ridge-runner, he applied for a seasonal staff position with the school. While finishing college, he has spent the past two summers leading youth in the woods.

Not only is Nate from a long line of American ancestry, he is also following others who have served their country and then turned to helping children in the woods. Charlie Benton was one of the first minority interns hired at the Wilderness School. A physically huge man, he had been shot up badly in Vietnam. In fact, when he took off his shirt, it was evident that his chest was riddled with scars from where medics had patched the bullet holes. A Vietnam vet who was also part of the Black Horseman of Keney Park in Hartford, he rode horses and had a lot of wisdom to share. The children loved him. Charlie died a few years ago, and so it was only from my interviews with Tom and Nancy Dyer, who both worked twenty-day expeditions with Charlie, that I learned of this good man and his contributions. There are those in this country who at times will besmirch those who answer the military's call to service, but in answering the call those who answer learn the value of service to others and so they stand and give back.

Rather, the better term is *pay forward*. *Give back* implies that something was taken from somebody who needs it back when, in reality, things given as gifts, in kindness, as charity, and intended to improve another or society are usually given without a thought of gaining it back. Such acts are done to improve another being, to help move him or her forward; to give back would stop moving the improvements forward. The expanding matrix or web of those who have benefited would shrink if the gifts were returned to the original giver. The world and, specifically, children at-risk need those gifts continuously paid forward. They need people like Charlie, Nate, and others who answer the call to serve.

While at the Wilderness School, I witnessed the fact that sometimes the call to serve comes late at night. I woke up one night at the Wilderness School's base camp to the sound of voices coming from the Officer of the Day office. All contact between base camp and the field staff when they are on expedition in the woods with students is made through a staff person assigned to be Officer of the Day or that officer's backup. I dressed and walked over to see what was happening. What I found was not just those two but three or four other staff members, working and trying to help.

It seemed that one of the students needed to visit a clinic or hospital to be checked medically—a simple task, yet it becomes complex when it involves an extraction from the trail. The team decided to reroute a logistics van that was returning after spending a day paddling with another crew. Being closer to the trail, it was easier and quicker for it to respond, canoe trailer and all, than to send a van from base camp. However, the driver was a newer staff member and needed directions. Shannon (the course director) was on her knees on top of the desk, consulting the large road map handing on the wall and a topographical map to determine the best way to redirect the van while Ricky, the Officer of the Day, was checking the topographical map to see how hard it would be for the sick student to hike to the trailhead.

About the same time, another crew's staff called in with a question about a situation that might be developing in the field. Based on an observation and some hearsay from a couple of students, he was concerned and was asking for some guidance. Fellow staff members Nate and Kayla (Officer of the Day backup) were off to one side, reviewing the instructor's manual and looking at a new incident flow chart that had just been designed by another course director, Nicky Wood, in an effort to come up with some options.

Meanwhile, Micah, who works as a logistical staff member (but is itching to be a field instructor) stopped in to see if he could help and, more important, learn. Together they—the staff assigned to the Officer of the Day system *and* those available and volunteering to help—formed what Aaron, the WS program coordinator, calls "spur of the moment response teams." He explains it as follows:

> An issue from the field is presented through a phone call and the response team comes together—some are assigned this duty and others join in because they are in the room and feel they can contribute. They begin to process the issues from the field and problem solve— "This is what they're feeling and trying to relate." The group begins trying to draw potential wisdom and solutions from their own past experiences. They see what the Wilderness School manual says or what the incident response chart on the wall says….teamwork can be so spontaneous. But yet they're so confident when they're doing it, which means the training has got to be really good.

Sitting in Front of a Profound Teacher

Paying forward is a key element for those who work to help youth. Scarred by life's experiences, saved by the wilderness's therapeutic magic, many a student has returned to help others. Marc Smith Sacks grew up in sunny Southern California. Unfortunately, his life was not always sunny. A survivor of sexual abuse, he lived in a house that was the epicenter of drug abuse and dealing in his neighborhood—not just recreational use but very heavy, hard-core drug use. Marc remembers a summer camping trip with his dad to Yosemite Valley when he was ten years old. His folks had been divorced since he was two years old, so he looked forward to these summer trips. It was while they were looking at the valley walls that he had this jaw-dropping feeling that he explains as

> awe at the miracle of nature. I was sitting in front of a profound teacher. It wasn't just a bunch of trees, cliffs, and rocks. There was something more. There was something very ancient about it that was beyond even the human wisdom. There was something bigger than that and just feeling that there's this wisdom there—this old, old wisdom that was in the rocks and trees and that it would teach me. It was interesting; it almost felt like it was making an offer right there. There was nothing, no exchange, no verbal exchange, no, nothing audible or anything like that; but it almost felt like, "Oh I'm here and I will always be here for you. If you ever need me I'll help you."
>
> From then on, I think I had a profound appreciation for the power of being in nature. So, in that sense I was hooked; from then on I wanted to be outside. I want to do outdoor things.

Then a fortunate twist of fate in the form of an IQ test stepped in. Marc tested in the top percentile and was moved to honor classes. It was there—among students from better surroundings, doing better things with their lives, "creating great lives"—that he realized that they really were not different from him except for what they did and the lives they created for themselves. They weren't better than him, they weren't smarter than him, and they didn't have anything special. He was torn between his old neighborhood and his new life. He didn't know what the difference between these two worlds was, but he knew it wasn't big.

It was after a neighborhood brawl as he stood looking in a mirror at his shirt covered in someone else's blood that he became disgusted with himself. He began to ask himself *What am I doing? What am*

I creating? What good am I creating in the world? He knew that he wasn't creating anything and that his parents weren't either, so he decided to disassociate from his neighborhood friends and develop his honors class friendships. He believed that in attempting to change his life, he didn't have the confidence, the skills, or the strength to stay even loosely connected to the home crowd without regressing. He quickly realized that to survive and move on, he had to break clean.

It took Marc most of his young adult life to figure how to be an adult, how to be responsible, how to set goals, how to be disciplined. Without a role model, he thought he was behind the eight ball. It took him nine years to finish his four-year college degree. It was only toward the last years of college that he had people willing to help him.

In 1996, he did a semester of research in the San Juan Mountains through the Sierra Institute—a summer of backpacking through the mountains accumulating data. It was awesome but led to some big breakdowns.

> I came to some big realizations about some of those things [that], when you grow up in a situation, you don't see all the things as unique; you see them as they were, as reality. So spending that much time in Nature, I think, was like this powerful mirror that said, "Look at your life. Look at what you've been through. Look at what you've kind of been ignoring for all the years."

He started remembering things from his childhood that he had blocked out, really disturbing images and experiences. It was his survival mechanism to block them out, but then they came back. He had to deal with them. He was sitting in front of a campfire when they hit, and he totally melted down in the presence of his fellow researchers.

It had something to do with being in Nature, a really

good place for that to happen. You know, it was a really good place for me to take a good look and get a clear look at what was happening, the story I had lived and the story I was creating for myself. So I was again reminded: "Oh, Nature is a teacher."

The following summer, Marc got a job leading wilderness trips for a camp in central California and found himself drawn to the toughest members, the "ones with the biggest problems and who had the biggest chips on their shoulders." They were mirroring his problems, tendencies, and behaviors that really "pissed people off." But he found a joy he could relate to in a been-there, done-that sort of way. Yet in some ways it was on-the-job training, and he didn't know what he was doing. He just knew he was "drawn to do the work and cared about it."

Following that, Marc spent some time with Outward Bound before coming to the Wilderness School in 2000. And it was at the Wilderness School that he learned the idea of appropriate challenge.

We let each kid know up front that "We're gonna do our best to give you the best challenge that'll take you to your edge, to let you find out what you can do and not do. But part of being your leader is to stand in a commitment that we will make sure that you have what you need to do that."

Sometimes that means being really creative about finding the right resources, the right scenario, the right agreements, the right standard. It's unique to any trip. The point, I think, to all of this was to teach the kids how to be a leader in a challenging situation not to just sit down and complain about their experience but actually to problem solve and to declare, *This is where I'm headed, this is what I know, these are my assessments about the situation, this is what I know I can do and I can't do. How am I going to figure this out? I got my head share. I can't do this on my own. Maybe I need to ask someone for help. Maybe I need to come up with a different plan because my strategy is not working.*

It was in 2001, during his second year at the Wilderness School, that Marc and Jason worked an expedition together. Jason and Jeff Bruno were to be the instructor team, with Marc serving as the course director. But Marc got called to substitute for Jeff, who left and returned three times during the twenty days for health reasons. It was a tough crew that challenged them every step of the way. It became even tougher with the instructors changing on an emergency unscheduled basis. Marc remembers challenging one lad with the threat that he was crossing the line and that if he didn't behave, he would be removed from the course. It produced a result that was opposite of the intended one, with the kid screaming that he was going to kill Marc. Looking back later, Marc saw that

> Jason was the one constant. Each one of those kids that came on the course had a transformation. You could see it from the beginning to the end. They were an inspiring group. I would say that group was a real success. [It was] a tribute to Jason in his steadfast kind-hearted perseverance with them because they were a lot a work, definitely. They all had problems of their own that were not their fault. I could see that from my own experience.

Today Marc is a leadership coach. He trains business executives to be leaders by use of the outdoors.

A Day at Base Camp's High Ropes Course

I had my own experience with being a role model when I joined the Old Saybrook, Connecticut, youth group at a ropes course. OSYG returns each year to the Wilderness School for five-day program made up of middle schoolers who are about to enter eighth grade. Brenda Partyka, their coordinator, is a Wilderness School alumnus and uses this time as "a chance for the kids to learn responsibility, build self-confidence, decision-making and teamwork." These lessons are the three Rs of outdoor experiential education: respect for self, respect for others, and accepting responsibility for one's own actions. One of the girls wanted the group to talk to her as she worked the various elevated elements (a detailed explanation follows). It wasn't that she wanted us to "talk her through" by way of giving her instructions; actually, she seemed fairly comfortable and competent on the elements. Rather, she just wanted to talk! They were a friendly group of about seven students, and we all participated in asking her silly questions. We turned it into a game of who could ask the silliest. At one point, I remember her saying, "I can't believe I am up here talking about sunspots! This is cool." I guess she was looking for a distraction as she did well on her own.

When it came time for lunch, I was preparing my sandwich when Dominic, one of the OSYG youth, invited me to sit by him. We chatted about school, what he liked to do—rather general, harmless stuff. I didn't remember having any specific conversation with him at the ropes course before then, but he must have felt at ease with me because then he asked if, when it was his turn to do the elements, I would talk him through it. I agreed, but just as lunch ended, he got a bloody nose. Whether he would be able to take his turn became questionable.

So I headed back to the ropes course and ended up working the zip line, helping spot and holding the ladder as each student climbed down after finishing the final element. I was about four hundred feet away from the slanted pole walk that starts the course when I heard several people shouting my name. Dominic was ready to walk the pole and asked, "Where's John? He promised to help me."

As I turned the corner and headed back up the path, I saw Dominic already in the harness, standing there, waiting for me—me, a sixty-five-year-old man, untrained in the hard skill of ropes coursing.

What did I have to offer this young man? Yes, as a ski patroller, I had an understanding of the equipment and what was needed because we used much of the same equipment and procedures for evacuations of skiers should a chairlift stall. But I was neither current in that skill nor trained by the Wilderness School, so what could I offer?

I asked Dominic if he was ready, and he nodded his head. Then he turned and told the belayer he was set to go. He waited for Matt Shove, who as the logistics staff was the belayer, to recheck the gear and give his "on belay" acknowledgment. Dominic then called out, "Climbing," and proceeded up the slanted telephone pole. The belayer and the student were connected by a rope that passed overhead. There was a wire above the element that had a wheel and pulley so that the rope could move as the climber did. Thus, the belayer was standing on the ground, the rope left the belayer's harness, ascended to the overhead wire's pulley, where it turned and headed down to the student's harness in a clean direct line.

As Dominic started up the slanted pole, the remaining crew formed up on both sides of the pole for initial support. Because of rope stretch and wire sag, there was an area in the beginning of the climb when the belayer was powerless to react; we were there if Dominic should slip. His crew and I divided into two teams and lined up on both sides of the pole, facing each other with Dominic between us. With arms raised, palms facing him, and hands cupped with fingers together, forming "spoons, not forks," we were his support. We were his "belaying ninjas."

He did well covering the pole's thirty-five foot length slowly but fairly sure-footed as it rose about fifteen feet to meet the tree. Once he reached the midpoint of the pole, our job was done. He was on his own, with just he and the belayer connected by the rope, acting as a team. Next he climbed about eight feet up the tree using the staples that had been placed previously, but he did something nobody else did that day. Somehow, the person before him had gotten the belay rope incorrectly placed on the wrong side of the foot wire. The Burma Bridge was a three-wire element in the shape of an inverted triangle, with two chest-high wires for each hand to hold and a foot wire for the feet to share. Normally, the climber enters the tree's platform from the near side between the foot wire and the hand wire, but not Dominic. When the last person across the bridge had released the belay rope, it was sent back down on the wrong side, on the far side of the foot wire. If Dominic were to continue with it in that position, it would create a friction point with the foot wire and significantly encumber his movement, as well as unduly wear the belay rope. Instead of being a clean, direct line from the pulley to his harness, the rope would come from the pulley, turn under the foot wire, and then come to Dominic's harness. He was never in danger, but having the rope under his foot would have made the climb harder than it needed to be. Matt directed Dominic's route up the tree so that by crossing under the foot wire and entering the platform from the far side, he corrected the rope's position. He did it flawlessly. Then he started across the Burma Bridge. Everyone was cheering him on, offering encouragement, shouting up positive words to help him. Nobody had believed that he would make it up the slanted telephone pole. Not only did he do it, he was now on the Burma Bridge, twenty-five feet in the air!

The Burma Bridge offers a wire for each hand and a third wire for the climber's feet. The basic technique is to stand erect, look forward, and stay balanced while placing one foot in front of the other. Slowly, he made his way across its sixty-foot length. He stopped a couple of times, took deep breaths, recovered his balance, and continued on. He finished the bridge and switched his belay to begin the Postman's Walk.

The Postman's Walk has two wires, one overhead for both hands and a foot wire. The technique is to sidestep your way across the seventy-five-foot length while leaning into the top wire. As the belayer stands to one side of the element, the key is to lean away from the belayer and thus use the belay rope as a stabilizer, a third point of contact. It was there that Dominic decided to stop. He wanted to come down. So Matt brought him down, and everyone in his group, as well as the instructors, ran up and congratulated him, slapped his back, and gave high-fives all around. He turned and looked at me, his eyes bulging, his body shaking, and his palms sweaty and scratched; we shook hands. Nobody had thought he would make it up the pole. He had done that and more.

After every activity, the group circles up for a discussion of what they learned from it. When it came time for Dominic, he looked up and said, "I couldn't have done this without my new friends … and *John!*"

It blew me away! Actually, our connection blew all the instructors away as well. I mean, they are the pros, they are trained, and they live to do this with the students. And yet here was this sixty-five-year-old man making a connection on the fly. As word spread through the staff about how he and I connected, I kept getting compliments about how unbelievable it was, a young kid and an old guy making a connection. What was most obvious to me was that this meant that, at my age, I could still be entertaining. But more important and of a more lasting value was the realization of how we can easily overlook seemingly simple interactions that can be powerful to others.

Why is age such a factor? Why do we separate the young from the elderly? The crew will do a service project at a retirement home on what is called an expedition day, but a day? Before my grandfather came to live and die in our house, I used to visit him and his brother on my way home from school. Each was a short visit, but he always had a story to tell. Why, as a society, do we believe that such a separation is good?

What is really interesting is a picture that Brenda Partyka, OSYG's outdoor program coordinator, has of the group. It was taken when one of the first students did the Burma Bridge and has the rest of the group seated off to the side on some logs. While I really don't remember doing anything special with Dominic early on, in this picture we are seated relatively close to each other. So the connection didn't just happen; it took time to develop.

When I told this story to Billy, my older brother, he said that my success was based on what the family had always thought—that I was vaccinated by a phonograph needle, giving me my gift of gab. In my sales career, I had never thought about meeting in the present, being present, being in the moment. Looking back now, I see that I was. In the process of trying to figure out what product would work for the account, I was meeting him where he was. In thinking about meeting a need or filling a need, I was working in the present. It's a different business with different jargon, but still it was the same human experience of one person trusting in another for help and support, I think. And, I think of Dominic. What a guy!

But there is another reason, a reason that serves Dominic well on a daily basis. Dominic does not live with his folks. He lives with his grandmother and his great-uncle. I think he has learned that he can find help and thus can trust people regardless of age when he sees that they care. The support that he received from his great-uncle Angelo gave him the confidence to ask me for help.

Maybe this is a good spot to say what outdoor educators are not. They are not clinicians, nor are they therapists. While they are trained in the group process in anticipation of what they will experience in the field, they are not degreed as group therapists. What they do not do is clinical therapy. If you have the mental image of folks in white coats, then that is exactly what they are not. In fact the white coat itself is probably more a TV fiction than reality, even when it comes to real clinicians. Those whom I have met in dealing with young adults dress much like you and me. But it is not their dress that sets them apart; after all, a white coat would get messy rather quickly on a hike down a muddy trail. The psychiatrists and psychologists are skilled and trained to prescribe medications, procedures, and treatments to benefit the child. They assess, counsel, advise, evaluate, review methods, and do research to determine the proper treatments and services needed. Also, they usually do their work in a hospital, professional office, or clinic setting. It would be hard and expensive to get them to do one-on-ones in the woods, although it is done. You will find them working as a team in a multidisciplinary approach with social workers, hospital staff, "the family doctor," and others, including outdoor educators. Clinicians, group workers, cowboys, improvisational masters, and Trail Walkers—soul friends, is this how we shall define them? Or is there more?

The outdoor staff are "guides and guardians," to use Dave Czaja's words. They are highly trained in the hard skills needed to live, not just survive, in the outdoors: hiking, camping, cooking, paddling, rock climbing, whatever. They can teach such skills and then step back and let the crew members do it themselves. They are great when working with groups; they let the members run the crew (leader of the day), perform the daily tasks (cook, water, scrubbies) and move the crew down the trail (navigator), but always under their watchful eyes.

I saw it when I visited the Aviators, a Wilderness School crew, on the Appalachian Trail. Each day, a different member of the crew is assigned the job of leader of the day. His job is to wake up the crew, call and run "chow circles," ensure that everyone is on task during the day, "bombproof the camp" after meals and before bed, remind the crew to drink water, and motivate the crew, to name a few of the "LOD's" responsibilities.

Andy was LOD when I visited, and he was on his game. He made a list of what he wanted to say when he called the circle. Because each member in the circle crosses his arms in front of him and then holds the extended hand of the person on either side of him, Andy strategically placed his notes at his feet so he could refer to them as needed. He called the circle, got the guys quiet, and worked through his list: cooks report, double-check who had water duty, scrubbies (kitchen cleanup crew), and bear hang, which involves hanging their food from a tree to prevent the bears from feasting on their provisions. I sometimes wonder if the name should not be changed to critter hang because, as Nancy Dyer proposes, "The bears would get it if they wanted to." Andy asked if anyone in the crew had anything to say, kept the guys from talking out of order (first foot in gets to speak), asked the instructors if they wanted to say anything, asked for a quote (a reflection), and then closed the circle with the crew in unison saying, "Peace and chow!" Andy did an excellent job, and yet this was only day three of the expedition; he was buying in early. The sooner the crew members buy into the program, the sooner the changes can begin. It is the natural progression for groups to form, storm, normalize, and perform before adjourning. Over a twenty-day expedition, the crew may storm several times and thus have to "renormalize" several times as well. The goal is getting them through all that so that they can come together as a cohesive group. The sooner they buy in, the sooner the awakening and the sooner the intentional internalizing of what they learned can happen. It is a constant challenge, as Matt explained to the staff during training, when he used this metaphor:

> Take a rock and tie a balloon to it and hold it. The balloon is freedom and the rock is responsibility, but they are tied together. The leader of the day has a lot of responsibility, and they start to get a grasp of that freedom stuff and that they can own that time. Sometimes you've got to rein that back in, deflate the balloon a little bit. It's challenging.

It is a challenge for the student to learn the proper balance between freedom and responsibility that lasts a lifetime. And it very much refers to the challenging role parents and other adult mentors perform: to rein in the child by shortening the string or to deflate the balloon. That is the role of the guide and the guardian.

Outdoor educators are highly trained in two sets of skills. "Hard skills" are what it takes to hike, to paddle, to camp, to build a fire, to rock climb—to perform the physical activities required in the wilderness. "Soft skills" are the people skills of empathy, of being in the moment, of being nonjudgmental, of processing and being attuned to what the group's needs are. Thus, they are skilled in working with groups. With a high rate of return for the seasonal staff, they have become a highly experienced and skilled family of outdoor educators.

The Wilderness School's nationally recognized instructor manual uses Tuckman's (1977) five stages of group development: forming, storming, norming, performing, and adjourning. Actually, the manual shows five different models with differences merely in labeling the stages. The models and experiences are used, according to the manual, "to meet normal developmental needs, to help prevent social breakdown, to facilitate corrective and rehabilitative goals, and to encourage citizen involvement and responsive social action."

It allows the staff to know where the group is at any moment and how to plan and react accordingly. Understanding that all groups develop certain characteristics as they form aids the staff in anticipating, planning, and reacting to the behaviors of the group and individuals. Combining that with an understanding that each stage has its own characteristics provides the staff with the information they need to move the group forward. It gives the staff a way to read the group and formulate what the next steps need to be.

Or as Aaron Wiebe, program coordinator for the Wilderness School, said, "The staff was forever chasing the eye of the storm."

The group development process has predictability but also volatility. Sometimes instructors work through a difficult process and recover to a point of calm with the crew, but shortly afterward, predictable or not, circumstances within the group may take an unexpected turn. Nancy Dyer further clarifies this point.

> Even within Tuckman's general framework, environmental challenges and student behaviors can make an anticipated calm time in the course become a raging storm. By the end of the course the expectation is that the group can weather most storms.

The analogy of weathering storms reminded me of the experience that Ricky Harris, Wilderness School instructor, had when he was a student on his Wilderness School twenty-day expedition. Read how three situations compounded the storm. (The two girls' names are fictional.)

> Rayella was particularly disruptive in the group. In fact, she was separated from the group and was "off course," meaning that an instructor hikes and camps with the student but at a distance from the main group.

It allows for one-on-one discussion, which hopefully will guide the student back to recommitting to the goals she initially set for herself while on the course. It was while the group was crossing a road that one of the boys decided he had had enough; he was done, finished, going home. He dropped his pack and ran off down the road. With only two instructors, it was thus necessary to bring the girl back into the group so an instructor could take off after the runaway, thus leaving the nine students and one remaining instructor to halt and stay in place until the runaway and instructor returned. After several hours, the runaway returned, energized and recommitted to finishing the course which at that point was day seventeen of the twenty days—close but yet so far in meeting their goals, schedule, or working together.

With a few hours of daylight left, the instructors decided it was best to shorten the mileage, establish a campsite, get the kids fed, and then reintroduce the girl to the group. In the best of plans, a student is reintroduced into the group in a more detailed, thought-out process, but time and circumstances dictated otherwise. And so while sitting in circle, allowing everyone to discuss their "I" statements and what they could do to help the group, Rayella turned to Aesha, a younger girl next to her, and whispered something that caused her to explode into tears and sobs. With that, Aesha's older and protective sister, also in the group, rushed to comfort her. Having just lost their mother, the two sisters were on the expedition to help them process that loss, and everybody in the group knew that. Over twenty days, everyone in the group knows just about everything about everyone else; it just happens, kids talk. Once calmed down, Aesha was able to tell the group that Rayella had whispered something to the effect that Aesha's mother did not love her and that she was the reason for her mother's death. *Bam!* The whole group was in an uproar. The group had sort of adopted Aesha as their own younger sister. Now she was being attacked, and the group would not accept that behavior. The older sister was now bawling, others in the group were very vocal about how Rayella should not be talking to the sisters that way, one boy went off in the woods whacking a large log against a tree, which caused the log to split apart and go flying like a broken bat out of a batter's hands and toward the group.

I [Ricky] was beside myself and went off looking to let that frustration out. I sat on a stump for a while and then began to kickbox with a tree—bang, bang, bang. Meanwhile as the group raged, Rayella was laughing, saying, "That's exactly what I wanted to happen … to disrupt all this Kumbaya-ness."

Finally, the instructors brought them all back into the group. They got them to process and accept the fact that things happen, that this is what happens when people get upset, and more important, that the need was to move forward. In an amazing show of skill, patience, acceptance, and understanding, the staff brought the crew together and held them, as Ricky put it, "in a really good spot." It was such a good spot that they could hold it together, and, in the end, the entire crew graduated.

The staff is trained in what Dave Czaja calls the "ethics of safety first," be it physical, emotional, or mental safety. On a twenty-day expedition, there are many real and perceived risks in the activities—paddling, whitewater, rock climbing, high ropes, and zip line challenges. That's not to mention the environmental and social risks a student could experience, such as the bugs, the coyotes that howl at night, the friction that develops between children in the normal course of events, and of course personal insecurities like homesickness. As guardians, the staff has to get the crew to trust them by letting them know that the instructors will not let them get hurt, that they will do everything they can to provide a safe environment. Thus supported, the students must learn to manage these real and perceived risks and to trust that their course leaders are responsible adults who will teach them and protect them. Trust and respect between student and instructor are critical. In the ethics of safety first, the students must feel safe.

On day seventeen, the Aviators, a Wilderness School crew, went to St. John's Ledges for a day of rock climbing. Devon S., during the first couple of days of the expedition, was overpowered by a prescribed morning quarter-dose sleeping pill. While the rest of the crew would be standing around waiting for the next activity, Devon would be sitting and almost asleep. The medication prevented him from doing the high ropes and zip line on day two. He wanted to participate and actually tried the slanted telephone pole, but it was too much for him. The staff was concerned that he would not be able to fully and safely participate if this continued. So the first challenge was to discuss with his physician if the medicine could be discontinued. He agreed, it was withdrawn, and Devon responded.

The second challenge was his fear of climbing. Now, off the meds, he was like Spiderman on the rock wall. He had a great time. When he was asked why he did so well, he said, "At first I was kind of scared, but then Greg (WS instructor) said he would be there for me and I believed him." He believed, he trusted, he did it—case closed. In the words of Dave Czaja, the three points of effective leadership are "trust, motivation, and skills." In this situation, they played out as follows:

- Trust: Devon trusted Greg when he communicated his commitment to Devon.
- Motivation: In showing that he cared, Greg motivated Devon to succeed.
- Skills: Devon had been taught the necessary rock climbing techniques to be successful.

Because of the precautions, the equipment used, and the procedures in place, the actual risks are extremely small when compared to what the children will perceive as risk. Standing at the edge of the zip line, harnessed and clipped in, a child might fear the line breaking, the harness coming undone, or the anchoring trees falling down when in reality the line is designed to hold not just the child's hundred pounds but twenty times that or more. The plan is to have an appropriate challenge that is as challenging as possible but not impossible and not overtly dangerous.

Lifestyle, Calling, Ministry

In my research, a theme kept recurring, whether it was in a book I was told to read, even if for a different reason, or in the interviews I conducted on this journey. Those who have been involved in wilderness education the longest seemed to readily accept the distinction, while those who were younger in age and time spent "in the business" were less likely and almost embarrassed by it. Let me explain by giving some examples of what I call the Secular Ministry of the Wilderness.

In his book *Ghosts of the Fireground,* Peter Leschak recounts his life as a forest firefighter, managing a helicopter response team whose job it was to be the first eyes and the first firefighters on the ground. Although raised Catholic, Leschak left the church to study in Texas to become a Christian minister. After he decided ministry wasn't for him, he spent twenty-one seasons becoming a minister of the "fireground." He said that he was

> a secular priest ordained by training, experience, and most importantly, the willingness to accept the mantle of command.... It's the nature of our society that I'm considered unworthy of huge financial reward for that risk.

Eric Blehm's book *The Last Season* recounts Randy Morgenson's twenty-six summers as a backcountry ranger at Kings Canyon National Park. Prior to his last season (I won't tell you here so you can read the book), he had been a legend to his fellow rangers as well as the hikers who crossed his path. It wasn't a job; it was a calling. It was his ministry. He was charged with "protecting the people from the wilderness and the wilderness from the people." For those twenty-six summers, he patrolled a twenty-square-mile section of wilderness that became not just his home but his temple. He educated hikers, cleared unapproved campfire sites, marveled at the beauty of the surroundings, and wrote and pleaded to save the wilderness from overuse. He didn't just search and rescue lost hikers; he fought to preserve a simpler, more nature-respectful way of life.

Dave Cowart joined the Woodson Wilderness Challenge as their water guru. He had been guiding and paddling on the rivers of North Carolina for years before he ever heard about Camp Woodson and their need for a staff pro to manage the paddling segment of their therapeutic program. He knew it was special but didn't realize just how much until his father, a lifelong Methodist minister, attended a Camp Woodson graduation. As he was leaving, he turned to Dave and very emotionally exclaimed, "You have a ministry here!" At one time, Woodson had three staff members who each had a parent or relative that was a minister.

In the one opportunity I had to talk with Chelsea Ambrozaitis, a Wilderness School outdoor educator, she mentioned that her grandfather had been a minister. So it wasn't just North Carolina; it was Connecticut as well and I suspect that if I traveled the country asking that same question, I would find an interesting number of field educators with a family history of ministry.

"We think of ourselves as ministers," answered Dr. Thecla Helmbrecht Howard, EdD, known as Dr. T, when I posed that question to her and her husband, Anthony Howard, M.S., known as Mr. H. Danielle had introduced us after she met them at an Association of Experiential Education regional conference. They run Kamp Kessa and Sheltered Risks, which are equine wilderness programs, in central Kentucky. They use horses and the wilderness as the agents of change, along with a strong dose of ecocentrism to wrap their students into oneness with nature.

I have mentioned the seasonal nature of this profession. When Jason passed, he was between jobs. The Wilderness School season was finished for the year, and he was preparing to return to New England for a job in Maine at a boarding school with an outdoor component after a short climbing trip to Squamish, British Columbia. He was always on the move to the next adventure.

Besides the seasonal jobs, there is another element—year-round staffers who are able to have "normal" lives. They work for programs that rotate staff over the course of an expedition. This affords them time for a family life, but they are just as dedicated—maybe a little older but with the same love of the outdoors and desire to help others. They have found a way to cross over into the world of marriage, children of their own, a home, and expanded life possessions. Many of them still drive SUVs and pickups; the difference is that they don't carry all of their worldly goods in the back. They still have that desire, as Benton MacKaye described, "To walk, to see, and to see what they see." Ms. Janie at Woodson told me of her plans to hike the Continental Divide Trail once her husband sold their flag store. After thirteen years of working in the woods, she needed to get out and pick her own path.

Modern day cowboy, nomad, master of the improvisational, Trail Walker, secular priest of the wilderness— call them what you will. In the words of Singing Dove in the Gentle Wind,

> [Trail Walkers are] exemplary young men and women who walked with them [the students] on this journey, metaphorically and literally. They ate the same dried food, were cold or hot with them, hiked all day with them, and shared stories in the Sacred Circles they had each night.

In point of fact, serving as a wilderness educator is a calling and a response to a call. *Calling* implies that this is more than a job. To do this properly, it has to be a lifestyle. These educators have that adventurous lack of "the conventional," to paraphrase Aaron's quote that opened this chapter. It is not a job; it is beyond that. But it is an individual's choice to live such a lifestyle. With low pay; being away from home for long periods of time; being required to assume the mantle of educator, guardian, and guide and adhere to an ethic to do no harm, are they not ministers in a different setting? While they may not acknowledge or accept such a title, especially as they tend to travel an alternative path, they are nevertheless a denomination of teaching guides and guardians using the outdoors as their cathedral of change and growth. Their vestments are the climbing harness, the safety helmet of each specific activity, the safety vests and wet suits, the boots and shoes for each specific activity, and the fleece clothing that exemplifies their outdoor lifestyles. The greatest of their sacraments is, to use Cardinal Basil Hume's words, "The sacrament of the present moment." Their "bible," like the original, is a compilation of many books: an educator's manual; a logistics manual; a "here to there" manual showing routes with trailheads, emergency exits, and other contact information; a student manual; and finally a book of "revelations," or actually, files of accumulated quotes, tips, and knowledge gleaned from other programs, studies, and books deemed worthy to be included as supplemental educational back-up references.

They become ministers after all, as Peter Leschak wrote in *The Ghosts of the Fireground*, having "struck a wellspring of spiritual inspiration and practice."

Like those lost-and-then-found children who survive, succeed, and learn to believe in themselves, the educators come away from their experiences with a powerful transformation that can support them their whole lives. They often become the best outdoor educators because they have learned, maybe not consciously, "that they can only live fully by helping others to the same transformation." Every alumnus of a program with whom I have talked told me of tough, hard challenges. Amy Pine said, "I cried up every mountain I ever hiked for five years." These are really dirty, grueling experiences. Yet, with awe and amazement, they also said how rewarding, how freeing, and how deeply touching the experiences were. In fact, they, like Amy, "wouldn't trade the experience for anything in the world."

As I see it, outdoor educators, using Laurence Gonzales's words, "learn to function as a team, to value their brothers and sisters above their own lives and to protect them." They are selected and hired because they are already on the path, the Tao. They come with a wellspring already in their hearts and, in the process, "extend and deepen those transcendent qualities."

Jack Reacher Meets Shannon Zich

Empathy and Soft Skills

Jason was also very introspective—constantly challenging and bettering himself from within, and also inspiring me to be that focused on those eminent character priorities. I've always held your son in the utmost respect as a person. He was truly one of the most genuine, sincere people God has blessed my life with. Never concerned about the fleeting distractions of popularity or societal expectations, Jason saw straight through to the core of someone and bonded with them on a deep, true level. Now that's a gift.

> —Steve Scheper, Turpin High School buddy,
> e-mail, November 15, 2001

Jack Reacher is the protagonist in Lee Child's series of novels about an ex-military investigator. Before he retired, Reacher served thirteen years in the military police, including leading the Army's special investigative team. He was good at what he did and thus achieved the rank of major twice (but you'll have to read his books for that explanation). Now, he lives off his retirement sustaining a low-baggage—make that a no-baggage—existence as he somewhat aimlessly crisscrosses the country using buses and hitchhiking as his favored means of getting around. No longer employed to hunt out and stop trouble, trouble now finds him and he is reluctantly drawn back into chasing the bad guys and saving the nation. His creed and his key to being successful in finding those bad guys, both then and now, is as follows:

Success depended on empathy.
Think like them, feel like them.
See what they see.
Put yourself in their shoes.
Be them.

While Jack Reacher is a fictional character, Shannon Zich is the real deal. More than once, those who have worked with Shannon told me of her abilities to reach children and of her dedication to the process. As someone suggested, she could very well be the poster image of the quintessential outdoor educator, airline stewardess, or Zamboni ice-resurfacer driver, all of which, in fact, she has been. I was first introduced to Shannon through e-mails. At the time, she was a course director at the DCF Wilderness School who wanted to raise money, on her own, to provide a scholarship for a child to experience the school's twenty-day expedition during the 2010 season. A course director is the main support for the crews in the field and base camp. They are the instructors' and students' link to base camp. To be a course director, one needs to have been in the field to understand how the courses, the youth, the staff, and the programs operate and then needs to learn how base camp functions so that the field needs get met on a timely basis. They operate between two worlds, and they get things done.

An avid bicycle rider, Shannon planned to ride from her home in Wisconsin to Connecticut, or to put it another way, she planned to ride on two very skinny tires for twelve hundred miles.

> I so much love this place that I wanted to figure a way to pay the tuition to help a family send their child here. This place feeds my spirit, and I saw it as a way to give something back to the kids.

Dave Czaja, the school's director, suggested that she contact me for ideas on starting her own foundation (and to collaborate with and use an existing foundation such as Jason's). I was impressed with her initiative and offered the use of the foundation, gratis, in any way we could to accomplish her goal of benefiting the school without her facing the hassle and costs of creating a nonprofit from scratch. I was not sure how much time and energy I could offer Shannon as I was deep into the details and preparation for my Appalachian Trail hike, but I was willing to do what I could. Then, unfortunately, Shannon suffered a recurring back injury flare-up, and her planned ride was canceled for that season.

I finally got to meet her in person in June, when I arrived at the Wilderness School for staff training. That is when I found out how the wilderness affected her.

> I grew up in a small town, and we didn't have a lot extra of money to go to faraway places. So, most of our vacations were car camping trips. I didn't backpack until I was twenty-one. I loved our camping weeks and was always sad when we had to go home.
>
> When I was in college, I studied abroad in Australia. I took an outdoor education class, and my brain was blown open. "Oh, my gosh, this is amazing!" I was in a class about therapeutic learning, but it was more about hard skills. We did rock climbing, backpacking, and a final expedition/backpacking trip in the rain forest, which was really intense.... We went out as four students per team. We were given a map, a compass, and our food. They said, "Go here and we will meet you at this spot." None of us had much experience navigating or much information to go on, and I probably had the least amount. Even though we had a one-day workshop on navigation, it's not a natural skill for me. So, I definitely had to work at it and trust the other people to get it done.
>
> It was one of the most intense experiences of my life so far. It rained the entire four days. Water dripped from the trees, and it was about fifty degrees.

We were never dry. The rain forest grows so fast we couldn't find the trail. We were bushwhacking and had to crawl down on the ground. We had machetes and were trying to find the trail, trying to negotiate it all. We were borderline hypothermic the whole time—freezing cold, leeches all over the place. We hardly ate anything. We would get so cold when we stopped that we couldn't stop to eat. It was my first big backpacking trip. It was so muddy; we were hiking up these hills, falling down on our faces in the mud. We were filthy muddy. At one point the other girl (there were two guys and two girls in our team) had such bad blisters on her heels [that] they were bleeding. She was barely moving along. So it became almost "to each his own." We all had to survive this on our own. The boys went up ahead, and I felt like, "We can't leave her alone back here." So I hung back with her and we did the best we could. At one point, we got just enough separated—she was far enough back behind me that I couldn't see her and I couldn't see the boys up front. I fell down again for the sixtieth time in the mud, and I was in tears. I was crying, I was scared, I was freezing, and my legs were so bad. I just couldn't go on; picking up my legs one after the other was so hard to do.

I had this very poignant realization that there was no way that anybody could rescue me. We were deep in the rain forest, the canopy was far too thick for any helicopter to come in, and we were off course so even our instructor didn't know where we were. The boys were not going to come back and get me, and there was no way the girl could help. I was like, "Wow, I'm the only person right now that saves my life or doesn't."

And I was so cold that if I had laid there any longer, I physically wouldn't be able to get up. I was shivering so much; I was probably past the point of shivering, and it felt really dramatic at the time. I don't know, but this big light bulb went off, and it was, *Get your ass up and get going.* And I did and I made it. It was one of the most powerful experiences that I think I've had to date. At the end of the trip, [when I was] debriefing the instructor, a burly Australian mountain guide, [he] started crying. He had been so worried about us; he had never had a course that was that challenging, with the weather that chilly. It was really intense, and he had the realization that people could have died or gotten really hurt. So it was like tears of relief that everybody made it, got through it. I had an all new level of trust in myself after that. I can do things that I didn't think I could do.

It was Shannon who ran the staff training workshop on empathy and nonviolent communications. She wasn't preaching to the choir but reinforcing what they already knew. While empathy is the key to building any good relationship, it is the critical basis for the therapeutic relationship. It is what these educators build on. The workshop facilitators discussed the importance of being nonjudgmental and "being in the moment," a phrase I heard more than once while at the Wilderness School. Just being there for the students is so important because it gives them a much-needed steady presence to help them feel wanted, valued, and a part of the group. When I asked Shannon to define "being in the moment" or "being present" she responded,

> I think being in the present is a combination of many subtle things that add up to being physically present and mentally aware and connected to the situation and people around. It's a combination of choices and mental discipline around thought processes that ultimately guide the ability to be present on a daily basis. It is a state of mind as much as anything else, I think, which

leads the process of how a person is "present." There is a lot of empathy involved, but it is much more than that, especially with students. Consciously feeling empathy helps me to stay present with them and guides the process of what that looks like. If I have the majority or all of my focus on the present moment in time and am not dwelling on the past or worried about the future, then as an instructor I will be more aware of the nuances and needs of my students.

For example, I wake up thinking about what is happening for me after my summer is over. I'm worried I don't have a job lined up. I'm daydreaming about where I'd like to go and who I'd like to meet. Meanwhile, my student wakes up just having had a horrible dream. He is grumpy and despondent. If I'm spending a lot of mental focus on my worries, I might not even notice my student's mood or, if I do, maybe I will feel irritated with him for it. If I am focused on the moment at hand and I have set aside my distracting thoughts, I'm more likely to notice and then I can draw upon my empathy to feel a sense of concern for him and respond kindly and supportively.

Another example is that I have been canoeing all day with my students and I have been dwelling on a breakup in my past. The more I think about it, the more I feel bad about myself and depressed. I arrive in camp pretty spent emotionally, and now I have to deal with tired, wet, hungry kids who are unmotivated to do anything. I could easily go through the motions of getting camp together and taking care of them, but if I am truly present with them (in my mind) with my actions, I can help nudge their energy into a more positive place. Instead of going through the motions, I can dig for some energy and be a deliberate, powerful role model of how to behave when life isn't perfectly comfortable. I can go over to where they are setting up their tarps and tie some knots with them, ask some questions to get to know them better, joke with them, laugh, and listen. Or it could be more subtle: I could go over to them silently and be a calm presence, not trying to change their energy, and just help silently and maybe give a little smile or acknowledgment. Either way, they can feel that I am with them. I could be "there" and not give a feeling of being present at the same time. I think this is what happens when instructors get burnt out. We are going through the motions, but there is no passion or love behind the actions. We don't feel "present" to the kids. Another shot at an example: being in a conversation when someone is just sitting there emotionless versus them looking me in the eye, nodding their head. The second makes what I am saying feel valued and appreciated and understood. It feels like that person is present with me and focused on me. Being in the moment is listening with your whole body, I think....

I'm trying [to] capture a clear, concise description of the subtleties of being present. It's tough! The subtlety can surely be felt better than described.

I've been thinking about you this summer, John, and hoping you are continuing to carry your contagious positivity and zest for life to the lucky people around you. Wow! Light bulb ... as I type that, I realized that *you* were a fine example of a very present person when you were here last summer! Wow, as I think back to that time, I really noticed that about you. I think passion for what a person is doing is a key ingredient in truly being present with people. It's full engagement in what is happening in that moment and in that time and place. And that is just what you demonstrated!

Carl Jung noted Swiss psychiatrist, thinker, and the founder of analytical psychology, wrote that even before considering theories and methods, the most important aspect was a genuine relationship between two human beings through which "any suffering should be shared." Very quickly, the students come to realize that the staff is cold, hot, wet, and tired—in short, just like they are. They quickly realize that they are "equals" in their experiences, and in that equality they reach a level of just being fellow human beings, the most basic and reassuring denominator.

An essential part, writes Father Lou Guntzelman, a Catholic priest, author, and newspaper columnist in Cincinnati, Ohio, is true listening, emphatic listening. He writes

> Listening is not only hearing words, but "hearing the speaker's feelings" along with the words. Hearing only a flow of words is like hearing the words of a song but not the music that enhances them....
>
> It's to have someone listen to the story of our life, take us seriously in a nonjudgmental way, and understand.... Our deepest inner experiences can only make their appearance in the world—and eventually be accepted by us—when someone else glimpses them and understands. By doing this, another person validates our own experience of ourselves....
>
> But what good is all the talk if no one listens?
>
> Our hearts experience the failure to be listened to as an absence of concern. It implies that no one is interested in walking over the bridge between us.

Sometimes being present can mean standing up. When Amy, Jason's younger sister, was a high school sophomore, she noticed that a young lad was being bullied by a bigger kid. She kept noticing that the young man sitting next to her in general study hall was always a bit shaken up—hair messed up, clothes disrupted, books torn apart, face reddened—and so one day, when she thought he might be crying, she asked this eighth-grader if there was a problem. It was then that he explained the problem with the bully and that he hadn't told anybody about it. Days later, she noticed the bully heading right for the boy. But before the bully got there, Amy stepped in to block his way and got thrown to the floor. She picked herself off the floor and threw a bag of candy at the bully. What did the nearby teacher observe? Not the bully's being out of his assigned seat or Amy's being thrown to the floor. Amy was observed throwing something, so she got sent to the office. Once there, she explained what had been going on, and then the school got involved. The parents were called in, the bully was suspended, and most important, the bullying ended. Ask Amy about it today and she will say it was nothing; she hardly remembers it. But it speaks volumes to her ability and her willingness to reach out and help another. When the young victim really needed someone to listen to him, Amy was there. She has always had the trust of her friends as the one they could talk to, the one with whom they could discuss what was happening in their lives, the one who would listen without being judgmental.

When folks are judgmental, negative, and demanding, children withdraw and, for that matter, so do adults. Try it yourself—be negative and you will see people withdraw right in front of you. Being nonjudgmental, listening without agreeing, and using their words to talk with them is what Shannon calls "sneaking in the back door."

Some of the crew members will be on board right away, while others need time to settle into the program. Confrontation doesn't work. If you were to ask them if they were scared, the immediate response would be a macho "Not me!" And then they just get more defensive. For many, just the admission of fear would be a sign of weakness and could instigate a loss of respect from others. By watching their behavior, Shannon told the staff, they could try to figure out what the children were really feeling and thus subconsciously communicating. Once the staff figures that out, the child's needs can be met and the behavior improves. Sometimes it works better than other times, but it is always better than doing nothing.

Needing a Tougher Shell

Sufi was a sixteen-year-old girl who Shannon met when she worked at another program. Since the time she was twelve, Sufi had been under supervision because she struggled not to hurt herself. She would cut herself; she had scars from head to toe, literally. Sufi had no qualms about cutting herself but would get concerned if an instructor, therapist, or other student showed up with a bruise. Sufi saw others' lives as having value, but she couldn't see her own value. She was sweet, gentle, loving, intelligent, and well spoken—in short, a caring person to others but not to herself.

Shannon's position was one that rotated every eight days. Eventually she left Sufi's group and took on a different group of students. She would check in on Sufi, but what she would find was not encouraging. Sufi eventually went to a boarding school, but the closer she got to eighteen and being released from care, the more that hope for a life-changing revelation dimmed. Sufi haunts Shannon's mind even today. Shannon wonders what happened to her. Shannon searched to understand how someone with such great human qualities could see value in others yet not in herself, how harming herself was the only relief she could find for her pain. Sufi forced Shannon to make a decision—if Shannon wanted to help others, if she wanted to stay in this profession of helping youth, then she needed to survive, and to do that she needed to build a harder, tougher skin. She had to learn how to empathize and how to be tender, gentle, and loving while not allowing the pain and agony to enter. She needed a way to protect herself from the daily trauma of her chosen profession.

I was faced with a similar issue earlier while visiting Woodson Wilderness Challenge that remains clear in my mind. The graduation ceremony had ended, and folks were leaving, saying their thanks to the staff and wishing one another well. The mood was happy, festive, and positively charged, so it was heart wrenching to see one of the graduates being prepared for transfer back to his juvenile development center. There he stood on the back ledge of the van, assuming the position of hands together, held out in front, as he was being bound and shackled with leg irons, wrist cuffs, and a leather restraint belt around his waist. He had just walked out the door of what was probably the single most joyous celebration in his young life, high on the feeling one gets from a successful accomplishment, only to be brought back to the harsh realities of life. He knew when the program started that he would be going back to the center and he knew the terms and procedures required, so he might have been better prepared than I and even the staff were to see him so treated. I know it affected the staff as they discussed it during their follow-up session. Although WWC is an adjudicated program and this possibility exist for many of its students, it is hard for the staff to accept; they see their work being torn down. All of us that day needed tougher shells. That experience helped me understand what Anthony Howard wrote about the paradox in which these wilderness educators find themselves: needing to care authentically while being emotionally detached.

Planting Seeds

Where Shannon originally thought, *I can help kids solve all these problems,* she realized she couldn't. But that, at the very least and actually more important, she realized she could just help to plant seeds to help children meet their needs. As she explained it, the basic seeds, according to Maslow's hierarchy of needs, are survival, love, belonging, power, freedom, and fun. Love grows with having a sense of support, acceptance, and belonging; creating friendships; caring for others; and being involved. Power represents the ability to make a decision and have choice over ourselves, and it is earned by developing skills and competence. Fun allows for laughter, pleasure, enjoyment, and most important, learning. Freedom reflects independence, liberty, autonomy, and choice. Over time in the supportive nourishment of the therapeutic environment, these seeds can germinate and start to sprout. The sooner they take hold, the sooner real change happens.

Some call it empathy, others call it sensitivity, but neither is considered a very manly attribute; rather, they are truly human attributes. As parents watching our children grow, Rosemarie and I worried for their future and for their development. Were we doing enough? Were we doing it right? There were two instances when I had a chance to see Jason's human side more vividly. The first was during a trip in 2000 to visit him at work at the Wilderness School. He and I took a hike not far from the school in Peoples State Forest, which sits just south and east of the village of Riverton, Connecticut, with its famous Hitchcock Chair Factory. We hiked out onto a rocky knob called Chaugham Lookout (elevation 1,110 feet), exposing us to the Pleasant Valley area and the west branch of the Farmington River (elevation 505 feet), a National Park Service–designated "wild and scenic river." Standing on the knob, with a bright sun and a couple of white cotton-ball clouds floating above us, we could see fly fishermen casting in the river as kayakers paddled downriver. It is without a doubt one of the prettiest spots in Connecticut; it is close to where I went to Boy Scout camp, and it is in the home state of both Rosemarie's family and mine. Jason knew all that. And the educator in him knew that for a young kid who has never been able to see past the end of his block, the chance to stand on this outcropping would be awe-inspiring. Jason turned and remarked how beautiful it was and wondered aloud, "Would you and Mom ever consider retiring back here?"

This from someone who had hiked and climbed in majestic places like the Front Range of Colorado, Big Sky Montana, and Yosemite, to name a few. Jason understood that life wasn't based on a question of numbers as in the size or elevation of the mountains or the volume of the rivers' flow or the depth of the valley. He realized that it was more significant than that. He realized that the real worth of life was more intimate; it was a value that changed with each person, and he was looking at it not through his eyes but through his parents' souls.

The second instance was the following summer when Rosemarie and I visited Jason at the Wilderness School for a graduation ceremony. Graduation day is a joyful and emotional experience that all parents of both students and staff should experience. Each crew member is introduced to the audience by one of the field staff who has spent the past twenty days with them in the woods. It was in watching Jason introduce and talk about his charges, hearing him explain what each had gone through and the personal development he had witnessed, that Rosemarie and I saw the development of confidence and sensitivity. And in it, we heard him say, *I know what I am doing, I love what I am doing, I have the compassion to lead and to help others. I will be okay.*

Such focus and compassion for others is the trademark of a true leader. I met one in Great Barrington, Massachusetts. PJ Haley is this amazing lady who works at the Eagleton School as the garden manager. Becky Mitchell, the school's director of marketing, invited me to visit after seeing my request for outdoor experiential facilities to visit in her National Association of Therapeutic Schools and Programs newsletter. Eagleton School is an experiential school dealing with children with autism, Asperger syndrome, and pervasive development disorder. Haley, as she prefers to be known, uses her garden to reach these students. Hopefully, in the very near future, she will take the time to write about her experiences and the powerful effects her philosophy has. For now, I am pleased that she agreed to allow me to include her and her program in my journey.

At first, some students are reluctant to tend the garden; she lets them sit and watch. But eventually, as they see the other children getting involved, they become involved too. As Haley explained,

> For me, an organic garden isn't only about not using chemicals; it's about becoming fully integrated from the inside out. They have to integrate the learning at their own pace, their own way.
>
> This particular kind of kid—they've got so much going on. You know, if you get abused the night before, beaten and left in the street or gone hungry, you're not going to care about the math lesson the next day, at all. But if you're free in the garden, who knows what might happen. You might become curious. The garden

is what we are. The whole process of the garden is what we are from seed to harvest. I've always said that I don't care what their problems are if I could have them for one season and they [could] experience the process of seed to harvest. Certain things will correct and certain things won't come to light for them for maybe ten years, but then it will sprout. Whatever it is, whatever they have been to have stimulated from being in that process, it's a way to stimulate an individual through them being in a process rather than trying to outline the process in the dimension on a blackboard and say, "Here, take it into your head or your eyes, but not your heart, not where you feel it." What I'm after is some independence, and through that they will eventually understand the interdependence of the whole deal going on and they will leave the program much more connected to themselves and the process and processes in general.

Can't Do It without Him

Bear Mountain has the highest mountaintop in Connecticut, but it is not the highest point in the state. That distinction belongs to the south slope about two hundred feet below the summit of Massachusetts's Mount Frissell, which marks the tri-state border of Connecticut, New York, and Massachusetts. I had gone to Bear Mountain with Betta Hanson, course director, to visit her crew, the Aviators, as they called themselves. It was one of her scheduled visits, and we were bringing mail, a new prescription for one of the crew, other stuff, and in general just checking in. I had stopped to take in the view when I heard a voice behind me saying, "My ankle's better today." I turned to see Jon K. coming toward me. He was short and stocky with a bandana over his head, and I remembered chatting with him during gear issue on day one. I asked him what had happened, and he proceeded to explain that he had hurt his left knee the day before and was favoring it when he slipped and hurt his right ankle. In a putting-the-cart-before-the-horse kind of way, I found myself backing up and asking about the knee. Everything was getting better, he reported, and he was glad because he didn't want anything to spoil his time.

I asked him what he liked so far, and he told me about the unscheduled cold water challenge. It seems the crew had stopped by a creek that was running really cold. On a dare, Jon and two others jumped in to see who could withstand the chill the longest. They didn't just stand in the creek; they sat in the water. "I told myself nobody was going to beat me," he boasted. And nobody did. Eventually, the instructors said thirty minutes was enough and that they needed to get back on the trail if the crew was going to make camp before dark. But the three wouldn't budge. Nobody wanted to be the first to leave, let alone appear to make the first move to leave, so a tie had to be negotiated and they agreed to exit the water together.

Now, if you are making a list of enjoyable things to do in the woods, bruising a knee, getting a swollen ankle, and sitting in cold-running mountain stream water for long periods of time are three things you probably wouldn't even consider for the list. But to hear Jon tell it, it was "the neatest stuff." And I learned all that from him because I was there. I didn't set out specifically to talk to Jon. In fact, as an invited onlooker, I was trying not to be in the way. But because of my presence, the moment developed. By choosing to be there, to listen, and to be in the moment, it happened.

Rosemarie says that children, all children—whether from her special ed behavioral class or "traditional" classes—want to talk. They want to be recognized. I guess I could have said something to Jon about the possibility that he could end up catching a cold or that he should be more careful when walking, or I could have called him out for being out in the woods with the bugs and all to begin with, but what would that solve? I mean, what was there to solve? Jon was having a good time, making friends, and finding out how much "pain and hardship" he could handle. He was finding out who he was and, yes, just being a kid. Not a bad day in paradise. Later, at graduation, Jon said, "My highlight of this expedition was the competition that I did with two others and the fact that *all three of us won.*" [author's emphasis]

Notice that, for Jon, this wasn't an ego victory but a shared victory. He was not egocentric. Part of his highlight was that all three had won. He proved his mettle and at the same time acknowledged that the other two had as well. All three were in the moment. Sometimes the moment lasts longer.

When you look back at the great male characters of TV from the late 1950s to the mid-1980s, two men stand out for a mannerism they both displayed—combing their hair. In fact, a song memorializes one of them and his need to groom: "Kookie, Kookie, Lend Me Your Comb." Neither man was the main character of his respective show. Kookie was a valet, and Fonzie was, well, he was The Fonz. So I am happy to say that the art of hair care is alive, well and attended to by Johnny S.

Howie, his social worker, brought Johnny and his dad, John, to the Wilderness School to drop Johnny off on day one of his twenty-day expedition. Howie mentioned that Johnny had some issues that he thought would best be handled in a nontraditional therapeutic wilderness setting as the traditional stuff didn't work for Johnny. Howie had seen other clients go through the twenty-day program and it had worked for them; he was hoping it would work for Johnny as well. Johnny was receptive to coming, and as Howie said, "You can't do it without him."

To be successful, each child needs to buy in and want to be there. The staff call it the challenge by choice. Johnny, in choosing to come, assumed the responsibility for his actions and his participation; there would be nobody else to blame.

One of the main activities on day one is gear issue. Before coming to the program, participants are given a list of what to bring and all has to be checked and then packed into their issued rucksacks. Their instructors and the logisticians help sort through everything to make sure everything needed is there, that it fits, and that the unapproved stuff, like cigarettes, are left behind. Johnny seemed to be having a problem with a new flashlight, so I stopped to lend a hand. As much as Johnny tried, he could not get it to light. As he tried, his frustration grew and everything became, in his words, cheap this and no good that. He had two flashlights and when he tried the second one, it shone. The problem was solved, and he was happy again—or at least it seemed so for the moment.

He was also part of the Aviators, so when I made it to Bear Mountain, I got to see him again. Rather, I got to see how much he was involved. The crew members see everything—they don't miss a trick—and so it became quickly apparent to the crew that Johnny cared for his hair. Johnny may be dirty, covered in mud, unwashed, wet, and cold, but his hair—ah, it was picture perfect. How did he do it? He became a persona all his own. Often when he entered a group or walked into camp, he wasn't recognized by way of a grunt of recognition, one of those guttural, one syllable sounds that guys so often use. Rather, it was clearly an imitation of Ed McMahon's famous *"Hereeee's Johnny!"* He did his thing, carried his load, and they accepted him. However, it was Nick K. who noticed that Johnny wasn't getting any mail from home.

The school encourages two way correspondence—from the folks back home to the students and from the students to the folks back home. The base camp staff tracks the mail to determine who is getting it and who is sending it. To those deficient on the receiving list, the staff will write encouraging letters to let them know that others do care. For a kid away from home, whether for the first time or not, think how it must feel to be left out, "forgotten." It bums a kid out and makes him feel excluded. What does it say about the parenting skills of those back home?

Nick and Johnny had never met before they arrived at the Wilderness School. On day one, they hit it off. Each had come from different parts of the state. Where Johnny was of medium height, a little chunky, and a bit quiet, maybe even shy, Nick was the "ladies man." Tall, blond, athletic, and trim, he had personality. So while on the surface the two didn't have much in common, they bonded.

Nick then did something that will be remembered and talked about at the Wilderness School for years to come. He asked his mom to write to Johnny. A kid with his own issues took the time to think about another member of his crew. Nick didn't just return something he found that Johnny had lost. He didn't just give him a hand with setting up a sleeping tarp. He took the time to realize Johnny's situation, thought about what he could do to help, and then acted on that plan by asking his brother to ask his mom to write to Johnny. And being the family that they were, Nick's grandmother started writing to Johnny as well. Some days, Johnny got more letters from Nick's folks than Nick did. The crew gave Nick some razzing over that, but they all knew and they all respected Nick for what he was doing.

As the twenty-day expedition was winding down, Johnny was concerned about where he would be living upon his return. It seems that his dad was very inconsistent as a parent, having issues of his own. As much as he tried, he didn't have a handle on what he should be doing, like writing to his son while at the Wilderness School.

Nick and his family made plans to stay close to Johnny and involve him whenever they could. If you asked Nick, it was no big deal, but to the staff it spoke volumes about Nick and his family. To Johnny, it meant a lot.

In his book *Anam Cara,* John O'Donohue writes that a "friend is one who awakens your life in order to free the wild possibilities within you." *Anam Cara* is Gaelic for "soul friend." That is Nick to Johnny; it might embarrass Nick a bit if you say it to his face, and he might not admit it. Maybe at his age, he may not see the importance of his relationship, but it is important nevertheless. In the frustration, turbulence, and uncertainty of Johnny's life, he found a friend and a family who offered calm, who offered support, and who offered Johnny a chance to see another side of life and be part of a supporting family.

Empathy is derived from the Greek word ἐμπάθεια (empatheia) but adapted from the German word *Einfühlung* (feeling into). It means "the ability to recognize and share feelings of another in such a way that one is driven to help." It requires a presence, like "putting one's self in another's mental shoes." One is listening for feelings and needs unique to that individual at that moment.

True empathy requires listening with the whole being: the hearing that is only in the ears is one thing. The hearing of understanding is another. But hearing of the spirit is not limited to any one faculty, to the ear, or to the mind. Hence it demands the emptiness of all the faculties. There is then a direct grasp of what is right there before you that can never be heard with the ear or understood with the mind.

—Chinese philosopher, Chuang Tzu

To be a good listener, Father Guntzelman writes,

> We need compassion and empathy…. I will detect unspoken aspects such as the emotions that vibrate in their voice. I'll note their body language, eye and facial expressions as well as the speed that accompanies their words.
>
> You become a mirror by reflecting back what is being said without attempting to one-up the speaker. You make no value judgments. It is important to remain nonjudgmental because then there is no need for forgiveness. By mirroring you restate in your own words the emotions you are hearing. It implies you not only understand and validate those feelings and that you are interested in helping. Empathy precedes compassion.

I don't know if I can pinpoint a date in my life when the importance of empathy in human relationships was ever really discussed or taught to me. I think it was a way of life demonstrated by my parents, and as such it percolated through them to us children. I definitely know that at age twenty-four, I did not have the awakening that Jason did after his second season at the Wilderness School, when he wrote,

The Things That Have Worked:
Fair, firm, friendly
Calm, cool, collected
Being straight, telling it like it is
Talk like you're in a conversation with them, not at them

These words were his way of reminding himself to create that positive, empathetic environment in which the students knew he cared and that he could be trusted, and in creating it, he was acknowledging their dignity. Jason had arrived at the doorstep of adult (higher-level) thinking as a kind and caring person, making a plan to be empathetic.

There is a story—maybe more urban legend than fact—that Dave Matthews, while on tour, has gone incognito as a person down on his luck and played his guitar for the public on a local street corner. The story goes that he opens his guitar case to accept donations from people passing by, but very few stop, as they are all unaware of whom he really is. Rumor has it that he video records these scenes with the intent of splicing this footage with concert footage of screaming and cheering fans, juxtaposing two very different responses as he plays the very same songs. Empathy forces us to look past what we expect to see, to step away from our own concerns, and listen, smile, and make eye contact with the person who is really there. As O'Donohue writes, such a soul friendship is "an act of recognition and belonging. Soul friendship cuts across all convention and categories. You are joined in an ancient and internal way with a friend of your soul."

These simple acts of looking directly into a person's eyes when speaking to that person, smiling at them, being non-judgmental while listening not only acknowledges and validates the other person's identity, but as Aaron said, is critical to being supportive.

We want to be as supportive as possible, we want to listen, we want to hear where kids are at, we want to anticipate maybe what's going on with the child, maybe they don't have the words for it, maybe you can guess for them: "I am guessing you're really nervous right now. I'm guessing because the van [is] leaving and you're really nervous about whether this is going to work or not. And that must be really scary." That guesswork is called empathy, and you're building language when you're talking to students that way. You're building their language and their ability to process in the world.

It works by having open conversations, leading with curiosity versus judgment. It's a practice of curiosity, being curious about the other person, showing a genuine concern for them. In asking them they open up. It is a willingness to try and hear and understand who a person is. If you're safe from judgment, you know judgment has consequences and if you are safe from that then you're gonna feel a lot more willing to disclose who you are, you'll be more willing to show vulnerabilities and share opinions. You get to explore things; you get to wonder about things. When you can share those and receive validation and hear discussion that's a very powerful thing. But that's a culture we create, we model, and we try to give the students the tools through our dedication 24/7 to that ethic.

Something Like an Equal Footing

The skillful wilderness educators have just that kind of empathy. The key is to put it into action quickly. When children with little or no outdoor skills or experiences leave home and enter the woods, they are out of their comfort zones, they are on edge, and they begin looking for direction and support. For some, there is little wiggle room as jail is often the only alternative. The sooner the educators can make that connection, the sooner the wilderness can do its thing. As a Wilderness School alumnus, stand-up comedian and team/leadership development guru Roy Charette said,

When they are out here, they realize they are in a setting that they don't understand. And so they have no choice but to be hypersensitive to what they're being told, how they're going to be safe, what to do and what not to do concerning bugs, in rain and setting up a tent, in cooking meals, and so unless they pay attention they're not going to be able to function properly and they realize that very quickly. They come out here and they say, "Okay, I am so uncomfortable and my anxiety is so high, I have to listen because the people who actually know what they're doing are the only ones who have control of this situation." It's because they feel out of control that this works so well.

Outdoor educators walk the walk, talk the talk, and *wow* the students with their skills while accepting the students by sharing that information and by placing the students on an equal footing. Everyone needs to paddle, everyone needs to rock climb, everyone needs to belay, and everyone needs to be on an equal footing. As she writes of her own growing up with an abusive mother in *Home to the Wilderness,* Sally Carrighar appreciated such acceptance, which she received not at home but at school.

> For any child, this first contact with adult minds on something like an equal footing can lead him into his own age of enlightenment. For me they were more, and I remember all those teachers with gratitude.

Has anyone with such a wealth of knowledge and "cool" skills ever given children with needs this much attention and support before? In the giving comes the trust; in taking the time to explain, instruct, and share the relationship that develops, the personal growth is allowed to happen. In the acceptance of that transfer is the beginning of the therapeutic relationship. Alone in the woods, away from home and the "security" it offers, away from the chaos and frustrations of everyday life, the student becomes open to new trust, new confidence, and new hope. The beginnings of a new perspective develop. As Jeremy Poore of Stone Mountain School in Asheville explained,

> The key, is to take everything away, bear everything, take the clothes, take the jewelry, PlayStation, cell phone—take everything away and what is left is the kid, how they act, how they try to fit in, what defense mechanisms they use. All these things become very apparent because not only are you out there in a simple but very complex environment, but you are quieter, with less distraction and wearing the same clothes.... You are just out there, and your interactions with your team leaders and teammates become the most important things of anything you do.

Beautiful in My Skin

This concept of friendship, whether it is the Celts' *anam cara* or the Buddhists' *kalyana-mitra* (noble friend), is not egocentric. O'Donohue writes,

> Intimacy is the secret law of the universe. The human journey is a continuous act of transfiguration. If approached in friendship, the unknown, the anonymous, the negative, and the threatening gradually yield their secret affinity to us.

One of our Anasazi Wilderness scholarship recipients wrote the following about her experience:

> I started to define myself through my actions, thinking I would never be any other way and I was only bound to let people down. That perception of who I was was

part of the reason I never let anyone get too close to me. What I didn't let myself remember was how much I used to do for other people when I was younger. I could barely even remember that person. Now I see that that person is still there. At Anasazi, I thought about my entire life from the very moments I was brought into this world. I thought about everything I had done from that point on and had a sudden realization that I was all of those things, not just the person I currently had decided to define myself as. I remembered my pure, innocent soul before I had even known what a line of cocaine was or what it felt like to let a boy touch me even though it made me sick. I caught a glimpse of that soul again that was still there, buried deep beneath it all. I felt it begin to surface day by day as I strayed further away from all the things that had clouded over its brightness for the past four years. My soul was finally feeling everything.

A successful therapeutic wilderness program is a program of change. Over the length of the expedition, the soul friend helps to create a new opportunity to grow and develop. Such new possibilities allow the old selves to be discarded. The same scholarship recipient wrote this following the completion of her Anasazi Wilderness expedition.

I knew I was making bad choices, but I almost thought it was out of my hands and that that was just the type of person I was so it was inevitable that I did the things I did. At Anasazi, I saw all of that in a different light. My attitude took a turn permanently after experiencing how essential it is [to have] a positive attitude in order to succeed. Even though I wasn't always in that state and I would lash out and become discouraged on the trail, a new outlook on every situation was something

I gained there and took home with me. Now, I have an overall heart at peace with what is going on around me even if it is hard or frightening. I now realize that I have the opportunity to step back and look at it however I choose.

It is, as Joseph Fletcher writes in *Situational Ethics*, "other regarding, yet secondarily, it may be self-regarding. But if the self is ever considered, it will be for the neighbor's sake, not for the self's." It is an attitudinal, altruistic kind of love that in the Judeo-Christian philosophy is called agape (uh-GAH-pay) love.

It is what, in Fletcher's words, "is due to all others, to our various and many neighbors when we 'know' them or not." Thus, an empathy based on agape "provides for the greatest amount of neighbor welfare for the largest number of neighbors possible." This is a much deeper sense of friendship than is in the two other and more emotional kinds of love recognized in our Judeo-Christian heritage. *Philia* is a Greek term meaning "a mutualistic friendship" wherein the intent of the benefit is shared equally by both parties, such as in a brotherhood and in a buddy relationship. *Eros*, on the other hand, refers to an affection that is both egotistic and romantic (sexual).

Agape refers to an unconditional, nonjudgmental, self-sacrificing, intentional, willful, and beneficial love for the good of others. Such a soul friend allows others to grow and open themselves to their own "wild possibilities" without concern for equal payback. In my interviews with the instructors, I found that the reality of getting back more than they gave, while never a goal, was always the result. Also, while they all hoped to make a difference, I sensed a surprise regarding their accomplishments in the degree of difference they make.

One Anasazi scholarship recipient summarized it eloquently.

I was immediately accepted and loved. Trail Walkers were like parents to me. They took care of me and loved me as if I was their own child. At first, I was so surprised that they could care so selflessly about someone they just met and without even knowing their past. They knew nothing about me or the things I had done that had harmed people or how I had harmed myself in so many ways; they didn't even ask. It's because at Anasazi, that doesn't matter. They see you for who you are. That acceptance gave me so much confidence in myself because I was reminded of my goodness and reality hit me that I wasn't stuck in the horrible things I was doing. I was truly seen, and even being dirty for weeks and in the most unattractive clothing I could ever imagine, I finally felt beautiful in my skin.

Grape Jelly Changed His Life

As a course director, Betta is the main link between her assigned group and the base camp. Course directors are responsible for coordinating the happenings in support of and in response to issues that arise while crews are on the course. To be proactive, she regularly visits the crew to see how thing are going. It was during such a visit that she overheard Gordo (name changed) expressing his dilemma. He hated strawberry jam, not just the brand the school used but all strawberry jam. He just didn't like it with his peanut butter or anything else for that matter. In the woods, there are not many alternatives, so he passed on the strawberry jam and ate his sandwich without any embellishment.

Betta's next trip to the group was also a resupply day. She had made a note and requested a swap—jelly instead of strawberry jam. So she called Gordo over as the cooks were unpacking the supplies and showed him the new jelly. He was ecstatic. Amazed that somebody had not only heard him but had actually listened and done something about it, he kept identifying Betta as his mother because nobody else but his mom had ever done anything for him. Somebody actually did something kind for him.

The streets harden children. Nothing is easy; nothing is safe. Just when children think it is safe to let down their guard, they get hurt. They learn to take care of themselves and not depend on anyone else. You see it at the Wilderness School on day one when they first assemble in the parking lot and play basketball while waiting for the other students to arrive. What would be a foul in a game of friends could be cause for battle in the street. One boy bumps another, and you see a sudden, momentary check between the boys. They need to make sure that things are cool and that this is a safe place.

Gordo came to realize that the school and the woods are safe places. He found that the staff was there to protect him. He could wear his slippers and not his running shoes. For maybe the first time in his life, he found a place outside the confines of his home where he could feel safe, where he didn't have to look over his shoulder, where he could relax, and where he could let down his guard. His life was changing, and he showed it by wearing his slippers at the base camp.

After his course was completed, Gordo returned to the institutional residence where he was living. As one of the older residents there, he was a leader who was looked up to and respected; he had influence with the students. Each year, a staff member from the Wilderness School visits the institution to explain the school's programs and hopefully identify interested students. Shannon saw Gordo on her way in, and they chatted about his course and how he had been doing since then. She invited him to sit in on her presentation and speak if he wished.

Shannon worked to get the class excited about the opportunities at the Wilderness School, but that day's group had a hard time focusing. The group didn't want to hear it—that is, until Gordo stood up. Turning to the students, he told them directly that they all should be going on a Wilderness School expedition. He told them how it had helped him, how he had met people who were kind, friendly, and willing to help him be a better person. Their leader was speaking, and they listened.

John F. Hunt

A Banner Pick

Empathy even finds its way into the business world. Mike Wolfe and Frank Fritz are antiques collectors, also known as pickers. In fact, they have a show on the History Channel called *American Pickers,* which I watch occasionally. It follows them as they search the back roads of this great country to find people who have collected stuff, maybe too much stuff, and now are willing to part with some of their collectibles. It was during such a trip that they stopped at Bushkill Park, a closed amusement park in Pennsylvania. The new owner was trying to bring the park back to life but had encountered a setback. Flood waters had destroyed the bumper car ride, and a considerable amount of work and money was needed before it could reopen.

Mike and Frank prowled the grounds as they always do, looking for what they call "rusty gold," treasure to them but trash to the owner. They found two old, broad, canvas circus signs. They were the kind of signs that circuses used years ago to announce their offering of extravaganzas. But the signs, though big, were worn, torn, faded, and littered with holes—not much to look at, but in the hands of the right person, they could be a treasure. They negotiated a price of four hundred dollars, shook hands, packed the signs into the van, and went looking for an expert to appraise the find.

They found him and a surprise in New York City. Once there, they unfurled the signs and hung them on an outside chain link fence to check them out. Based on the expert's appraisal, they were able to sell them online for ten thousand dollars! They pocketed the cash and headed back out for more pickin'. But along the way, they realized that before they could go searching for more deals, there was something they had to do. They went back to the closed park and gave half the money to the owner. American Pickers, American businessmen, American entrepreneurs—call them what you will; they were just doing their job. They didn't have to go back, but they did. They could have headed down a different road looking for more deals, more treasure, and more profits. Without a strong emotional intelligence to offset it, reason would have said, *Keep on driving. You're businessmen. You shook hands on it. Now it's yours.* But Mike and Frank talked it over, agreed that there was a greater need to be met; turned around; and headed back with a present for the park. They made a purchase, made a sale, and made a huge profit. Then they made a five thousand dollar donation, and more important, they also made a friend.

American Pickers, "A Banner Pick," *History Channel,* Season 2, 2010

There were three distinct episodes with Gordo—grape jelly, slippers, and institutional visit. I was given this information by three different staff members; each gave me a different part of the story. Yes, Betta's initiative to get him some grape jelly started the ball rolling, but if the field staff hadn't been on their game, if they hadn't been open, if they hadn't met him in the moment for those twenty days, and if they hadn't given him that chance to believe in himself, it all would have gone to waste. The subsequent interactions of each staff member were as important, if not more important, than the first staff interaction with Gordo, as well as all students.

Empathy can even find its way into being "cool." When Jason was about fourteen, he visited Andy Tomlinson, a high school buddy, at his family's cottage in Harbor Springs, Michigan. Jason suggested that Andy's younger cousins be included in their activities, so when they biked into town to get their daily dose of Michigan fudge and ice cream, it wasn't just the two cool high school dudes but a gang of happy kids. As Marsha, Andy's mom, wrote, "He was such a gentle leader but firm in his beliefs." Empathy—he had a way of making others feel at home around him.

The Quiet Mind, the Smart Heart

Balance of Influence

Life has been likened to a bottle of muddy water; as long as it is kept in motion, it is impossible to see anything but swirling particles of mud. Given time to rest, however, the mud settles and the water becomes clearer. Given time to rest, we gain a different perspective of ourselves and life in general. A life that is too busy for "time out" is merely a form of existing—not living.

—*Year of Grace: A Daily Companion*, The Sacre Coeur Center for Healing and Spirituality

Trust me, putting your job ahead of your heart is a mistake. Risking our hearts is why we are alive. The last thing you want to do is to look back on your life and wonder, if only.

Mike Royce, *Castle*, 2011

I've always admired Jason's spiritual connection with the outdoors. He always got something extra, that sense of completeness and joy, out of simply being with nature. I have always envied that. In his world of unknown goals and destinations, the one constant in Jason's life was obvious.

—Steve Scheper, Turpin High School buddy, e-mail, November 15, 2001

As I met with and interviewed those who work in outdoor experiential education, I began to sense that our humanity has been pulled apart in two directions. One part has been pushed aside at the expense of personal growth and development. Our ability to think and reason, as best exemplified by the studies of mathematics and science, makes us different from all other creatures. Over time, this ability has become the overriding character of and driving force in our culture. Unfortunately, this has reduced us to being virtually one dimensional, and in the process we are diminished. This struggle has made life too flat, with no vertical or added dimension. Yet it is as important to human development today as it has ever been. It is the part of our humanity that best reaches those in need and is therefore the part that the wilderness educator draws from and awakens to achieve growth. Maintaining the proper balance between heart (emotions/art) and mind (reason/science) has been a constant and, some would say, losing challenge throughout the history of Western civilization.

In their article "Notes from the Margins," Anthony Howard, M.S., and Thecla Helmbrecht Howard, EdD (aka Mr. H. and Dr. T.), cofounders of Sheltered Risks Inc., write that the natural world teaches us about diversity, which is critically important for our creativity. It is our ability to create that allows us to evolve.

> The most creative places in the natural world are found in the margins that exist between the larger biological systems. For instance, the wetlands that exist between the ocean and the land are fertile crucibles whose extraordinary biodiversity leads to natural evolutions.... It's in that 'gooey-gooeyness' that we develop direction, order and new life.

Chet Raymo, PhD (professor emeritus at Stonehill College, my alma mater), in *Skeptics and True Believers* (and *Honey in the Stone*) uses the metaphor of knowledge being an island in an infinite sea of the unknown. He writes that what is known as truth and fact, what we call knowledge, is an island or solid ground. Scientists stand with one foot on solid ground and one foot in the water that's lapping at the shore, searching for truths in the wetlands of the natural world. Once they find a new truth, something that can be proven, tested, and verified, it gets added to the shoreline, expanding it. Sometimes what has been affirmed as truth gets tossed back into the sea to be tested again as newer truths prove the old one false. It gets replaced, and the island enlarges.

There have been times in my life when I have had one foot in the water, searching for truths in my life. When I was in second grade, my family and a group of doctors were concerned that I might die if my hemorrhaging of blood did not stop. St. Raphael's chaplain administered last rites; I was an island in the unknown.

Eventually, the bleeding just stopped. I had transfusions and consumed the worst-tasting "milkshakes" known to man for the battery of X-rays and tests I would undergo. The cause was never confirmed.

It wasn't until my senior year in college that I was diagnosed with an ulcer, and a consensus was drawn on the probability that I had had a bleeding ulcer in second grade. In the early 1950s, ulcers were an adult ailment blamed on job stress, drinking alcohol, and bad, greasy, or spicy diets. Children weren't considered to be under stress, so why test an eight-year-old for ulcers? Today, we know better; stress is not the cause.

Part of the shoreline, part of what we know as fact, has been thrown back and reshaped because today we know that it is not adult stress causing ulcers but a bacterium (helicobacter pylori) that lies dormant in a person's stomach lining and for some reason (still unknown) awakens to cause havoc for some while not for others. Even the dietary restrictions seem to have been altered over the years. Whereas milk was once prescribed, it is now on the "Avoid" list along with alcohol, coffee, spicy foods, and large meals. Now the suggestion is to eat multiple small meals.

There was actually a time when, before a party, I would drink some milk to coat my stomach. It was a bit of a trade-off: milk for the ulcer, scotch for me. One night as I was downing a glass of milk, a friend who was in medical school walked in and launched into a

The Grandeur of the Grand Details

Science contains wonderment within its cold reasoning. Consider deoxyribonucleic acid, or DNA, as it is more commonly called. When I was in high school, Coach Joe B. taught us about the X and Y chromosomes as we generated matrices of their various combinations. Years later, the DNA molecule was discovered as making up those chromosomes. That discovery opened a new area of research and study. Of all the molecules on this planet, DNA is by far the most amazing. Of the human body's ten thousand trillion cells, 99.999 percent contain a complete set of our make-up: tall, short, skinny, fat, bald, wavy hair, left-handed, or right-handed. It is all there in a code that spans 3.2 billion letters. The number of possibilities would be written as a 1 followed by three billion zeros—too long to write out in this book. This is incredible enough, but there is more.

Each cell contains twin strands about three feet in length, which means that about twenty millions kilometers of this stuff is bundled up inside each one of us, more than enough to stretch to the moon and back dozens of times. You don't see it and you don't feel it, but it is there.

Each DNA strand is three nanometers in diameter (three billionths of a meter). A typical cell is fifteen micrometers in diameter (fifteen millionths of a meter). Thus, each strand, because it has less volume, fits into the cell quite easily. We also know that at a specific time in the cell's existence, the DNA strand will replicate itself just that once. And all of this is accomplished by only 2 percent of the DNA, as the rest is called junk DNA, so named because no one knew the purpose or function for it. That is, no one knew until recently, when it was proposed that the junk DNA is actually the "middle-management team" of life. The junk tells the rest of the DNA what to do, when to do it, and how to function.

Whereas science previously focused on controlling or manipulating the individual genes, it must now first understand and then learn how to deal with these middle managers as well. Thus, the shoreline gets larger and the ocean expands as well. In the explanation is the miracle.

References:

Bryson, Bill. *A Short History of Nearly Everything.* New York: Broadway Books, 2003.

Raymo, Chet. *Skeptics and True Believers.* New York: Walker and Company, 1998.

"Researchers Find 'Junk' DNA Key to Health and Illness," *The Cincinnati Enquirer,* Sept. 5, 2012.

long discourse on how my veins would be closed by calcium buildup. He never asked how much milk I drank a day or what my daily diet was; he just fired away. Well, I do admit that even today, the scotch does taste better without the milk.

Thus, the island gets bigger, and the shoreline expands. But here is the really interesting part: the ocean never gets smaller! Every discovery expands what we know but also expands what we do not know even more. It opens new areas of inquiry and new mysteries. In short, there are things we don't even know we don't know—and we may never know.

We live in an amazingly enchanted world but fall short of understanding and appreciating its wonder due to the diminished role played by our hearts with its emotions, art, and spirituality. As Antoine de Saint-Exupery wrote, "It is only with the heart that one can see rightly; what is essential is invisible to the eye."

It is in the wilderness, the natural setting, that we begin to reconnect with and strengthen that part of our humanity.

"The Unsilent Silence"

Spirituality is best nurtured in the silences around us and the silences within us. And one of the best ways to do this is to shut off the sources of the noise that is all around us in our culture and simply be quiet. And one of the best organized ways in the Department of Juvenile Justice, in North Carolina, where that happens is the Woodson Wilderness Challenge, where there are prolonged hours of silence with only the wind blowing and the silence of one another's presence. Speaking theologically and magisterially, it is in the silence that I believe we experience the presence of God.

—Robert Randolph, clinician chaplain, North Carolina
Department of Juvenile Justice, interview, April 22, 2010

The silence of the wilderness draws us back into our inner selves, into our spiritual selves. In that silence, the mind quiets; the heart takes control. Our senses are no longer overcharged, and we begin to hear things—new things, like what Jerry's campers heard—that were there all the time. We also begin to learn more about ourselves because the silence allows fears, anxiety, and emotions to come out and to be addressed.

It is silence that we fear. Blaise Pascal, famed philosopher, scientist, mathematician, and writer, wrote that it was not the vastness of the universe but "the eternal silence of the infinite spaces [that] terrifies me." It wasn't the size of the universe that bothered him but that it could be and was so silent.

The stillness of the woods, the stillness of the night, reminds us of our "human solitude," and that frightens us. We are masters of avoiding who we are and the confrontation about what is going on in the depths of our being.

There is an old saying that claims that the cure for loneliness is solitude. When we no longer fear solitude, we realize that we are not alone. We find that we are in a presence that is neither stressful nor boring.

The author Pico Iyer wrote,

> In silence, we often say we can hear ourselves think; but what is truer to say is that in silence we can hear ourselves not think, and so sink below ourselves into a place far deeper than mere thought allows. In silence, we might better say, we can hear someone else think.

I remember a radio show host once talking about the evils of silence or "dead air time" in his business. It seems that he had turned the in-house speakers off so he could talk to a caller and forgot the time. The music ended and was followed by pure silence; it was the ultimate sin in broadcasting. Somebody paid for that time, and it couldn't be wasted on silence. Noise is our security blanket.

The call of nature is the call to enjoy her silence. It is a call to leave the noise, chatter, and distractions of everyday life behind. It is a call to an awe-inspiring place surrounded by the sounds of silence.

However, the silence of the wilderness is not all that silent. I remember waking one morning to the sounds of what seemed to be two hawks dive-bombing the lake just outside my tent. I had stayed the night alongside the lake at Woodson's base camp. At first I thought that I was dreaming, but then I realized that the sounds were real and I was missing an extraordinary aerial show. By the time I got the tent flaps and, for that matter, my eyes opened, the hawks were gone. Their screeches were something I had never heard before or since.

In the wilds of Alaska, Steve Prysunka hears a pod of whales singing a song that has been passed down through the ages and will be picked up and carried by other whales. For us everywhere, just like for Steve's children in Alaska as well as for Jerry's youth in Georgia, there are more sounds to hear if we only stop and tune in. Water cascading over rocks, the wind rushing through the trees, coyotes howling at night—sounds are everywhere in what Chet Raymo calls the "unsilent silence."

It involves more of a tuning out than a tuning in. We tune out the normal sounds of everyday life—cars, school bells, music, phones, and electronic games. The endless stream of chatter that is everywhere around us that we are conditioned to expect needs to be tuned out. Then, once the mind is quiet, we can hear the other world.

Sterling Wharton (Outward Bound New York City instructor) told me that, oftentimes, a student would say, "I never slept where there's no noise. I'm always used to hearing cars honking or the subway passing overhead. I'm not used to being in the outdoors where it's totally quiet."

There comes a point when the fears begin to subside the longer we are in the woods, when what scares us loses its impact, and when we begin to realize that we can survive. It happens because the perceived risk is its own fiction. What first appears scary isn't. To paraphrase Willi Unsoeld, we pass from adversity to become joined to the woods.

As guides and guardians, using the ethics that prioritize the child's safety first, the staff allows the child the experience of finding him- or herself while in a safe, trusting environment. It's as Roy Charette (Wilderness School alumnus and former field educator and program coordinator, as well as CEO of TrainingPath) explained.

> I think one of the things that allows the environment to work in working with teenagers is that it's uncomfortable. Because, if the students are in comfortable setting, then they will attempt to control that setting based on their previous experiences with home and community.

When Marc Sacks spoke of his realization of "sitting in front of a profound teacher," he was speaking of transcendence; it was his "aha moment." Beyond the physical matter—the trees, rocks, plants, and flowers—around him, there was an ancient power "beyond human wisdom" that was there to teach him, to help him grow. He couldn't put his finger on it, but he knew he needed to be outdoors to learn more. It took him many years of living with nature, including some messy emotional breakdowns during highly charged campfire discussions, but in those moments of discomfort, in the darkest of the night, and in the dancing of the flames, he found his strengths. Highly regarded and respected for his skills as an outdoor educator, he continues to work in the outdoors.

Code of Behavior

Spirituality adds dimension. It adds verticality; it adds fullness to our reductionist culture. As Father Tom Kreidler said over lunch one day,

> It's part lifestyle, part attitude; it's a totality that puts together the spiritual with the temporal. And the

operationalization of that is that it's not always about us. It is how we lead our lives and the reference points we have within that.

In her book *Home to the Wilderness*, Sally Carrighar expresses her belief that the wilderness touches on these reference points when she writes that there is a certain "integrity—'reliable adherence to a code of behavior.'" She writes that all the creatures of the woods acted so that the code was not broken. They knew and could depend that all would act accordingly. They are the surviving species because they followed the ways that worked. The only question mark was man; he can and does break the code.

Have you ever watched a flock of birds in flight? Have you ever seen a flock of birds alight on electrical wires or land on a roof ridge? In all those sudden turns and maneuvers, have you ever seen birds collide? I haven't. How do all those birds know what will happen next, instantaneously? Could we put that many humans in cars in an open space and expect zero accidents?

Carrighar writes,

> Once the wilderness code was ours. Once we were a species that survived in a wild community, among our animal neighbors, because our species too was one of the morally fittest. And when we became more human, when we emerged into the state of cerebral thought and language, so that we could find words for our moral standards, we did not have to look further for them than our biological background, our inherited customs and usages. Even before we had any religious feeling we must've been moral people. Only later would we have attached those standards, those wilderness values, to our dawning religious consciousness.

In different parts of the world, the religious impulse takes on different forms, but almost everywhere the long-known social rules are incorporated. For many centuries, these religions have provided a code of behavior that is very similar to the wilderness code. Now we in the West seem to be losing our willingness to follow religion's guidance. Is the biological behavior still in our genes?

Willi Unsoeld was a member of the first American team to scale Mount Everest, and he did it on the peak's west ridge, a route that had never been done before, has not been done since, and may never be repeated. His philosophy can best be explained by his hunger for experiencing the sacred in nature. In "The Spiritual Values of Wilderness," he writes, "For primitive man, things were alive or infused with life, were viewed religiously as of some ultimate worth. With modern man we've lost this, this religious view of nature."

Building on Rudolph Otto's *The Idea of the Holy,* Unsoeld also wrote,

> There has never been a sacred anything that lacked mystery. The mysteriousness of it is the sense of something more, of a hiddenness beyond which you can't go.... When you step into the wilderness ... there is a mystery in nature which I think is one of its great attractions for us. Then add the complexity of a problem in nature to resolve and you can learn to believe in yourself. There is the hiddenness of organic growth, of how a seed decides to be an oak tree. No matter how much reference we have to the genetic coding of RNA, DNA, somehow it doesn't come out totally explained.... I am, of course, greatly impressed with the mystery of mountaineering.... So you go a little farther and you never know until finally you reach the summit and then you know. Except, how about getting down? So there is a continual mystery that I see as directly correlative to the mystery of the sacred.
>
> The sacred has never been anything else.... You don't mess with the sacred. Allied with this power is

a certain fear. We used to talk about a fear of God; ...
I mean the kind of existential fear, the fear of radical
dissolution, of being nullified by the overpoweringness
of the sacred.

He continues by saying that the mountains and the wilderness
hold a sense of "overwhelmingness" based on their "raw power." Man
is attracted by a fascination in their mystery and power. From this
comes a sense of unity with one's surroundings, which leads to "a loss
of a sense of self." This loss builds up to "a sense of totality. A sense
of all." And finally joy.

Deep down at the very core beyond question, beyond
analysis, beyond words, it's pure joy.... You go to nature
for an experience of the sacred. ... to re-establish your
contact with the core of things ... in order to enable
you to come back into the world of man and operate
more effectively.

It is interesting to note that another word for *reestablish* is
reconnect, which comes from the Latin *re-ligare,* the origin for the
word *religion*. In short, religion is the reconnecting with and respect
for what is sacred.

Rudy Brooks is the bureau chief of prevention for the State of
Connecticut's Department of Children and Families. He believes that
the use of the wilderness saves lives, as well as saves his department
and the state money by preventing youth from entering the system.
He came to that conclusion based on his own personal experience.
Over his years as an administrator, he has participated in many
executive and leadership developmental programs. He remembers
an Outward Bound Course in Colorado where he climbed Mount
Massive (elevation 14,421 feet).

That mountain took everything out of you going up
and coming down. I mean, it took every ounce of

physical and emotional strength you had. And it was such a, almost like, a religious experience when you shared that with—I think there were twenty of us in the course.... We spent a week out there, we got up every day, we ran, we jumped in brooks and the icy baths; we ate well with lots of grain and fiber. It was just a great experience.

And you look at the mountain and then you say, "I'll never be able to do it." But once you do it, it's like, "I can't believe I did that. I didn't believe I had that much in me to do it."

And so when you see kids trying ropes courses or trying to get over that wall or doing things where they have to challenge themselves both physically and emotionally and challenge themselves to work together, once they accomplish it and you just see it in them, you see it in their expressions, in their eyes, as you see it in how they feel about themselves to have been able to work together to accomplish something, it's just a wonderful experience.... Kids can only benefit from it; families can only benefit from it.

If you think about it, those are powerful words from a modern-day bureaucrat! At a time when government is imploding under the burden of special interests and political correctness, it is reassuring to find someone who is not afraid to recognize the sacred and the power of the sacred to help him achieve his mission of saving children before it is too late.

Sandy Newes, PhD, discusses grounding a sense of self to the wilderness.

I believe boundaries get enmeshed between people, and they can't unplug anymore because they don't have a solid sense of self and they don't have any innate ability to ground.... And that may well be what wilderness does better than anything else.... [It] allows you to be more firm in that boundary when you are with other people, to be able to separate yours from theirs and to be able to know what your gut is telling you. If you don't have a gut to trust, how are you really going to know ... what is or isn't a healthy decision?

Freud wrote, "Everywhere I go I find a poet has been there before me." What the poets, the mystics, and the ancient peoples knew is what Western culture dismisses—that heart and mind, feeling and thinking work together and that living is not reduced to just thought and reason. There is more to be gained by combining the two because, in so doing, the whole human being, the whole human self, is present. Have you ever noticed that many people who are considered experts in one field are often the dumbest in general? What we laugh off as the absent-minded professor stereotype is actually a mind divorced of common sense, unable to function beyond the focus of their expertise. Daniel Goleman, in his book *Emotional Intelligence,* identified the condition and named a chapter discussing it "When Smart Is Dumb."

Blood on the Floor

Graham Brown, in his online review of emotional intelligence, writes, "Once learning is embedded in the heart, as well as the head, the lesson is converted to wisdom. It is common knowledge that we learn much more easily subjects for which we have a passion."

To prove that very point, Dr. T asked me to think about an episode that I could clearly recall from years past, like in my childhood. The fact that I could remember something that far back and not something more recent explained how passion aids in our ability to learn. Think about it yourself for a minute. Pick an episode from your youth that you can still vividly recall. This was my response.

One Sunday morning when I was in second grade, I woke up with a terrible pain in my abdomen. I went to the bathroom and proceeded to vomit blood, a lot of it. My aunt Doris, who was a nurse and lived above us, was summoned. The doctor was called, and he directed us to meet him at the hospital. So I was bundled into my dad's first car and off we went straight up Chapel Street to St. Raphael's Hospital and its emergency entrance ramp off Sherman Avenue.

Once in the emergency room, I was the center of activity; people poked to test the pain's sensitivity, pricked my fingers for blood to test—in short, they did a great job of adding to the discomfort. It was while they were preparing to hang the transfusion bottle on the mobile stand that the bottle fell. It was glass and it broke, spilling blood all over the floor and everybody's shoes. I remember that as if it were yesterday.

We then discussed how amazing it was that I could remember something so far back in such vivid detail but not remember more recent events as well. It is because, through that entire hospital experience, I was wired, I was alert, and all my senses were tracking. I was totally involved; my senses and my emotions were running the show. My emotions were then and are now the foundation of my learning. They organize my mind. Dr. T explained further.

> They are the organizing premise of your mind. So if you have experiences that get the juices flowing and if you have experiences that trigger things, you will have memories. You will have a rich gooey, gooey-ness about you that will create love and generatively. But those emotions are what do it. So you want to have kids at risk or people at the edge, out of control a little bit, not always in control because that's when the learning happens.

In the chapter "Leading from the Heart," I described how Anna resolved a standoff between herself and a student by speaking Spanish. I used that example to show that working on the fly, improvising when the textbooks fail to specify a procedure, is a characteristic of wilderness educators. It is based on what Jason Michaels of Warren Wilson College called "being emotionally intelligent." It is an accumulation of what Goleman calls "other characteristics." It's not reflective of a person's IQ but is a very important "key set of abilities such as being able to motivate one's own self and persist in the face of frustration; to control impulse and delay gratification; to regulate one's moods and keep distress from swamping the ability to think; to empathize and to hope."

When I attended the AEE's 2010 Best Practices Conference, Ed Spaulding of Northland Adventure explained that "changing one's life will change one's thinking quicker and better than changing one's thinking in order to change one's life."

Sometimes the mind needs to be quiet so the heart can be smart.

Five *As* and One *T*

Trauma and Other Causes of Behavioral Dysfunction

It's our nature to dance on the edge of chaos. If there was no chaos, we would make it or find it.... Because if there was certainty and there was predictability and everything was all cut and dried, you'd be bored out of your gourds.... We are looking always for the new thing; we're always looking for ways to dance on the edge of chaos.... Rightness and wrongness become the borderlines.
—*Meet the Real Creator–You*, Fred Alan Wolf, PhD (Dr. Quantum)

I was just attending the big outdoor trade show in Salt Lake. I was talking business (yeah, right) with a retail buyer who mentioned that he worked at Gray Wolf Ranch (WA) serving at-risk youth.... Warren Wilson College came up, and his eyes got real big. He said, "Yeah, yeah, I worked with this awesome guy from there. You may know him ... Jay Hunt? We worked together in Montana. Then he stayed with my wife and I when he got sick in Yosemite."

I smiled because the mere mention of [Jason's] name got this guy elated. We sat down, and I explained all the recent events to him. He was obviously shocked; he asked me to hug him, and then we just swapped stories. He came back by several times during the show and asked that I pass his e-mail [address] on to you.... He is Steve Sutorious real nice guy with a mutual appreciation for the finer human beings who pass through this world. Stay in touch.

—Tyler Stracker, college and climbing
buddy, e-mail, February 10, 2003

There are two points that strike me about Tyler's e-mail. First, I think it refers to the depth of camaraderie, bonding that happens from working together for a relatively short but intense time period (in this instance twenty-one days) in the woods. Second, it refers to something that I have never experienced in my business career.

In my earlier life as a sales rep, I attended many trade shows over the thirty-eight years prior to retiring in 2010. I attended shows held by my customers in their attempts to reach out to their customer base in the areas of hardware, paint, and locksmith services. I attended the extremely large and very international National Hardware Show in Chicago and followed it to Las Vegas, chasing both my customers as well as my factories. I have practically worn out shoes scooting among the three sites for Auto Week in Las Vegas. There have been housewares shows, paint shows, and home center shows as well as locksmith, power tools, and rental yard shows that I attended multiple times over those years. I met many people along the way, saw numerous product demonstrations, and rotated through too many sales meetings. I would stand in a booth and try to talk as folks came down the aisle. Some would stop in; some would walk on by. When they stopped, I would talk—some would listen, some wouldn't want to hear a pitch, some would ask a specific question, and almost all followed the "Buyer's Rule of Thumb": budget the time or the money spent in a booth and then move on!

Oh, I chatted and joked with those who stopped, and I occasionally even remembered them at another booth or at the next show. But I never witnessed such a scene as Tyler described above. I never experienced or witnessed two adult professionals create such a bond. I never saw two men emotionally hug in a booth at a trade show. As I read the e-mail, I wondered what it was about Jason, what connection he made, that even eighteen months later, the experience of working with Jason for a brief twenty-one days had produced such a truly deep and emotional response. It tells us all how well he connected deeply with the people he met along the way.

The Matchmakers

My mother called me one Sunday afternoon after she had had a chat with her pastor. He had noticed us when I took her to church the previous Sunday and wanted to know who I was. After she explained that I was single, had a job, and lived on the other side of town with some buddies, he suggested that they combine forces and get his friends' daughter and me together. So I called Father and agreed to an introduction the following Friday night at St. Brenden's rectory.

When I arrived, she was already there, and we got a chance to visit with Father and take a tour of the rectory. It seems he was a former Marine and, for a hobby, had a shooting range in the rectory's basement. He had some cool guns and was quite skilled at their use, as evidenced by the targets lying about. It was decided that the young lady and I would go out for pizza for our first date, and we left Father at the range—ah, at the rectory.

Our dating ended before it began one fateful afternoon. We found ourselves looking into each other's eyes when, suddenly, my entire body went into fright overload. Flashing across my mind was the good Father, in his shooting range "vestments" of shooting vest, earplugs, and shooting glasses, smiling while sighting me in the crosshairs of his Colt .45 revolver. First fright and then flight took over. Jumping up, I grabbed for the door to leave, only to walk into the living room closet! Now I was in a sheer panic as I found the real front door and headed for my car. I think I muttered something about just remembering I needed to be somewhere else, a family event or something. Whatever it was, it wasn't coherent. And that is just the physical/electrical side; that doesn't even consider what my Catholic upbringing was driving through my conscience over the matter.

Looking back on it some forty years later, it's pretty funny. But it does show how much our emotional brain does control our lives. Normally our senses, running on autopilot, feed the sensory thalamus with whatever information they pick up by way of sight, smell, feel, taste, and sound. From there the information is sent via separate pathways to the amygdala, which controls our emotions; the hippocampus, which acts as our database; and, finally, to the cortex, the judgment center. If it wasn't for the cortex, we wouldn't be human. We would be—well, let's not go into that as the apes might get insulted. It's the reason we can think and reason. It collects all the data, reasons, evaluates, and makes decisions. It's a top-heavy brain but has served us well for years as it continues to simultaneously receive input from different sources. Science is constantly investigating how the wiring of this system works as every new experience creates a new wiring pattern built upon all previous experiences.

When the amygdala receives sensory experiences, it tags them with emotions and passes that information to the hippocampus, which, in turn, feeds the cortex along with the information sent from the sensory thalamus. Everything is running just as smoothly as silk—except for when the amygdala determines that a threat, danger, or trouble is happening. Then the amygdala short-circuits the system and, in effect, takes over. The pathway between the thalamus and the amygdala becomes a superhighway, while the pathways feeding the hippocampus and the cortex get shunted or hijacked. In an incredibly short length of time, the amygdala has the body on emotional high alert even before the cortex can make a decision. The word *emotion* is based on the Latin *emovere,* which means "to move out." That is what the amygdala does; it moves the body. It gets the blood pumping to the legs to facilitate running, adrenaline is produced so the body is able to perform unusually hard tasks, the body becomes edgy and ready for whatever is coming, and the pupils enlarge for improved vision. Have you ever experienced an adrenaline rush? All this is done before the cortex's frontal lobes have analyzed what is happening. It's an amazing system that has preserved our species since before we stood erect. It places the amygdala at the forefront of our defenses.

Sometimes it goes into overload and isn't able to stabilize on its own. Children who are traumatized by their experiences at home, on the street, in school, or in life in general often become hardwired a certain way so that they, like Gordo, are always on edge, always on guard, always looking, always checking. Or the child may become just the opposite—so hardened that nothing moves him. In the first child, just the slightest disturbance can cause him to erupt, while in the second, not even a building falling down next to him can get a reaction.

A child traumatized by life experiences doesn't carry visible trauma scars. You don't see a scar from mental trauma abuse like you do the scar of a knife battle. They are there but run deeper. You know that they exist only after the fact, when you piece together the pattern of the acting out, the withdrawal, the sudden drop in school performance, the change in "friends," as well as a host of other social and psychological traits that combine to build the child's defensive wall.

For Gordo, it meant always wearing his sneakers so that he could run, so that he was always at the ready and able to escape. If he were playing basketball and unintentionally bumped into a player he did not know, there would be a momentary pause and a stolen look at the other player to make sure the bump would not turn into a fight and that everyone was "cool." Every time he left his parental home, he was unable to relax. So it was a truly major turning point when he realized that he could wear his house slippers in base camp, in the woods. Even though he was looked up to and followed by the other members of his transition home, he was always on guard there. The trust and safety he felt in and with the Wilderness School expedition crew allowed him to be himself.

Emotional trauma can result from a single event, like the death of a parent, or from a continuum of adverse experiences that beat one down. In either scenario, the brain stores the event in detail to be prepared to act appropriately in future events. It hardwires itself to know what to do in the future. While at first glance, my episode with the good pastor may seem to the reader as an overreaction, there is more to the story. In fact, there are two additional episodes that provide some history.

For several years prior to that experience, I worked for an insurance company that had its local office in a medical arts building that stood across from downtown New Haven, separated by the Oak Street Connector (Route 34). Our first-floor offices had these huge window walls that gave us views across the connector and into the city beyond the Knights of Columbus Headquarters or into a small shopping center and the beginnings of the Yale–New Haven Hospital complex with its many buildings. The tower stood on its own block and at the foot of a changing community. It was during a sales meeting that we became distracted by a woman's screams. Looking into the parking lot, we saw a young lad dressed in a kelly green tam-o'-shanter and brown leather jacket snatch a purse and run across the parking lot directly in front of us. Many of us immediately left the meeting to help. But our problem was that to get into the parking lot, we first had to go into the lobby and then out the main doors. We had no direct exits. By the time we got into the lobby, the victim was coming inside emotionally distraught and crying about how men in the building just watched but did not help. While we wanted to help, we were stymied by the building's layout. At the moment it was best to be merely supportive.

A few weeks later, I walked over to the bank in the small shopping center across the street from the office. Its parking lot had a line of cars parked along the perimeter and then a double line of cars, parked end to end in the middle, before getting to the building itself. As I approached the double line of cars, I noticed the bank door opening, and a person clad in a green cap and leather jacket flashed out the door and headed into the parking lot to my right. *Looked familiar,* I thought. Then the bank door opened again, and the head teller yelled something about stopping the runner as he had just robbed the bank. Thinking it was the purse snatcher and maybe there was a chance for payback, I quickly turned to head him off as he exited the double line of cars. That's when it turned ugly. Yes, he was dressed just like the purse snatcher, but he was taller—much taller. The purse snatcher had not turned to bank robbing; it was somebody else. That much I noticed as I angled to meet him. But what really got my attention was when he turned, looked at me, and said, "I got a gun." He then proceeded to draw from his jacket pocket a small pistol. Oh, this was not the purse snatcher! He kept running, and I opted to let the police handle it. Fortunately, my description of him, along with others from the bank's staff, and some really smart police work that comes with knowing the streets allowed the police to catch him the next day in another part of town with the money, the gun, and wearing the same clothes. Being on the wrong end of a gun was a picture that got filed away in my brain, and I guess I became sensitized to that set of circumstances. It would wait, in suspense, until the danger presented itself again while I, in the meantime, went on with the rest of my life.

But what about children who are constantly under siege? How do they cope when it is their very nature to absorb all that is going on around them? That's how we humans learn, by absorption. Watch a young baby grab, hold, and then put things into its mouth. It is using all of its senses to learn. As the child gets older, it begins to focus better by sight, sound, and touch. It can make connections without orally checking objects out. The learning process never stops. If overloaded, and lacking the necessary maturity to make the proper judgments and the ability to properly handle, process, and file away each event, the underdeveloped brain shuts down. It hardwires itself into a defensive shell and basically stops developing. It's a result of trauma, pure and simple.

In short, as Sandy Newes wrote, "Trauma is relative to each individual's life circumstances. Being under siege is all relative to the environment a child lives in; i.e., opening up, thinking about being constantly yelled at or inconsistently being shown love, as opposed to be shot at."

What is so hard to understand about trauma is that the same event can produce totally different results in different victims. The first variable is whether the victims understand the trauma and what it means. Second, the victims are influenced by how those around them react to the trauma; they are impacted by their families' and friends' responses. A victim being told to "stand tall and tough it out" may respond very differently from a victim who is surrounded by people who are frantically yelling and crying. In the first instance, the victim may remain calm, while in the second instance, the victim may collapse under the pressure from those who should be supportive.

Even though, on the scale of physical violence, the first victim may have suffered a more severe and brutal attack, the disparity in the observed degree of violence is irrelevant. Whether hurt by abandonment, abuse, addiction, or apathy, an objective intensity scale reading is irrelevant. The effects are determined by how the victims understand the events and how those around them react.

I see how the trauma from the loss of Jason has affected me in two activities that I have enjoyed—music and skiing. I have always enjoyed singing and whistling, even making up my own lyrics and tunes—not that I have a voice of any merit; it's just that I enjoy opening my mouth and singing on my own or following a tune that I hear. After Jason died, something happened. I still enjoy singing, but I have lost my volume in church. Whether I'm at my parish church or visiting another, I can barely hear my singing. If I'm walking down a street, no problem, and whistling through an office building is easy. But when I attend Mass and try to sing, I open my mouth and it's as if nothing comes out. It has probably made the Mass more pleasing to those around me, actually. Nothing else has changed in my participation during the Mass; I just have no volume.

After Jason's accident, I had to walk away from being a member of the National Ski Patrol. I had originally joined the patrol at Perfect North Slopes, our local tri-state ski area, as a way of having an activity that the whole family could enjoy. I patrolled and they got to ski free; it was a great time. I had been skiing my since senior year in college and had taken first-aid training since Boy Scouts. It was a perfect combination. It felt good to do something I loved, like skiing while helping others.

However, my shock at the helplessness, at being unable to do anything, at being unable to use any of my training while we sat with Jason in intensive care for nine days really brought me down. I knew from the beginning that his medical situation was out of my hands, but to be there and not be able to help my own son as someone emotionally driven to be hands on was traumatic. I stopped patrolling because I didn't want to be called to a situation involving someone in need and find that I could not see the individual but see

Jason. I was afraid I would lose it; I could not jeopardize someone else's health.

Since then, I have skied on occasion along with my patroller friends. If they were called to help someone in need, I skied away. But last year, as Paul Gaffney and I were skiing together, a situation happened directly in front of us. I stopped. Paul attended the young lad while I positioned myself well uphill so as to block anyone from getting too close until other patrollers arrived. It felt good. I could survey the situation and think about what needed to be done while feeling unaffected by memories of Jason's accident. My first aid and patrol knowledge was still there, although a refresher course would be needed for recertification, but it felt right that I was there.

It's How You Deliver the Message

My generation grew up with the television. Everything about it was new and had never been done before. The screen was small, and the shows were live. My favorite show was Steve Allen's—anything with Steve Allen. His music, his writings, his "Man in the Street" segments, and his ad-libs were great. It was his "Letters to the Editor" skit that I really enjoyed. He would take a New York City daily newspaper and read the letters to the editor—but not just read them. He would "emote" them. With a broad-brim felt hat on his head and a card sticking out of the sweatband with the word *Press* printed on it, he would work himself into such a frenzy demanding the justice and the redress that the writer so badly sought and deserved. Oh, the outrage, the indignant how-dare-they-do-this attitude! Soon the audience was in an uproar, demanding redress themselves, and would roar their support whenever he asked for it. With his glasses falling off, his hat thrown down in disgust and then pounded out of shape, the paper long shredded and littering the desk, he could have marched the entire audience out of the theater and down to city hall right then and there, chanting all the way, "Get the axe! Get the torch! This injustice shall be avenged!"

But here is the thing—if you read the letter in a normal manner, it was nothing. It was harmless and inconsequential. So the garbage cans make noise. So the dog barks too long. So the parking meter doesn't work. Why the fury? He taught me that a message could be turned into a cause based not on what was written but on how it was delivered.

I was reminded of this at each of the two trauma sessions I attended during my journey. The reaction to the victim's problem by the people around the victim (family, friends, and support staff) can actually dramatically increase or decrease the victim's sense of trauma more than the problem itself. It's a two-edged sword. Once the abuse is revealed a child who does not initially fully understand what has happened to him or her (as in the case of sexual abuse), can be pushed over the edge by the response of those around the child. As the child comes to understand more fully that what happened wasn't right, then an internal reaction traumatizes the child. It's a no-win proposition unless those close to the child understand how they need to handle the situation. Mike Smith, a DCF Trainer and fellow Stonehill graduate, said during one of the trauma workshops, "Perception becomes the reality."

Causes of Childhood Behavioral Dysfunction

Abandonment, abuse, addiction, and apathy can scar a child for life. And there is little the child can do about it.
—Bill O'Reilly, *Who's Looking Out for You?*

O'Reilly's quote jumped out at me when I read it in 2004 or 2005. He did not develop the thought any further, nor did he explain the terms he used; he just finished the paragraph with those two sentences. But the alliteration was easy for me to remember, and I believed it covered rather cleanly many of the obstacles that youth face in developing.

Then, three pages later, he used the phrase "media absorption."

The more I thought about that phrase, the more I saw a larger focus develop. *Media* was too specific and I felt that *absorption* played a much broader, more basic and intrinsic role in conjunction with those first four *A* words that necessitated its inclusion as a fifth *A* word. I thought I could use all five of them within the foundation's mission and in this section.

As I learned more about trauma during my journey, I came to see its impact as well. I was first exposed to the facts of trauma at the AEE Best Practices Regional Seminar in Columbus, Ohio, in May 2010. While listening to the various speakers and participating in the workshops covering the issue, I got to ask questions and sensed a connection with the Five *A*s, as I was calling them. A month later, during the Wilderness School's staff training, I participated in a workshop presented by the Training Academy of the State of Connecticut Department of Children and Families. Matt Shove answered a question by using the analogy of children's being like "sponges" to refer to how they pick up or learn stuff, and Mike Smith (DCF Trainer and Stonehill graduate) jumped on the word and its relationship to absorption.

To date, I have not found any specific use or reference to "Five *A*s and a *T* of Childhood Behavioral Dysfunction" in any of Bill O'Reilly's books or in my discussions with clinical professionals in their respective fields of social work, child psychology, and education. In fact, such professionals have used other terms in our talks, such as *grief, loss, neglect*, and *internalization*.

In an effort to ensure clarity in the common language of trauma, each A word is defined and expanded on below.

- Abandonment is something a child might never get over, whether it's due to his or her parents' divorce or separation or one parent's desertion, death, or imprisonment. In the movie *Hook*, Rufio, leader of the Lost Boys, is mortally wounded in a sword duel with Captain Hook. As he lies dying in Peter Pan's arms, his final words to Peter are, "Do you know what I wish? I wish I had a dad … like you." He didn't want some overpriced sport sneakers or the latest video game but an understanding, supportive, loving dad. How deeply it hurts to not have a father is something I never really appreciated growing up.

Unfortunately, today's statistics show that men are abandoning their families all too often. David Blankenhorn's book *Fatherless America* makes this point convincingly. He believes the problem is, as the subtitle says, "our most urgent social problem." This challenge is being met head-on by men like Harold Howard of Cincinnati's Talbert House Social Agency. He is the director of the Fatherhood Project, which "assists men in their efforts to become the responsible, committed and nurturing fathers they want to be." Howard is intent on getting dads involved in their children's lives. And the problem is not new.

In 1947, when I was two, the man who married my aunt Helen left her and their two children. I never knew the man and to this day I do not to acknowledge him as an uncle. They were living in Texas at the time as he was an Army pilot. When World War II ended, so did the marriage, for whatever reason. After aunt Helen (my mom's sister) and her children moved back to Connecticut, ours became an extended family. We never did anything without them. Not only standard family events like weddings and birthdays but also Sunday afternoon drives and free time. I didn't appreciate it then because I thought they were cutting in on my time, my space, and my toys. (Remember, I was spoiled by having three mothers.) That was then, but now I understand. What my folks were doing was wrapping the three of them in love and support. Joey, my cousin, was a year older than me and, as I realized later, he always missed having a dad. My dad tried to help. They would talk, and Joey would show him his schoolwork. He was included in all we did, but in later years when it was thought the Army would "straighten him out," it became apparent that something was missing. Joey never got into serious trouble, but he never reached his full potential, either. Just when the family thought he was "on his way," he would regress. It wasn't until Joey died, in 1969, at the age of twenty-four that I realized how much off base I was and how great my parents were. Joey had reached out to my father, and Bill Hunt was doing all he could to help him find his way.

• Abuse comes in many forms—none of them good—and when repeated over time, it is potentially life changing. Physical, mental, and sexual abuse are the big three categories. It is well known and accepted that those who are abused grow up to become abusers. In order for the healing to start, the problem has to be identified and the parties separated. Such abuse may go undetected for a long period of time, even years.

At the AEE's 2010 Best Practices Conference, Bobbie Beale, PsyD, explained survivor's guilt to me. In many instances, witnessing the abuse of another traumatizes a child because the child feels guilty for not stopping the abuse even though, in reality, the child is powerless to stop or prevent it. She further explained that often times survivor's guilt is more traumatizing than the trauma experienced by the person abused.

As my daughter Danielle explained, many abused women develop, over the period of abuse, very negative feelings about their bodies. They view their bodies as being dirty and the very reason for their abuse. Initial programs using the outdoors to help them regain control of their lives backfired. It seemed that the dirt, the bugs, and the lack of a stable environment amplified this rejection of their bodies. In order to maximize the benefits of the outdoors, the programs needed to slowly introduce the women to the outdoors by way of short walks instead of sweaty, grimy hikes and by the use of cabins instead of tents. First, they had to be taught what normal living was. They needed to be shown how they should be treated. They had to be shown that their bodies were clean and not the problem. The problem had to be shown as existing outside of them.

- Addiction is too pervasive in our society. While the misuse of drugs has been with us always, it seemed to explode across the population in the 1960s and 1970s when we overthrew so many norms of the time, including protecting our lives. Parents and friends trapped by this insidious condition all too often turn children into addicts as well. US drug czar, Gil Kerlikowske, reports that after spending one trillion dollars on the War on Drugs, "In the grand scheme, it has not been successful. Forty years later, the concern about drugs and drug problems is, if anything, magnified, intensified." It has been a terrible waste of money and, more important, a tragic waste of human lives totaling in the hundreds of thousands. Prohibition during the 1920s didn't work to stop the use of alcohol, and today's prohibitions are not working with drugs. We don't have "the Great Society"; we just have more babies in the river.

- Apathy is a state of just not caring or loving. It is different from the behavior of the abuser, who plays mind games to gain control. Apathy is being there physically but not becoming involved. For a child who naturally desires to be loved, to be part of a family, to be part of a group, the lack of interaction is deadening. As Rosemarie often remarked about her special education students, they want to talk and be heard, but they don't have the chance. Sometimes the apathy of one parent is covered by the caring of the other parent, but if that parent leaves, everything changes.

  In discussing apathy with Jeff Bruno, an instructor at the Wilderness School, he told of a young lad he had worked with in another program. The boy's mom had been diagnosed with cancer, but that did not stop her from making every moment count. He had some of the greatest birthdays, and every day was a day she made special. But when she died, it changed. His dad was too tied to his business. He could not, would not, or didn't know how to take the time to be or provide that support. Although the boy was an amazing high school gymnast, he spent his time and money foolishly to avoid dealing with his mom's loss. With no support from his dad, he became more focused on flashy clothes and "good times." He had no coping mechanism in place to help himself.

Another boy, Vinny, was a short young lad who seemed to have a knack for finding gold. Because of his height, he might get lost in a crowd, but it didn't stop him. While he was on a Wilderness School twenty-day expedition, he found some string and a fish hook when the crew stopped by the Housatonic River. As the others played and messed around during the break, where was Vinny? He was off catching fish! No bait, discarded hook, string tied to a branch—Vinny was the kind of kid you just loved for his spunk and initiative. So it hurt the staff when they heard that he had run away from home. He had issues with his mother and her lifestyle. Kim, WS' program coordinator, ran into him in a McDonald's parking lot one day, so she stopped and asked if he was hungry. She offered to buy him a meal if he'd let her take him home or at least to an adult he trusted. She asked him what had happened, and he told her how he had wanted a puppy for Christmas. But Vinny didn't get a puppy for Christmas. It wasn't that Mom could not afford one; in fact, she gave a puppy as a Christmas gift. Who got the puppy? The puppy was a gift for her boyfriend! That one act told Vinny who his mom really cared about. Running away seemed the only thing to do. At least she couldn't hurt him again if he wasn't with her.

Vinnie's story reminded me of a radio talk show I heard years ago; the recommendations stayed in my mind because the show's host spoke to what parenting is all about. It was a show I had never listened to before, just one of those chance encounters that you can't plan. I wasn't looking for a discussion of family values but rather trying to fill some windshield time.

I drove from Las Vegas to Ely, Nevada, to make a sales call with a customer's salesman on one of his accounts. The drive was long, and I had limited radio reception. I caught a portion of a phone-in show to which a young, divorced father of two called to ask for advice. He was thinking of going back to finish his college degree and was also interested in developing a relationship with a divorced woman who had two children of her own. The analyst asked one question: "How old is your youngest?" He said, "Three." She then stated that until the youngest turned eighteen, he should not date or socialize and definitely not marry. She said he should focus on being the parent for his children. That was his sole and most important role and obligation.

I had never thought about it before, but her recommendations were rather straightforward and demanding. Then she explained that dating tells the children that they are no longer as important to him. Spending time at the woman's house tells them that their home isn't as good anymore. Watching their dad go off to visit the woman tells them that he sees her children as more important. And if he should marry and the marriage should produce offspring, then that tells his existing children that they are not as loved and that Daddy needs to find new children to love. Vinny would have told him the same thing.

Abandonment, abuse, addiction, and apathy are the first four of what I call causes of behavioral dysfunction, and I consider them to be external factors. The external factors happen around the child. A child with divorced parents may not be able to sustain a marriage in later life or may decide not to have children at all so as not to make the same mistakes. Children who are abused may become abusers, and a child born to a mom who is on dope or addicted to alcohol may be born with preexisting addictions or tendencies. How tragic to have to detoxify a newborn! And apathy seems like such a waste, such a hollow existence. The fifth factor is an internal factor.

Absorption is one of the most natural processes in a child's young life, and it is an involuntary one, like breathing. You may call it the child's natural curiosity about the surrounding world. In short, children are sponges.

The natural process of learning is to absorb: eyes see, ears hear, hands grab, and mouths taste. What child doesn't grab an item and bring it to its mouth? What child doesn't crawl to an item to pick it up, turn it over, throw it down, and repeat the process?

When I was at Mountain Crossings, I met Gray Wanderer, who was then hiking the Appalachian Trail after retiring from forty years in education. He told me how, years earlier, when their daughter was in Montessori school, his wife was concerned that their daughter was spending too much time playing with buttons—all shapes, all sizes, and all colors. So they went to talk to the people at the school. Yes, Montessori is experiential, they reasoned, but—really? Buttons? And for that long? They listened and decided to let the school continue the practice. Today, their daughter is a surgeon, a very successful, bright, and well-matured individual.

As I watch Addyson, my granddaughter, play with spoons, I see what Gray Wanderer saw in his daughter: intense focus, intense curiosity, and learning at her own pace. No bells ring to move her along; her learning doesn't get cut off arbitrarily. She is actively learning, and it is absorption at its best. But there is a dark side.

Nick K. had a great twenty-day expedition. He made new friends and befriended Johnny by having his folks write to Johnny. In his graduation speech, he spoke to each member of his crew individually, saying something specific to them, without written notes. He is a leader. Once he got home to his secluded, wooded valley view with only a couple of homes on the distant mountainside, Nick got involved in school, doing fantastic stenciling artwork. He met a girl; they began reading the Bible together and made plans to go on a church mission to Central America—really good stuff. But he has this impulsivity that can lead him astray. He gets so absorbed in the moment, in acceptance by his friends, in following the leader, that he forgets to think and just reacts with, "Yeah, cool! Let's do it, man!" And that gets him into trouble. Even with the best support, a loving family, and good friends wanting to help, he still needs to find his way.

Absorption, while natural, needs maturity and to be developed along with judgment, and sometimes that doesn't happen. Children absorb, but they do not have the skills in place to fully process all that they absorb. How can they evaluate, how can they define, how can they recognize when there is nobody there to remind them, to mentor them, to slow them down so that they can think through what they are processing?

Let me give you an example of the negative impact of absorption. It comes from the first scholarship that Jason's foundation awarded to Anasazi Wilderness. The mother wrote asking for help and told of how her husband of some twenty-plus years had come home one day and announced that the marriage was over and—oh, by the way—that their business was bankrupt. Two weeks later, she was diagnosed with breast cancer. She was left with no husband, no income, and a terrible diagnosis. While she and her older daughter could cope, her younger daughter, a 4.0 student, couldn't. And that's where the daughter takes over this narrative.

> I began to lose it, so my mom put me on antidepressants. I never felt the same as that young innocent girl.… I started doing things that hurt my soul as I couldn't feel them as deeply. I would let guys sleep with me as I just laid there with my eyes staring off into space. I started to use drugs regularly and experimented with some of the hardest ones out there that I had always told myself I never would do. My grades slipped tremendously until finally I got expelled from school, and still all I cared about was my lifestyle and the next night that I would be able to run away from my problems. I found little pleasure in things that used to bring me great

joy. I had basically lost myself in all ways. I was always on the edge and angry, completely shutting myself off from any form of connection to my mom.... I was stuck in a box that I didn't know how to get out of, and my only solution was to further deepen myself into negative things for my heart and life.

Dr. Quantum (Fred Alan Wolf, PhD) writes about "dancing on the edge of chaos. He implies that our lives work best when we "dance on the edge of good and the edge of evil." It's that area where we grow and develop or, for some, to crash and burn, hopefully to rise again. It is the eternal struggle of living. Some youth truly do struggle. Given the natural drive to grow, their natural curiosity, and their natural instinct to absorb, some of these children exist in the most chaotic mass of abandonment, abuse, addiction, apathy, and absorption.

It may not be the parents' fault. They may be loving, kind, supportive parents. And yet the children can be traumatized by the outside world or environment, as in the case of rape or bullying. But they are survivors. They show up to these programs designed to help with their baggage, not really coming from any place or going anywhere in the conventional sense, and yet offering "a pretty pure version of an adolescent," to use the words of Haley from the Eagleton School. They are very present, and in joining a wilderness expedition bring this very chaotic, disorganized energy and grab chance; they use what they have—the present—to move forward. Their ideas of the wilderness experience may not be fully conceptualized at the time, like Anthony K. Sr., who thought it would be a vacation from home. But come they do, and in the process they find that they can control and create something great for themselves. They come with the greatest potential for creativity and success. In learning to believe in themselves, they use that positive energy to create a new life.

Laurence Gonzales, in his book *Deep Survival,* writes about surviving in the wilderness against the forces of nature. He notes that some of those who seem to be the best prepared do not survive while others who are less fit do. At the same time, he writes that the same principles for surviving a shipwreck, being lost in the woods, and so forth are the same for surviving the chaotic situations of everyday life.

> It's easy to imagine that wilderness survival would involve equipment, training, and experience. It turns out that, at the moment of truth, those might be good things to have but they aren't decisive. Those of us who go into the wilderness or seek our thrills in contact with the forces of nature soon learn, in fact, that experience, training, and modern equipment can betray you. The maddening thing for someone with the Western scientific turn of mind is that it's not what's in your pack that separates the quick from the dead. It's not even what's in your mind. Corny as it sounds, it's what's in your heart.

$E = MC^2$

An Individual's Development and Potential

You never know until you try.
When you lose yourself,
You find the key to paradise.
                    —"Knee Deep," Zac Brown Band featuring Jimmy Buffett

I followed you for the first time right up that rock,
to gaze out on a vast Colorado plain.
And I knew then, what I know now,
that I would never be the same.
The adventures, oh, the adventures you had,
they were so grand,
You were living and breathing a philosophy,
that in the meantime I have come to understand.
That for this moment and every moment I do believe,
That I shall always follow my dreams
To achieve the impossibilities,
and to say, my friends, it's much easier than it seems.
                    —Jay Seals, "My Friend," eulogy poem, October 20, 2001

Jason was Jay Seals's "window into climbing." First, it was the indoor climbing walls of Cincinnati and then bouldering at Red River Gorge in Kentucky. Jay got to experience Colorado climbing when he accompanied me on the road trip to visit Jason that I mentioned earlier. It was a beautiful, clear, sunny day, and the experience of the climb and the view from the top really excited Jay. I mean "really excited him" as in he continued to talk about it even after we got back to Ohio. It is those exceptional days, those exceptional experiences that stand out because of the profound impact they impart.

In today's compulsory, age-based public education model, movies are made and books are written about the exceptions to the rule. *Stand and Deliver* chronicles how Jaime Escalante turned underperforming East Los Angeles high school math students into state calculus champs only to be forced to have them take the test a second time because the testing officials didn't believe they could succeed without cheating. The "experts" didn't believe in the power of a teacher or in their own system.

A Smile as Big as the Moon tracks Mike Kersjes as he attempts to get his Grand Rapids special education class accepted into NASA's Space Camp, which previously had been open only to advanced placement classes. At first rejected by NASA and lacking the support of their own school administration, Kersjes and his students persevered and, in the end, won the respect of all, especially their competitors—the "normal" students.

Take the Lead explains how Pierre Dulaine, a New York City ballroom dance teacher, turned a detention class of teenagers into classic ballroom dance competitors. In each part of the movie, there is conflict and rejection—the high schoolers' rejection of themselves as good students, the rejection of Dulaine's initial request to do something different to reach them, rejection by the families for fear of having their children face even further exclusion, and even rejection by the "experts," the very professionals whose job it is to teach them. And yet in learning to believe in themselves and in their teacher and accepting the teacher's belief in the program, these students overcome and made something of themselves. These are educators who are not content with a job and the status quo. School wasn't working, and they knew they could make a difference. They were the few who stepped outside the system, to succeed while those who fail and play the system are many.

Each of these three educators saw potential in their students, even when nobody else, including the students themselves, could see it. Immersed in twenty-four/seven contact with the students, wilderness educators see change over the length of the expedition, whether it is twenty days, thirty-two days, or fifty-one days long. The potential for change is there. However, while personal growth can be measured, how do you measure or define a person's potential? Wilderness programs ask the students for goals, for reasons for being involved so as to measure development toward those targets. It is in working on those goals that students begin to see potential within their beings that they might never have realized existed. It is in the striving that potential becomes maybe not measureable but recognized

In his work *A Short History of Nearly Everything*, Bill Bryson uses Einstein's equation of $E = MC^2$ to show that humans have a very large potential. To review, E is energy (our potential); M is matter, of which we have a considerable amount, and, from what the nutrition specialists tell us, we, individually, seem to be doing quite well in gaining more of it daily; and C^2 is the speed of light times itself. Now the speed of light is 186,282 miles per second, which is no small number. Multiply that by itself and you get a number in the billions; here, we are talking about a very *big* number. Now multiply that number by a person's weight, and the result is that person's potential. Unfortunately, as Bryson writes, "We're just not very good at getting it out." Full potential is something most of us, if not all of us, don't reach. But the weakness in this argument is the elephant in the room, literally. The elephant has much more mass than a human, so his potential, according to this formula, should be exponentially that much greater. But so far, elephants haven't shown much potential; they haven't changed or "advanced." Except for the circus acts and the Internet videos of elephants that paint, all that mass hasn't produced a difference. The difference is our brains. Humans have two brains—an emotional brain and a reasoning brain—which together create our potential.

Part of the issue of the whole idea in the modern culture is with the model of real continuing community. In a village or community you

have elders, and in a community you have young people who are honored for the new fire that they bring, the new ideas, the questioning of the status quo. It's like that's not squelched and pushed aside. But what's in this for the broader vision of the culture here? They have something to add. And so the problem is [that] today, we don't have a lot of elders showing up.

—Jon Rousseau, Asheville, NC, interview, April 2010

All people are created equal, but they don't develop at the same rate. How many times have you been in this situation either as a participant or as a witness: A mother with her baby is asked, "How old is your child?" Then comes the onslaught of age-based comparisons: big for his age, so alert for his age, has such an abundance/lack of hair for her age, chubby for her age. Or mothers start comparing the "firsts" timeline for when their children slept through the night, crawled, walked, spoke, cut teeth. What does age have to do with it, really? Other than setting the child up for some negative comparisons or setting the parent up for a case of insecurity, the only people gaining from age-based comparisons are the professionals, such as doctors, teachers, self-help gurus, and so forth. And there are a ton of them, so it must be true. If you walk through a bookstore, you can get the feeling that you don't know anything and can't do anything on your own.

Let's look at it another way. Have you ever watched planes take off? They all form into a line heading for the runway, planes of all sizes and types—big, little, gigantic, medium-sized—one after the other, forming up for their turn to take off. Each gets its turn to stand at the start line, fire up the engines with the brakes straining against the power and the urge to go, and then, once the brakes are released, shoot down the runway. Somewhere along the runway, its wheels leave the ground, it takes off, and the plane becomes airborne. Something similar happens in an expedition crew as it struggles to turn itself into a functioning unit, with each member finding a role to play and a need to fill. Once the crew is performing (airborne), they still need to hold together as support for one another so as to keep the crew performing (maintain altitude).

But here is the thing—some planes, like a Piper Cub Special, leave the ground in a length of 350 feet while others, like a Boeing 747-300, need 10,450 feet to leave the ground. With all of our science and technology, why can't we make them all take off in the same span of runway? Why not save on land and pavement by making them all take off in a fixed space? We ask that of children. We ask them all to "take off" the same. And like the laws of physics that control planes and their takeoffs, so too are there natural forces that make each child take off differently. Through no fault of the parents, the environment, or society, children take off differently. But no child flies solo; once airborne, each child requires a unique support system.

In her book *No-Talk Therapy*, Martha Straus, PhD, outlines developmental runways:

> Consider the many different kinds of "runways" children must go down en route to adulthood: physical, cognitive, emotional, and social. Children "take off" at different speeds along the unique combination of developmental trajectories. For example, some kids who are very bright and cognitively advanced are also very immature and emotionally delayed. Some who are physically mature are socially awkward. Some kids have enormous discrepancies in development, while others seem more all-of-a-piece.

We hear talk of young children as still carrying "baby fat." Others are said to be "highly coordinated" or "advanced." I spent my childhood days short or underdeveloped, and I didn't even know it. It wasn't until after I graduated from high school that I had my final growth spurt. It didn't mean anything to me then, but it felt good about thirty years later. I was attending my high school reunion and enjoying reliving the success of our senior year high school football team, which had been undefeated and recognized as state co-champs. I had been a team manager all fours years, so it was fun to finally get back and reminisce with the guys. During the social hour, I had a chance to talk to Buddy

Chernovetz, our star quarterback, and it really hit home. He stopped suddenly in midsentence, looked me in the eye, and with his right hand creating an imaginary level line between his eyes and mine, said, "I don't ever remember talking directly to you. You're not the same kid." My secret was no more. When the guys weren't looking, I had grown taller. It had just taken a while. In short, as Dr. Straus writes, "Chronological age is seldom very informative."

And like planes, once we take off, we need help to keep going. Planes don't fly themselves, and neither do children. Ground control, pilots and copilots, navigational beacons, maintenance crews, as well as others work to keep the planes airborne. The energy expended to get off the ground is only part of the total effort. Children, who develop differently on different runways for mental, emotional, physical, and cognitive skills need the support of family and community once they get going. If the family or the community isn't there, the child has trouble. Life gets tough.

When I was growing up in New Haven, the sheriff had a bus called the Jail on Wheels. He would park it on the city green near the water fountain for tours. It was outfitted with a bunch of stuff like pictures, a jail cell, and an electric chair. But what I remember most is a sign that said basically, "Anyone asking you to do something wrong is not a friend." You have to choose the right people to be your friends or the trouble never ends.

George Carlin does a routine about aging in which he points out how a child uses half-years—"I'm four and a half, going on five." Then, somewhere around age ten, we drop the half-year. When we get really old, we might bring it back, saying, "I'm a hundred and a half." When you're young, you can't wait for the next birthday, and when you're old, you hope for the next day.

Somehow the years in between young and old don't get tracked the same. Nobody says he's forty-five and a half, and tomorrow—well, tomorrow is just another day at the office. We separate youth because they are too young and our elders because they are too old. We put students into compulsory age-based schools and our parents into "rest homes."

What does age have to do with learning? It doesn't any more than the color of one's eyes or the length of one's hair. The comment, "My, you're big for a blue-eyed boy" doesn't make sense. Is a child a slow learner or learning at his own pace? Is a child a math prodigy or just learning at his own pace? Why do we force students to learn at an arbitrary pace when they have their own internal clocks? Education's concern for age-appropriate environments and expectations continues to force children to act outside themselves.

The ancient cultures believed we humans are born with the power and genius we need. In her book *Home to the Wilderness*, Sally Carrighar writes about asking an Eskimo mother "how she taught her children the difference between right and wrong. She said, 'We don't teach them. We just remind them. When they are born, they know.'"

I watch it happen each day I babysit my grandchildren—Addyson, my granddaughter, and Boone, my grandson. There are things they do that make me wonder, *How do they know?* For example, I was watching Addyson crawled to the desk and used its side panels as support to stand up. But when she crawled to the empty desk chair for the first time and reached for the seat, she stopped when she felt it swivel. She didn't use it. Where did she learn that a moving object does not offer her the firm support needed to stand up?

Or how can Boone get so much pleasure out of a book he can't read? He will take a soft-sided book, shake it, bend it, fold it, suck on it, point at the words and pictures on the pages even if upside-down, grab a tab, wave the book in the air, and repeat all that for what seems a very long time, and all the time he is gibbering in delight. If he relates the book to having fun now, how much more fun will he have when he learns to read? Where do students learn to hate books and reading?

Recently the Milford (Ohio) school board, much to its credit, publicly announced the results of an internal study comparing the district's students' performances to the US Department of Education statistics. While their results were in line with the national trends, the article's title suggested the question that resulted: *Should boys be taught differently?* And that leads to the bigger question—*Do we even know how to teach them effectively?* The survey showed that more males are identified as "gifted" and yet get more Ds and Fs while also making up 70 percent of the learning-disabled population. Why do schools force students to learn at the same rate when their own results, as well as the national data, show that they do not learn well that way? Children want to be happy, and they want respect and the approval of peers and adults, but so many come out of school thinking they are failures. We don't "remind" them how to be good; we just make them failures, just more babies in the river.

Even for parents who are involved with their children, it can be a struggle. School systems seem to be more interested in fitting the child to the system rather than adapting the system to the child and his or her needs.

Lori Bauchiero is my niece by marriage. Dillon, her son, is developmentally delayed due to a history of sudden and severe seizures. Drugs have a short duration of effectiveness before his body adjusts, which then necessitates new drugs and new testing to determine the correct dosage. He has an uncanny memory and a fascination for keys and key blanks. In fact, I gave him a copy of the Ilco Key Blank Directory, which contains key blanks and is considered the locksmith bible, and he constantly reviews and compares its pictures to keys he finds. Everybody entering his home is asked to show him his or her key ring. He does relatively well in school. In fact, he qualified for the National Junior Honor Society's Honorable Mention designation for children with disabilities. To get it, he just needed his school to nominate him. In a meeting with the school district's special education department head, it became apparent that she wasn't even aware of the program and didn't see the need or the benefit to do the work or make the effort to recognize such a student, a special education child, in such a way, regardless of the effort he made to succeed. In a competitive business environment, even an entry-level marketing person would see this as a chance to let the public know how well the system is doing, but it is not so in forced public education that looks not to the parent but to the government for approval. Sometimes schools come across as believing that the parent is the obstacle to their control of the child.

Lori persisted, and eventually Dillon was recognized. To complete the society's service requirement, he was given his own school keys and placed in charge of opening select school building doors. And that wasn't Lori's first involvement. When Dillon was in elementary school, Lori initiated and coached Unified Sports, a Special Olympics program. As Dillon moved on, Lori continued to coach and promote participation by other schools in the district. By working with the Connecticut Interscholastic Athletic Conference and the Special Olympics, both Dillon's elementary and the local high school were recognized for the outstanding programs they developed. Dillon has moved on to high school and continues to learn in spite of the forced age-based public school system. But Lori stays involved because Dillon's needs do not go away and the staff loses sight of its teaching mission.

As hard as it is to believe, in some school systems, a child has to fail before services can be provided. They even have a name for it—testing out. Mark Gloekler is a friend and sales manager for Ilco. His daughter was having difficulties in school due to an auditory issue called central auditory processing disorder. Her auditory nerve doesn't work properly. Children with CAP tend to have low self-esteem because their hearing disorder hampers their socialization skills. They quickly learn that they are different from those around them.

Mark and his wife decided to home school their daughter after being told by the school that she could only get the help she needed if she failed first. So we instill failure. Does that make sense? What do you think failure would do to her already low self-esteem? Many "normal" children have confidence issues. A child with a disability such as CAP has an added burden, and then the school needs her to fail! Wilderness educators strive to make the experience as authentic and rewarding as possible without imposing phony and negative parameters.

Joe Juliano is a high school buddy of mine who has been an

educator since graduating from Niagara University in 1967. Joe began his career teaching middle school English and retired as the director of fine arts for the Hamden Public School System in Connecticut. All that training and "insider" experience didn't help his son. Brian had a calculus teacher who bragged about not giving As, saying nobody would earn that grade in his class. Brian understood calculus, and if his success as a vice president of Yahoo! is any indication, he probably understood calculus better than the teacher. In a conference, Joe told the calculus teacher, "Well, then, you are doing something wrong. If you're going to give grades, and I don't think you have to, but if you're going to give grades and then say to a kid that you cannot achieve the highest grade in this class, then what is the point?" As Joe saw it, "Brian and the other kids in the class were being put in a situation where this guy was in effect testing his ability to trick the kids into not being able to succeed. Really stupid idea."

It is all about the learning experience. Brian, like many others, not only learned but also figured out how to take his knowledge to the next level. All the teacher was offering was a class with no future.

But that doesn't have to be. In the fall of 2010, my wife moved from a self-contained special-education classroom with students in mixed grades to a "regular" fourth-grade class. She taught reading to two classes with a total of forty-two students. Three other fourth-grade teachers acknowledged that her class of twenty students was the most challenging as they seemed to have short attention spans and lack focus. She struggled all year with the concern that she was not getting through to them. At the end of the year, they were required to take the national standardized tests. Of the forty-two students who took the test, thirty-eight passed (a rate of 90.05 percent, compared with the district-wide rate of 88.8 percent and statewide rate of 81 percent that year). Two failed by the slightest of margins, and they were mainstreamed special education students! Of the remaining two who failed, one child had been losing focus for the previous several weeks and was experiencing some life changes that affected his performance. The last child's failure remains a mystery—perhaps it was just the wrong day to take the tests.

Our reductionist system places too much emphasis on the left brain at the expense of the rest of our natural wisdom. You wouldn't raise a horse that way, so why would you raise a child that way? Paraphrasing Dr. T and Mr. H, if you keep a horse in a small pasture, keep it idle and away from other horses, and don't let it access either the wisdom of the herd or the wisdom of its nature, you will end up with a horse that doesn't know its place in the world and that interacts in very unnatural ways. Does that sound like an adolescent child in trouble? Does that sound like a child who cannot relate to the world around him or her?

When you look at the historical records of those who have been involved with the formation of the American public school system since the late eighteen hundreds to now, you see how successful they have been in achieving their goal—the separation of children from parents, family, community, and church. The desire first expressed in 1650 and then really advanced since 1850 has been the scientific management of youth by "a central elite of social engineers." The fear of the turn-of-the-century mass migrations and a concern about how to integrate them produced a system designed not for creativity and independent thought but for control of the mass population. Today's results are not the fault of bad teachers or inadequate funding but rather the simple realization that, as John Taylor Gatto writes in *The Underground History of American Education*, "It's just impossible for education and schooling ever to be the same thing."

We have placed students in small pastures, small boxes called classrooms, and we tell them to be quiet, to listen, and to behave. We control their attention and movements by a bell system, and we restrict their peer association to those in their class, thus prohibiting them from learning from their elders. We all learn from those around us. Have you ever thought about how much information children pick up on the bus or during recess from the other students and from elders, who have experience? Successful solutions are often found by thinking outside the box. Unfortunately, we keep children inside the box. We look for improvements by spending money, but studies show that that method hasn't produced any positive results. And we fight over class size, which has been resolved.

A *Wizard of Id* cartoon made the point. When the duke informs the king of the demands for smaller classes, the king replies, "Repeal the child labor laws!"

When you realize that the use of child labor laws, which have some benefit, grew at the same time that children were being forced into age-based compulsory public schooling and that our national literacy rate has dropped since then, the questions must be asked, what have we gained?

If you think I am wrong, then consider that since the 1970s, the federal government has assumed more control of our schools, has replaced both the states and the local authorities as the central player, has increased spending by a factor of two, and has added more regulations, and yet student performance has stagnated. Reading scores have remained relatively flat. There is no correlation between spending increases and student performance. We just have more babies in the river.

As Anthony Howard writes, "To understand what wilderness educators are doing educationally, one needs to understand the mindsets and approaches they are up against."

Sometimes, you have to step back and view the world differently.

The Homecoming Queen and Educator

The Wilderness School's Logistics Department is in charge of all the very technical, hard-skill events. They provide the equipment and back up the field instructors for paddling, white water days, rock climbing, the ropes course, setting ropes on a rock face, and hauling the canoes to the river. If they were in the arts world, such as the theater, they would be the behind-the-scenes people, the gaffers, hauling the equipment, hanging the lights, and setting the rigging. The technical or hard skills are the same in several other industries, and thus former wilderness educators like Jason's good friend, Scott Ring, can continue to use those skills as he splits his time serving as part of Yosemite's search and rescue team, gaffing at Las Vegas theaters, and most recently rigging for the Alaskan pipeline. But what they leave behind is the depth of impact that the wilderness provides that is not found elsewhere using the same skills.

While I was visiting the Wilderness School, some of the staff got tickets to Cirque du Soleil, which was playing in Hartford. During the performance, one of the gaffers was setting up rigging for the next act and tied off a piece of apparatus directly in front of us. Shannon immediately turned to Don Pelletier, the head of logistics, and across the six of us between them exclaimed, "Don, he tied a bowline!" It was a perfect example of transference—taking a hard skill, in this case, tying a bowline knot, which the Wilderness School staff uses in the wilderness, and using it somewhere else such as in the theater, in a commercial application. No one said anything negative, so I guess those in the audience close to us were appreciative of Shannon's additional in-depth commentary, although they most likely did not realize that her observation was actually an affirmation of the Wilderness School staff's skills.

I met Liza Wilson at the Wilderness School in 2002, the year after Jason's death. I was in Connecticut to visit family and took some time to visit Tom Dyer, then director, at the school to talk about what the family could do to help. Liza came to the Wilderness School originally to do research for her bachelor's degree in sociology at St. Joseph's College in West Hartford, Connecticut. Her thesis studied

> how different types of education (specifically outdoor experiential education, or OEE) affects gender role socialization (specifically teenage girls). And my research showed that OEE is extremely effective for a girl's self-esteem. Being given the unique opportunities that living rugged in the wilderness offers helps girls feel that they can do anything. Get dirty, make fires, set up shelters! OEE empowers girls and helps them with self-esteem.

As so often happens when one is exposed to the power of the

outdoors, she returned to become part of the seasonal staff working the summer programs. She said, "When I shadowed the courses is when I decided that was what I wanted to do!"

She was in logistics during the two seasons that Jason worked there. Leading his first twenty-day expedition proved to be a challenge, so he stepped back and spent the second half of his first year in logistics as well.

Across the front of Jason's pickup is a string of bells stretched from visor to visor, which he got from Liza. So I had a faint memory of the "Bell Lady." In fact, we still have both the truck and the bells. We reconnected this year after Marc mentioned her as a possible interview source, and I found out the rest of her story.

High school was good until Liza got her first grades; something wasn't clicking. Where previously she had performed well in school, high school really shocked her system. In fact, she revolted. While she knew everybody in school and could hang out in any crowd without feeling the need to assimilate, she went funky. Maybe it was the fact that she had lost her dad in a work-related accident when she was four years old. She loved her mom and loved her spirituality but at the same time felt disconnected. She started dressing in black, everything black. She dyed her hair black and wore black eyeliner. Liza got her hair shaved underneath and kept long hair on top; she wore Doc Martens footwear and listened to new-wave groups the Smiths and the Cure for music. She was part of that hardcore punk movement that committed itself to no drugs or alcohol and, in deference to her mom, she got no tattoos and piercings. She was, you might say, a high school stand-out if for no other reason that she and only one other of her "punk" crew attended that high school; the rest went to the town's other high school.

When you hate high school, have no school spirit, and are not involved in any activities except skateboarding and going to hardcore shows, not much is happening in your life. That is when Phin, her friend, classmate, and the other member of her crew, got the idea to nominate Liza for homecoming queen. What started as a joke grew with the help of classmates to get her on the ballot. Then it became a cause; it became a fight against the "anointed ones": cheerleading captain, class officers, and most popular girl, whatever. Plus, just the thought of funky Liza being driven around the football stadium to the cheers of one and all had to resonate with a few. And so on one chilly October Friday evening, a few years ago, Liza, who had never been to a high school football game, let alone the stadium, had the time of her life being driven around the track as the homecoming queen of Bristol Central High in Bristol, Connecticut.

Not many homecoming queens climb rock face walls or paddle rivers, but Liza continues working with youth through the adventure-based offerings in Connecticut, using skills she first developed at the Wilderness School.

Jason's first year at the Wilderness School was a time of doubt. Leading his first twenty-day expedition was a challenge, as it normally is for new field staff. He doubted that he had the means to connect with the crew, thinking that his whiteness would be a hindrance and that the crew members would not respect him.

In thinking about her job that year, Liza wrote,

> A lot of what our job is on resupply is to take those instructors aside and talk to them and pump them up and be like, you know, you can do this. You have this power, you are great, you can get through this twenty.
>
> We're saying the same things to the kids that we're saying to these instructors. It's not easy for anyone to be out there for twenty days. So to be the one in charge and feel like you're not holding it together, I think it's so scary. When you have people depending on you—I know that was part of Jason's thing, just kind of working on himself like what's going on with him, so to be out for those twenty days was certainly an eye-opening experience. That summer was one of the hardest summers I ever had. I was there nine years.... That summer we graduated the least [number] of students ever.

Aaron Wiebe said of that year,

> I was a course director, which means I was doing some
> intervention work. I was available to come out, to visit
> the crew, to help them out, to give them support, to
> try to get kids back on track or, if the determination
> was they really needed to go home, then to facilitate
> or help facilitate it. The situation was this: Three kids
> were wild, and the crew was stopped along a cornfield
> on the river. The canoes were on the river bank. They
> were so wild and rambunctious. They had no regard
> for any of the policies, the rules, the instructions, and
> they had decided that they didn't need to fulfill any
> of the programs expectations.
>
> They just really had a disregard for everybody;
> they were walking all over the kids, walking all over
> the staff, probably making threats. This was day
> twelve, and in spite of numerous efforts to redirect
> and support these students, it had been going on for
> long time and building up to this. At one point, I
> think I was checking in with Jason. I could tell he
> was exhausted, and I think he … was dealing with
> an emotional crisis of his own. He was doing some
> deep personal questioning; I think he was dealing
> with that scary sense of, "Am I really the person for
> this?" This is kind of a deep self-doubt, and I think
> having a deep self-doubt certainly impacted his ability
> to feel energized on the course. I think it's a deep,
> deep worry; he was really anxious and saying, "I don't
> know if I'm cut out for this. I don't know if I have what
> I need to do this." It was just one of those moments.
> It was really powerful. I can really feel the gravity of
> what he was feeling and how heavy it was for him.
>
> I gave him as much encouragement and support
> as I could and let him know that it is demanding work

and is hard for everybody. The decision was made for the students to be removed from the course. Jason got back in the boat with his remaining crew and kept going on. After the course, he ended up meeting with the current program coordinator and saying he didn't want to leave the program but needed to take a step back from his instructing role. He went to work with Logistics for the second part of the summer. The following year, he came back to face his doubts and began to experience more confidence and success in the role of instructor. His experience of challenge in many ways parallels that of a Wilderness School student's—getting pushed to limits, experiencing a point of deep personal challenge, receiving empathy and support, coming back to face the challenge and to discover a deeper level of capability within himself. Perhaps the struggles in his first year created another source of empathy within him that allowed him to become a better instructor in that he had more ability to make the connections with his students. Self-doubt crosses cultural boundaries and does not discriminate. The self-knowledge, born from experience, that self-doubt can be overcome contributes a quiet confidence that is offered to students in our belief in them.

While I was in Asheville, I got to talk to Jeremy Poore, Stone Mountain School's program director. I was drawn to the school because Jason and a few classmates at Warren Wilson had done an after-school mentoring program there. It was one of Jason's first exposures, if not the first, to working with youth at-risk in the outdoors. Their project involved building a climbing wall on Warren Wilson's campus and then, over several weeks, teaching climbing skills to the Stone Mountain students. Once they were deemed ready, they moved to the wall for hands-on experience. As Jeremy explained,

All of us here who do the work at some point early on realize we have just as many questions as the kids do. In working together, the dynamics that we see, every time we identify a pattern someone has, or … a defense mechanism someone has, we have to turn that mirror upon ourselves and the more we can do that the more effective we become. That's what really keeps me in it. I love to give; I am a giving person by nature and at the same time I was realizing I was getting a huge amount out of being there. Many times I was finding myself in the woods thinking, *Wow, I am getting paid right now.*

Not on the difficult days, but sitting around on the top of a mountain around here—and this is a very beautiful area as you know—sitting on top of Mt. Pisgah or Mt. Mitchell looking out into the woods, beautiful robin's-egg-blue day, thinking, *Wow, okay, I can see how healing this is for me to be here. These kids who have never been anywhere near anything like this—it's got to blow their minds.*

So we would build on that, pick special campsites that had beautiful sunrises, wake people up to see them, and really get into sharing this area.

As tough as co-leading his first Wilderness School twenty-day expedition was, as frustrated and in doubt as Jason was, Bonnie Dyck, his co-leader, wrote,

I remember co-leading that twenty-day trek with Jason. He had so much to offer to the field. He had highly tuned intuition and a genuineness about him that helped him to easily connect with the young people. I also remember that at the end of the trek, Jason told me that I was a mentor to him in this field. This is one of the greatest compliments I have ever received, and I have thought about it many times over the years.... I myself had a mentor at Wilderness School (Jane Lohman) who helped me to get through my first trek and develop my skills in helpfully responding to troubled youth. I felt honored when Jason shared with me that I could support him in a similar way. No positive feedback I have received over the years has touched me as much as this statement from Jason.

It Doesn't Work if It Isn't Authentic

Sometimes kids don't have to say anything at all to do important work and feel better. There is a freedom in realizing it can be therapeutic to spend days shooting hoops with Nerf balls and watching teenagers explore their backpacks.
—Martha B. Straus, PhD, *No-Talk Therapy for Children and Adolescents*

Dave Bocchichio met Liza Wilson in middle school. If the teacher arranged the students alphabetically, they sat as far apart as B is from W. But sometimes, like in Italian language class, they ended up next to each other. Dave was a jock and not into the funky black dress, hard-edge lifestyle that Liza flaunted, but when they talked about enjoying the outdoors, they connected. They went different ways in college but kept reconnecting. Today, they have three beautiful children. Liza is a stay-at-home mom but still helps out at climbing walls and other outdoor activities when she can.

Dave teaches at East Hartford's alternative high school. There are days when he can sense that a student is upset about whatever is going on at home or in the neighborhood. His students are those who, as he says, "bombed out of regular school and are sent here." For example, one girl came to the school but didn't fit the mold that Dave is used to seeing. She was intelligent and beautiful, not from the fringe of society like so many other students who have felonies and have even done time. So he asked her, "What's going on?"

"I think I've been watching the news too much lately," she replied. "It's just so depressing; you know, things are really messed up." She said that she wished she could do something to make the world a better place but didn't know what to do.

Dave loves working with these students.

> Because these are kids that just can't follow some path that somebody laid out for them. It doesn't work if it isn't authentic. They say "screw it," and they walk away. And then they come to us, and I love it because they're like the rebels, but they're warriors and they want to make a difference. But they never really felt like they had any power.

And they have survived. They have blocked out early trauma, misfortunes, and failures in life by way of an inner survival mechanism. They are survivors who have learned to survive in many instances all on their own. Laurence Gonzales writes in *Deep Survival,* "Balancing emotion and reason can be like teetering on top of a big ball, requiring touch, timing, and a continuing shift of weight and energy."

Dave gives them chances and opportunities. A grin grows as he gives me an example.

> We will ask for workers to help some UConn football players run a twenty-four-hour overnight camp out in our middle school's gym: the middle schoolers are going to camp out, sleep, swim first thing in the morning, and participate in some adventure-based activities that my students will help oversee. The kids get excited and almost fight to see who will be picked to work.
>
> I was trained as a physical education teacher, but does it really matter in the grand scheme of things if this kid knows the proper form of how to shoot

a basketball into a hoop if he can't act civilized to
other people in the class? So I always focused on that
stuff like getting along and being respectful on an
elementary level, and then Liza got me working on the
ropes course and I saw how it helped build confidence
and gave the kids a positive boost. So I did Project
Adventure's Adventure-Based counseling, and here I
am; I found my niche.

The hard part is I have all these classes where the
kids come in and it doesn't from the outside look like
a normal class with an instructor.... We're out playing
cards, board games, and stuff and we're talking a little
bit about why, like my recreation and leisure class, why
it is important for people to have recreational leisure
time and what it does in stress reduction. I'm showing
kids all these studies I found online to support like it's
important for us to take some time, have fun together,
knowing what's the benefit of it all.

For David it is about getting his students to feel better about
themselves. It is about lifestyle changes that will help them gain
confidence in their ability to set and accomplish their goals.

A Foundation scholarship recipient wrote about the changes she
saw in herself during her "walking."

Confidence was another thing that I [struggled] with
in my life that I gained back at Anasazi. On the trail,
your mindset makes all the difference. If you believe
in yourself, it is ten times easier through it all.... It
also boosted a spark of motivation in me when I knew
I could do it.... Confidence and attitude go hand in
hand. Without a positive outlook, you cannot possibly
be confident. Negativity always caused me to believe
I couldn't do it, and then it seemed harder than it

actually was.… My attitude took a turn permanently
after experiencing how essential it is [to have] a
positive attitude to succeed.

I found another example of how confidence and attitude work
together when I was in Charleston, South Carolina, to help Danielle
with the 2010 East Coast Canoe and Kayak Festival. I volunteered
to pick up one of their guest speakers at the airport and got to meet
Wayne Horodowich. Today he is president of the University of Sea
Kayaking in Mill Creek, Washington, but for twenty-nine years
he was at the University of California, Santa Barbara and headed
up their outdoor program for twenty-five of those years. Born and
raised in Brooklyn, he was active outdoors as a scuba instructor, a
ski instructor, a canoeist with a claim to fame for putting a hole in a
Grumman aluminum canoe on the Delaware River. But all that was
only a prelude to when he moved out west to attend the University
of Oregon for a master's degree in anatomy and physiology. It was
there that he took an Outward Bound course in the Three Sisters
Wilderness, and he told me, "It literally changed my life."

He lost twenty pounds. His wife didn't recognize him, as he was
emaciated, exhausted, and exhilarated. He loved it and hated it. It
was his first time backpacking and he found his breaking point, but
by the end of the course,

> I believed and I still do there is nothing I cannot do
> or at least attempt to do. The only thing that is going
> to stop me is me.
>
> I got to a point where I could go no farther.… We
> had just finished our solo, where we do not eat for
> four days. As we're hiking along I had no energy left.
> Toward the end of the day, we took a little break and
> the crew leader says, "Okay, we're going to move up
> another mile because we want to climb this mountain
> (Broken Top) tomorrow."
>
> I said, "Richard, I can't go any farther. You guys

go up another mile, and I will catch up with you. But I just cannot go any farther." So he turned around and said, "We're making camp here." And I spoke to him a few days later, and I said, "How come you did not try to encourage me?" He said, "I've been watching you now for over twenty days, and when you told me you couldn't go any farther, your whole body said you couldn't go any farther. Everything we asked you to do, you've done; you're carrying around a seventy-pound pack, more than most people because of your size, and you just never stopped and [when] you said you couldn't go, you knew you couldn't.'

And I couldn't. I had no energy left.

When you are six-foot-seven, the world is not ready for you. Things like your tent, sleeping bag, pad, and, of course, your clothes are naturally longer and larger and therefore weigh more. Everything you do requires more effort. So when Wayne hiked, where weight is critical, he was already at a disadvantage. He was forced to carry more just to have the basics. Lightening his load wasn't possible. He had to carry it all and work his way through it.

Every instructor has to work his way through the challenges of the course. When Jason came back for his second season at the Wilderness School, he faced the same challenges again. Mark Sacks was with him on his second twenty-day expedition and relates,

In 2001, I partially led a course with him.... I think it was the day, the morning of the course [when] Jane Lohmann, program director, came up and said, "You're the course director, and now we need you to instruct it because Jeff Bruno is leaving school for medical reasons. Jeff needs to be gone for half of this course. He may be back or he may not. You might be leading this whole course."

There was this kid; I said something to him on the

second day. This was one of those groups that were really testing us early on. So I decided to push back and really, really call them on it and test them and set a firm structure with them because I wanted them to get past their kind of ego BS stuff and experience it for a couple days.... So anyways this kid was just going over the top and doing all kinds of inappropriate things and challenging us left and right, and I said something that really set him off. So he gets a hundred feet away from me, and he's just pissed. He was threatening me, "I'm going to kill you. I got something for you."

I think I challenged him; I probably said something like, "Look, you're way over the line. If you don't get your act together, I'm gonna kick you off this course," or something like that.

He was livid; he was not quite challenging me to a fight—but the very next level down basically, making a lot of threats. I [thought], *Crap, that's not what I wanted. Damn, that didn't work so well!* So [I was] trying to figure how to work this out with him and Jason [said], "Mark, maybe we're pushing him a little too hard for the first couple days."

And I [said], "Yeah, I'm just not sure with this group. I kind of feel we need to be hard on them, but I don't know." So we got into the final expedition, and Jeff Bruno was able to come back into the group. Bruno, I, and Jason hiked with the group for two days as a three-member staff, and Jeff immediately took such a good leadership role. He had, and I admire this so much, he had such better results with that kid than I did. Even in the transition day when I have worked with those kids for like twelve days or whatever it was, this kid and I were always right on edge with each other.

But that was a really special course. I remember

Jason coming to me after the course and telling me, "Wow, there's something about this course."

The way he said it was, "I got it. I really got what we're doing out here." And I remember those words. There was some context to it. It was around this idea of building an opportunity for these people to find the best of themselves and he was like, "Totally get it." He had this sense, I remember this, that like from this course on, he's—everything that he does from here on out with groups and stuff like that, he was going to have this new set of eyes. Oh yeah, that was really cool.

Each one of those kids that came on the course had a transformation. You could see it from the beginning to the end. They were an inspiring group. I would say that group was a real success. It was a tribute to Jason in his steadfast, kindhearted perseverance with them because he was the one staff member that was with them the whole time.

A World without Captain Hook

In the movie *Hook,* a grown Peter Pan has a climactic duel with his archrival, Captain Hook. A defeated and defrocked Hook looks up at Peter, who is prepared to run his sword through him, and asks, "Peter, what would the world be like without Captain Hook?"

Think about that for a moment. What if the entire world was good all the time? What if there were no villains, no bad weather, no school, no weeds in the garden, the grass grew to a fixed height and didn't need cutting—if whatever you don't like would not exist?

The answer to that is "Boring! Boring! Boring!" Those are the words of both Fred Alan Wolf, PhD (alias Dr. Quantum) and Father Tom Kreidler, my good friend and pastor, and I believe that many of their respected and respective brethren would agree. When science and religion agree, who am I to argue?

But really, if life was all good, all perfect, all kum ba yah, could we handle it? Is there any difference in the failures in the lives of the rich and famous when compared to the failures of the poor and unknown? In the cartoon strip *Zits,* Jeremy, the young hero, laments to his friend Pierce, "My childhood was incredibly bland: no drama, no heartbreaks, no triumph over adversity. Nothing but wall-to-wall-middle-class comfort and security!" Pierce replies, "Whoa! The suffering of never having suffered!" Finally our hero realizes his predicament: "No wonder I'm so cranky!"

In the book *The Price of Privilege*, Madeline Levine, PhD, discusses that "parental pressure and material advantage are creating a generation of disconnected and unhappy kids." The struggle and the victims exist on both ends of our lifestyle experience: the poor and underprivileged and the well-to-do and privileged. While it has been readily apparent just from following the news of drive-by shootings (to pick one example) that many poor people are murdered, it has also become apparent that many well-to-do children die at their own hands, from suicide. Levine writes,

> The various elements of a perfect storm—materialism, pressure to achieve, perfectionism and disconnection—are combining to create a crisis in America's culture of affluence. This culture is unmanageable for parents, mothers in particular, as it is for their children. While many privileged kids project confidence and know how to make a good impression, alarming numbers lack the basic foundation of psychological development: an authentic sense of self.

In the cartoon strip *Hi and Lois,* Hi enters a room as his son Chip watches TV. Hi reminds Chip that he is getting older and has to start making life decisions, to which Chip replies, "Can't you hire someone to do that for me?"

Some children of privilege are not grounded. With no sense of self, no sense of achieving by their own hands, they do not possess the tools necessary for growth.

> You fathers and you mothers
> Be good to one another
> Please try to raise your children right
> Don't let the darkness take 'em
> Don't make 'em feel forsaken
> Just lead them safely to the light
> — Billy Joe Shaver, "Live Forever"
> as sung by Robert Duvall in *Crazy Heart*

Singing Dove in the Gentle Wind, the mother of a Foundation scholarship recipient, wrote,

> What Anasazi gave her is a light in her heart and soul that reconnected her with herself, the person that I knew was inside. It is miraculous that this program came into our lives at the perfect time."

Our human nature seems to find solace in the struggle more so than in victory. Nobody is perfect; we are a mix of good and bad, or as Dr. Quantum would say, we are "dancing on the edge of chaos." We live with our feet straddling the line and, in some cases, scared by our ability to do good. Isn't that weird?

When I was a Boy Scout, we used to sing a song at campfire that involved using our flashlights. We would turn them on but cover them. Then at the proper moment, we would uncover them, raise them, and swing them around overhead as we sang, "I'm gonna let it shine, let it shine all the time." Each verse describes a challenge to keeping the light on (for example, "Hide it under a bushel"), but all are answered with a resounding "No! I'm going to let it shine." The world of the outdoors is all about letting each individual's light shine.

In her book *A Return to Love: Reflections on the Principles of a Course in Miracles,* Marianne Williamson writes,

> Our deepest fear is not that we are inadequate. Our deepest fear is that we are powerful beyond measure. It is our light, not our darkness, that most frightens us. We ask ourselves: Who am I to be brilliant, gorgeous, talented, fabulous? Actually, who are you not to be? You are a child of God. You're playing small does not serve the world. There is nothing enlightened about shrinking so that other people won't feel insecure around you. We are all meant to shine, as children do. We were born to make manifest the glory of God that is within us. It's not just in some of us; it's in everyone. And as we let our own light shine, we unconsciously give other people permission to do the same. As we are liberated from our own fear, our presence automatically liberates others.

We never get away from the chaos of living on the edge. There is an old saying that if you are not living on the edge, you are taking up too much space. It is on that edge that we learn. It is in the pain that we grow. It is the challenges that define who we are. Dr. Thecla Howard writes that discovery comes from the edge; life begins on the edge. Stand at the boundary of a wetland where different waters meet and look at the life that unfolds in nature's incubator. Turtles crawl out of the sea to deposit their eggs on the beach's edge and return to the sea to be followed later by their offspring. It is in this gooey gooeyness that we develop. The wetlands are sacred ground in Mother Nature's grand design.

Unfortunately for some, children especially, the problem is that the chaos comes too soon, too fast, and before it can be processed efficiently, and it overloads their lives. Some just don't have the skills or the maturity to handle the chaos and become withdrawn.

In the age of electronics, communications fail them. In a world where it seems that everyone has to be constantly connected, in touch with everyone else, where our lives exist in a constant electronic buzz, each adolescent believes the problem he has is unique, that nobody understands him, and thus that nobody can help. Many adolescents believe they are beyond help or that nobody is there who can offer help and support.

In *Hook*, as Maggie, Peter Pan's daughter, is being carried off the ship before the start of the final battle, she turns to face Captain Hook and says, "You need a mother very, very badly."

"I Couldn't See Past the End of the Block"

Anthony K. Sr. grew up in downtown Hartford, Connecticut, on Park Street. At the time, it was a rough neighborhood with gangs, fights, drugs, and crime—not a happy environment. It wasn't an enriching environment. When all you see around you is grief and insecurity, your life is negatively molded by those visions. The negativity smothers any hopes and dreams before a child can even realize such dreams exist.

I met Anthony at the Wilderness School the day his son, Anthony Jr., graduated. While no longer living in his childhood neighborhood, he believed it important that his son receive the same benefit he was given when he attended the Wilderness School as a kid himself years earlier. Anthony Sr. had been the beneficiary of a Wilderness School scholarship through the kindness of a neighbor "three houses down" who happened to be a teacher at the Institute of Living. She was a teacher not only for those in her classroom but also for the youth in her neighborhood as well. She found a way to take the neighborhood children on trips, like one to the Boston Museum of Science, to show them that there was more to life than what was visible from their front windows. At times some of the parents "thought her a bit weird," as Anthony related, because she provided opportunities; she opened eyes and, in the process, helped the children grow. It wasn't a job to her; it was a lifestyle, a calling.

When Anthony told me he couldn't see past the end of the block, he meant his life was being limited, defined, and shaped by forces that were not helping him to grow, to be what he could be, or to realize his potential. A helping hand, a guiding light, in the form of a neighborhood mentor opened his eyes. Initially, he thought of the idea of going to the Wilderness School as a vacation from the family, from the neighborhood, from the fear, from the crime, and from the terror. Through the help of a neighbor, he got into science, did a school project on aerodynamics, and placed first both at his school and in the city. He won honorable mention in the state finals. A kid coming from the projects never thought he could do it but became the only non-honors student to get first place in that competition at his school.

Today Anthony Sr. is happily married, works in electronics, and has plans for his younger son and a nephew to attend the Wilderness School. Anthony Jr. attends East Hartford's Synergy Alternative High School, is involved in their leadership program (with Dave Bocchichio), and is working with younger students, helping them in summer and after-school outdoor programs. He has been trained in adventure-based counseling with younger children and thus gives them an opportunity to do something meaningful in a supportive environment. He loves it and is looking to do more. Because of his father's efforts, he now can see opportunities for himself past the end of the block.

Earlier, I asked what the ancients had to get away from that caused St. Ignatius and others to advise them to escape into the wilderness for repair, especially when compared to the complexities of today, when folks face the explosion of noise, electronics, diversions, gadgets, and twenty-four/seven news, with our exposed risks of what we eat, drink, and breathe, all so prevalent in our culture. The answer lies in the comparison of a thimble full of water and a glass full of water. Both are full, maxed out. Both are doing successfully what they should be doing, holding the water. Humans, by our very nature, get consumed by our lives and our environment. The basic needs of food, clothing, shelter, and safety are the same today as in ancient times; the fictions we develop around our lives may be dressed differently but are still the same. So while we may have more stuff, have a greater library of knowledge, and even have ways of knowing what is happening right now on the other side of the world, we are, in some ways, no better off in handling that than the peasant who is being attacked by a thundering herd of Huns. Dead is dead regardless of the era. Throughout all of history, when all you know is being stressed and you can't see past the end of the block, it's time to step back. And the wilderness is a great place to do just that.

Feeling like Rodney Dangerfield

Validation

I could feel the strength of your blood,
when it was your hand that I shook.
And I could see the compassion of your soul,
when I took a deeper look.
You said, "Did you know that the stones we threw could melt away
like the snow?"
"If it comes deep down that you are afraid,
well, I'm telling you you're not alone."
I so admired your style,
when the day after high school graduation
you left your home.
Bound for the glorious Rocky Mountains,
on a bus, all on your own
> —Jay Seals, "My Friend," eulogy poem, October 20, 2001

R-E-S-P-E-C-T. Aretha famously sings about it. Rodney Dangerfield made the world laugh when he cried, "I get no respect!" People involved in the therapeutic wilderness have long fought for respect, as well. What is therapeutic wilderness? Well, ask anybody, and they will tell you it's like summer camp or some will look to the other extreme and call it "boot camp." In fact, it is neither but much more.

It is not a summer vacation camp, although for some, like Anthony K. Sr., the Wilderness School was a chance to get away from the problems back in the neighborhood. It is not the casual time of fun and games that summer camps are good at providing. That is not to say there cannot be an awakening; doing fun stuff can lead to change. If it wasn't for Camp Sequassen (Boy Scouts, New Hartford, Connecticut), I would not have learned to swim, and in accomplishing that all sorts of activities opened for me. I learned I had the chance to do so much more. Therapeutic wilderness programs are more concerned about personal life developmental skills than, say, swimming, leatherworking, and so forth. Therapeutic wilderness programs try to instill skills that help the student handle life challenges like anger, drugs, and abuse.

Nor is it boot camp. That environment is too harsh, too much in your face, too much emotional and mental tear down, too much deprivation. Why withhold food from someone who may never have had a decent meal? Why not give them more food, quality food? Why not make them feel like equals rather than a lowly piece of trash as some of them already feel? They may get wet hiking in the rain; they may sleep on the hard ground; the packs may be heavy; the trail may be steep, muddy, and slippery; and yes, they may have late nights working through issues. But they should do so as equals, safe, cared for, and protected, not torn down and deprived, as is the modus operandi of boot camps.

Three of the best things about outdoor experiential education are that it has great on-the-job training, an unbelievably beautiful work environment, and, as Aaron Wiebe, Wilderness School program coordinator reminds his seasonal staff, "It lasts all summer long." It goes every day, twenty-four/seven, all season long! I mean, what is there not to love about canoeing, kayaking, paddling, hiking in great surroundings, enjoying campfires at night, playing games, absorbing sunshine, beholding scenery, and making friends?

Each crew, each season, and each program is different and presents its own challenges. When Dave Cowart started, almost thirty years ago, there weren't specific college programs for this type of "work," he got "degreed in the field." He grew up Boy Scouting in the Great Smoky Mountains National Park. Then he became a river guide on some of the Tennessee and North Carolina rivers. When Woodson Wilderness Challenge (then Camp Woodson) needed a white-water guru, he applied and has been there ever since. He enjoys his experience-rich work, a point he knows that his friends employed in the more traditional indoor endeavors can't say about their jobs.

However, a problem comes with that enjoyment —it's too much fun. As an industry that is only some forty years old at the most, it has an image problem. Comments like, "You're playing in the woods" or "That's just a camp" shortchange the impact the wilderness has as a venue for changing lives. Legislators and others who hold the purse strings devalue the effectiveness of such programs. Even the staff has a hard time getting their parents, family, and friends to visit a graduation ceremony, let alone understand what they do. When Dr. Sandy Newes was at Penn State working on her doctorate in the '90s, she had to convince the department heads that it was, in fact, a viable field to study. "They practically kicked me out of school," she said. They told her, "You have no critical thinking skills! Have we taught you nothing?" She ended up "applying traditional clinical theory and method to it and talking about it from their (scholastic/clinical) perspective." At times, she felt as though she was "pushing a rock uphill."

The Tennessee psychology hospital's alternative living program where *Quartz* worked was closed. Legislators decided that the patients and staff were having too much fun. It seems one cannot have fun in the process of learning, growing, and maturing. Likewise, in North Carolina, the Eckerd Youth Alternatives camps have closed due to the budget axe. One of the last, in Candor, North Carolina, is where Danielle spent three years working with adjudicated youth.

For nearly thirty-five years, Woodson Wilderness Challenge was known as Camp Woodson. Tex and his staff operated as part of the North Carolina Department of Juvenile Justice and Delinquency Prevention. Several years ago, they noticed in their funding discussions that the powers above had been misled by the name and associated the program with summer camp, fun in the woods, arts and crafts, and so on. Woodson is nothing of the sort.

It is a rigorous therapeutic, adaptive Outward Bound program that requires tremendous effort and commitment both physically and mentally. Woodson had one of the best recidivism rates in the state with only 22 percent of its participants being rearrested, versus 65 percent of the general youth development centers' (YDC) population. In an effort to help the legislators focus on the success this program had in turning around young lives, they decided to change their name to Woodson Wilderness Challenge (2010). It worked for a year. Unfortunately, the drastic statewide budget cuts demanded by the current administration in 2011 forced their closure along with other programs. After 267 sessions of thirty-two day durations, serving over three thousand students, the doors closed. But not for long: private funding and support is beginning to build a new program (the Pisgah Center) to serve the needs of sixteen- and seventeen-year-old boys. The Pisgah Center will use the same base camp and basic philosophy that Woodson used for the past thirty-plus years.

Industry-wide associations are attempting to ratchet up awareness, but it is a long, slow process. The Association for Experiential Educators (AEE) was founded in the 1970s "to discuss ways in which education could be made more relevant for students," whereas the Outdoor Behavioral Healthcare Industry Council (OBHIC), founded in 1997, moves the industry to gain "the advantage of uniting to promote program standards and excellence." Both groups, as well as the National Association of Therapeutic Camps (NATWC) and National Association of Therapeutic School and Programs (NATSAP), share many of same members, so working together, they can make their missions known.

What complicates matters is that a new model by which to judge and thus validate the programs must be created. These programs are expensive, and the question becomes, even in a good economy, "Who pays?" The medical model of identifying an illness and then prescribing treatment doesn't work. A prescription for four days of hiking, one day of rock climbing, and two days of paddling doesn't mean anything. The closest model would be the psychological model of talk sessions, but even there it needs to be adapted for work with youth versus its basis in adult clinical work. Even though we provide more and easier means by which to communicate and have more social networks outlets, talking doesn't work for many of today's youth—if it ever did—activities do. Children, including adolescents, often believe that their problems are theirs alone, that nobody else will understand their situations, especially an adult, and that nobody will listen. If someone did listen, they would just make fun of them, and thus these children don't talk. As hard as it is to believe that it's true, even with communications' being empowered and expanded as they are by today's technology, communication just doesn't happen for many children, and such failure is the norm.

The sad fact is that the treasure of anecdotal evidence and personal testimonies is not acceptable. Our reductionist view of life demands facts—cold, hard facts. We know that by taking a child out of his comfort zone, providing safe and fun but challenging experiences, and making the child feel guarded and guided by supportive and loving staff, change will happen. We just don't know when the change will happen. It may be that day or sometime during the twenty-day course, or maybe it will come even years later. When the student has that all-important, personal aha moment, when he learns to believe in himself, when he says, "I can do this" and does it, then and only then will change happen.

I met Joshua Pearl at Adventure Links in Virginia. Duke Cutshall, the COO/CFO, invited me to visit after reading about my planned hike of the Appalachian Trail on the foundation's website. When he was seventeen years old, Josh awoke one night to find two escorts at his bed preparing to transport him to Second Nature in Utah. His family had decided that a crisis intervention was needed. They were tired of his acting out, his poor school performance, his drugs, and his abuse of himself and those who loved him. It was time to face and fight the devil. The experience made him "happier than any other time" in his life. But it didn't happen overnight. At first he was oppositional, as was his normal reaction to anything his folks offered. It took three weeks in the program for him to realize that he could take care of himself. He found a sense of control that he did not previously think he had. He was no longer lost and unable to cope but found an opportunity to change. But it still wasn't fun. That came after five weeks, and then he realized it was the "best time of my life." He finished the course and returned to his family with a renewed sense of purpose. Today he works in the outdoors and is paying it forward by helping others.

Documenting these results takes time. I was at the AEE Best Practices Conference in Columbus, Ohio, in 2010 when Lee Gillis, PhD, held a session updating the goals set at a conference held five years earlier. While everyone in the room recognized the effectiveness of experiential education, had personal experiences in which they witnessed change, and—by virtue of being there—bought into the concepts, they acknowledged that more work was needed to prove to insurance companies and other third-party payers the benefits and efficacy of such work.

When an insurance provider expressly excludes coverage of such programs, children have one less option for getting help. It's the unspoken "we don't send kids to camp" syndrome. Part of the problem may also be in how the programs are "sold." Prevention, intervention, and transition are the big three areas where these programs work best. As Sandy Newes says, "It may well be what wilderness does better than anything else." Working with a child before he becomes a customer of the justice system, before he gets involved with social workers, therapists, the court system, probation officers, and residential training centers (read *institutionalized*), saves money. Intervening while a child is "in the system" decreases both the time and money needed to bring release. But the longer a child is in the system, the more hardened that child becomes toward change. And regarding transition, the skills learned in handling others, in working with people, and in taking responsibility for one's own actions are skills that can be incorporated in everyday living "on the outside."

Dr. T and Mr. H relate how parents would cancel their children's participation in their equine program as punishment because the child had been bad, caused problems at school, or acted out at home that week. But those are exactly the times that children need to be in a program! Those are the times they need to be reinforcing the lessons of personal responsibility and respect for others. When would be a better time for a teachable moment than when the problem is fresh? But again, they say it's too much fun, it's like playing, or it's not school. And we have all grown to know that school is not fun!

Part of the problem in gaining and maintaining respect and validation might be the confusion caused by the proliferation of terms for this kind of program: outdoor experiential education, adventure programming, long-term residential camping, activity-based psychotherapy, adventure therapy, wilderness therapy, and therapeutic wilderness. They all mean something different, if only different shades on the some color chart.

Chelsea Ambrozaitis, a Wilderness School outdoor educator whom I met while there, interviewed fellow outdoor educators from the Wilderness School for her senior thesis entitled *Conceptualizing Success in Therapeutic Wilderness Experiences: The Creation and Maintenance of Instructor-Participant Relationships*. One of her points was that the Wilderness School was not a wilderness therapy program but still possibly therapeutic. She is right and at the same time wrong, depending on how you define it. It gets especially confusing when either term is substituted for the other. In wilderness therapy, students hike, camp, climb, and paddle in the outdoors with oversight provided by therapists, licensed clinicians, or social workers to the point that the professionals may periodically hike out to visit with the children in the field or even stay on course out in the field for the entire time. The field staff acts as guides and guardians and actively consults with the clinicians as needed.

In therapeutic wilderness, the woods are the venue of change. To paraphrase Steve Prysunka from Alaska Crossing, many of his charges have already been in therapy—one session a day for months, maybe even years. He wants them to have a different experience in a different setting. Getting the children out of their normal surroundings, away from the white-coat environment, and having them work on tasks together and individually and doing things they may never have thought they could do—in effect, quieting them down and refocusing them—gives them the ability to face and address issues from the totally different perspective of nature's consequences. They have the time to learn the skills needed to address their respective problems.

When Steve mentioned the hours of clinical sessions versus being in the wilderness, I was reminded of a point that Sandy Newes made during our lunch in Asheville. She calculated that a twenty-one-day expedition was equivalent to more than six years of weekly one-hour sessions, even factoring in sleep time.

In my mind, *outdoor experiential education* is an all-encompassing term covering a wide range of activities conducted for various reasons and purposes. Some reasons could be to have fun, to socialize with friends, and to counter that often-heard complaint— "There's nothing to do." Other reasons could be to become educated and to learn a skill. There are many companies and groups that offer such services; many call this adventure programming.

Then there is adventure therapy, which means that outdoor activities are used as a means of therapy (means of change). The purpose is developmental as in personal growth and life-skills enhancement. The idea of wilderness in therapy is a sense that you are purposely put into a situation where the natural world is in control. A sense that you are removed from most creature comforts. You are stripped down to the basics. Physical stress and weather rule the day. Food and shelter is lashed to your back. In this contract with nature a person is less preoccupied with the disruptions of daily living and occupied with a stripped down version of modern life. It takes one of four forms:

1. Long-term residential camping: This is not your two weeks at summer camp. This is months to a year or more living outdoors, with some classroom services and a wide variety of the traditional outdoor activities.
2. Activity-based psychotherapy: An example would be a one-day ropes course activity as part of a residential therapy program.

3. Wilderness therapy: This refers to an extended wilderness experience under the direction of a specific clinical plan.

4. Therapeutic wilderness: This type of program uses the wilderness as the venue of change without a specific clinical plan or on-going clinical oversight. The primary idea is that nature is nurture. The group becomes a significant part of the therapy in the sharing of the experience. As Tom Dyer writes,

> The wilderness is then the setting with the "out of doors" becoming the wilderness. This wilderness is a less remote out of door experience and can happen in East Hartland (CT). It is a relative term.
>
> The most important ingredients are the instructors who actually visit the real wilderness. And then share their beliefs and experiences (personal philosophy) while guiding the students in a more restrained setting.

What is interesting to note is that any outdoor activity, regardless of the original reason or purpose, may lead to personal growth and development. In learning to swim (a hard skill), I realized that a world of other opportunities was opened to me. Knowing that by working hard, I had achieved and in the future could achieve a goal gave me the confidence (a life skill) to develop.

People like Sandy Newes are working to merge the language of adventure therapy with clinical therapy so the two can understand and collaborate better. She calls it paradigm shifting, and it works to incorporate the good from both sides. On one hand, she trains the field staff to be better observers of "clinically relevant stuff," to better understand how the skill pieces fit and how they connect to the clinical process. On the other hand, she is also training the clinicians to think experientially so that they can integrate the wilderness into their clinical therapeutic process. In fact, she and Scott Bandoroff have formalized this training into a Clinician First Responder (CFR) class for field and industry personnel. Whereas most programs require Wilderness First Responder (WFR) and Cardiopulmonary Resuscitation (CPR) training, many develop their own emotional disturbance and behavioral guidelines, or crisis intervention guidelines, as some are called. As Sandy explains,

> One of the impetuses for CFR is that I came out of grad school and started at a wilderness program as a clinician and realized I knew nothing about wilderness therapy. I had been studying it in the books, blah, blah. But the next thing I know is I'm on call, and I got these really experienced field staff being forced to call me when there is a crisis in the field, around something like throwing rocks, and I'm sitting there with them going, "I haven't an idea." They don't teach you the magic phrase in grad school that's going to get you over, "I have no idea. What do you think?" But they were silent because of the power structure put in place. I was the clinical pro, and I was supposed to know, and at the same time there was this thing that you're not supposed to teach the field staff very much because they will take it and run with it.

Some states prohibit the use of the term *therapeutic* unless a licensed clinician or physician is on staff. In truth, the medical profession does not have exclusive rights to the term; the Greek term *therap* means "attendant" or "one who serves." The states' restriction of the use of the term doesn't help the child; it merely reinforces the power and authority of the clinical profession. It creates an additional cash stream for their members, which drives up the cost of care and creates a false image of their being the only effective source. Would we stop a mother from caressing her crying baby who has just fallen because she is not licensed? Is her care not therapeutic? The key is finding the right program for the child's particular circumstances, be it "a walk in the woods" or a clinical/medical approach.

In the book *Against Medical Advice*, Hal Freidman and James Patterson recount the Friedman family's struggle to help their son, Cory, overcome Tourette syndrome, obsessive behavioral disorder (OBD), and anxiety disorder. For thirteen years, they tried numerous professionals, sixty drugs, and a maddening matrix of combinations with little results but a living hell. Then, in what may have seemed to be a desperate turn, they enrolled Cory in a wilderness program followed by a boarding school that specialized in OBD. The wilderness changed his life, and the boarding school built on that awakening. It is a heartwarming story of a family's love and support and the refusal to give up or accept the norm. Maybe the book should have been titled *Success Even Against Medical Advice*.

A critical piece of the therapeutic process is the follow-up. After a child graduates from any wilderness program, be it a twenty-day, thirty-day, or forty-seven-day expedition program, there is a need for continued support. Some children go to boarding schools or other residential institutions while others return to their own homes and communities. Often, boarding schools provide that follow-up piece, but those going home face a challenge of finding the necessary support to build on the positives of the wilderness experience.

The Wilderness School does this well because the State of Connecticut requires the school to provide an experiential follow-up program, and the school's design incorporates both the expedition and the follow-up companion programs. It works because of two other conditions: all students are Connecticut residents, and the state is relatively small, which allows easy access to the school and staff.

Within the follow-up, there is a very critical aspect—that the local provider be fully aware of the outdoor experience the child has just completed. This hometown resource could be a twelve-step program like Alcoholics Anonymous (AA) or a clinical professional. The key to continued success and growth for the child is that the hometown provider needs to understand the process the child has just experienced and needs to provide care that builds on that experience. The hometown resource has to be on the same wavelength or the child may suffer, regress, or worse, fall back to his or her old ways and thus have a harder time recovering because of the lack of knowledgeable support. While it may be possible to find a local twelve-step program such as AA or Narcotics Anonymous (NA), or another type of support group or professional clinician, that group or professional may still not understand the wilderness aspect of the "treatment received" by the child. A resource that is once attuned maximizes the student's transition to home as well as future growth by building on the positives of what was, for the child, a major life awakening. It is a very tough process to find such knowledgeable support systems as the two professions 1) have their own separate terminology and perspectives and 2) are just now beginning to enter into a dialogue. It thus becomes necessary to train the local professionals in the nuances of attending to students who have completed such programs.

As he works to develop a specific follow-up for each of his clients, Andy Erkis, PhD, of Erkis Consulting in Columbus, Ohio, has a two-part mission: to find a professional he can work with for that child and then to expose the professional to the wilderness experience. It is a time-consuming process and a challenge he faces everywhere he works, whether he is with a family from Columbus, another major American city, or foreign places like Israel, Holland, or England. For the past year, he has been testing in Columbus a system of intense in-home care that provides three or four in-house visits a week and twenty-four/seven emergency care and uses the same language as the child's program used in the wilderness.

While many who work in the outdoors are drawn to do so by previous outdoor experiences of their youth, Andy came to it by way of an invitation from a graduate school friend. Frustrated by the ineffectiveness of the medical model to really help his oppositional defiant clients and by a stark realization he had: "Everything I learned as a psychologist didn't prepare me to work with those kids" (those for whom sitting in an office in therapy was counterproductive), he considered leaving his practice. But then he was invited to attend Second Nature in Utah. He experienced staff training and shadowed groups in the field. Compared to what he knew from working at a residential treatment program, the wilderness was "exponentially better for a wider range of kids." He saw the program as a "safe container" that, in exposing the youth to the wilderness's "amazing milieu" while "not allowing their old patterns to work," developed personal growth.

All too often, a lack of knowledgeable support becomes evident at the worst possible time. I had a chance to meet with Ed Raiola, PhD, department head of the Warren Wilson College Outdoor Leadership Program, while he was on sabbatical in Asheville. Ed told me of an incident that he had observed that not only had a negative impact on the experience at that moment but also could have caused a negative impact later in life.

Ed was going to a shopping mall that had a large indoor play area for children. One of the elements was a climbing wall, which was run by a young lad. A granddad was there with his grandson and decided to let the grandson climb the wall. The boy put on a climbing harness, was roped in, and started climbing. Now this climbing wall was a self-belaying top-rope wall, meaning that the belaying rope came from the top and that as the climber moved up the wall, the slack in the rope created by climbing higher was automatically reeled in by a mechanical system behind the wall. Traditionally, there would be a person belaying and observing each individual climber, but that wasn't the case here. When the boy started having difficulty, there was nobody there to help him, his difficulties begot frustration, and eventually he was hanging on the rope crying. The young lad who was overseeing the wall was too busy talking to a friend and failed to give the child any help, which begs the question: Was he even trained to help?

It appeared that for the young man in charge, this was just another day of work; he was just putting in hours before quitting time. But for the young child, it was his first experience, and whether he was nervous or confident, life allows that first experience only once. Will he come back? It is possible, especially if he sees some friends that he trusts doing well, he could very well be drawn in and move beyond the first bad experience. But worse, he could be turned off by it and other associated activities, maybe even to the point of voting against community initiatives designed for developing outdoor programs later in life as an adult.

In 1986 Steve Robertson was the champion of the Black World Championship Rodeo. A fireman with the New Haven Fire Department, Steve grew up visiting his grandparents' horse farm in Massachusetts. When I met him during my travels, he was with the Eagleton School, using his horses to help autism-spectrum students. No longer on the rodeo circuit, he told me of an experience he had with a young boy who wanted to be a cowboy. The lad started hanging around the rodeo's horse barns near LaGuardia Airport in New York City. He showed true interest and a willingness to work hard, so much so that Steve and some of the other members started training him, and he did quite well. Steve offered to drive him home one night after a rodeo, and as they got close to his neighborhood, the young boy took off his hat and put it in a bag. He was afraid to walk down his own street and show that he was different from the other youth. He realized that being different put him on the outs with street gangs, but at the same time, he was willing to do what he had to do to get away from the neighborhood.

I wish I had learned that lesson myself, as it would have saved me a hat. In the football season of 1960, I was a manager for our high school football team. That summer, I went out to Colorado Springs with a Boy Scout troop for the National Jamboree, which included one week at the jamboree and two weeks of traveling and sightseeing. Somewhere between Cheyenne and Jackson Hole, Wyoming, I bought a black cowboy hat. The headband that came with it wasn't good enough, so I bought a belt that had links in the shape of an eagle with a blue stone in the center of the bird's chest. I fit the belt to my hat and threw away the excess links. I felt like Sundance, a gunfighter–turned-marshal from the cowboy TV series *Hotel de Paree* (CBS 1959–1960). The show opened with the sun's rays dancing off the metal discs in his headband. I was cool—until, that is, I decided to wear it during a football game. That's when, after a bad play on the field, my hat ended up on the ground, being danced upon by a senior lineman whose only remark was something about cowboys not being welcomed. It was a lesson learned the hard way.

Another problem that faces outdoor programs is local zoning laws. I have found it interesting that, in the attempts to run wilderness programs, zoning laws have had a negative impact. The idea of offering a primitive wilderness experience runs smack up against the law. It's understandable to want to start the primitive experience at base camp. As soon as the students arrive, they should begin to be moved from their comfort zones. They should begin to sense change. So ideas like pit toilets, cold showers with solar bags hung over a wood platform, and other "roughing it" amenities fill the bill, or so one would think. But think again. Zoning laws don't understand or appreciate that roughing it helps in character development. Places like Kamp Kessa in Kentucky have been forced to change and alter aspects of their programs. Thus, in the end, the loss is some of the purity of the program. Maybe the overnight aspect at base camp is lost and programs move off site to have overnights in state parks or programs become day only. The challenge then becomes for the leaders to figure out how to maintain the awe and the mystery of the outdoors and how to move beyond comfort zones into the gooey-gooeyness of change.

Earlier, I used the term "a walk in the woods." There are many folks who, when they heard that I was preparing to hike the Appalachian Trail, asked if I had read the book *A Walk in the Woods* by Bill Bryson, a fun and yet thought-provoking book by a very successful and respected writer, except that is for the community of Appalachian Trail purists. For them, I get the feeling that there are two views. First, the book is kindling to start the fire that will heat the tar they are storing along with the feathers to be used should they ever see Mr. Bryson, and here I will paraphrase him, that far south again.

Second, to paraphrase what Winton Porter reports in *Just Passin' Thru*, there is a desire to tie Bryson stark naked to a board, cover him in honey, and leave him by the bee box near the river, just to sweeten him up.

The purist can't accept the fact that Bryson wrote a book about hiking the Appalachian Trail, their "church," but never finished hiking its entirety. In fact, he skipped parts and made fun of some areas and the folks he met along the way. The fact is that 80 to 85 percent of those who start the trail don't finish. He wrote a book more in tuned to those of us who start and stop, as well as the rest of the world, than for those who finish the thru-hike. In the process, he opened the Appalachian Trail to America in general. As the book's subtitle says, he helped Americans "rediscover America on the Appalachian Trail." We needed that.

I met and worked for Ms. Janet when I was at the hostel at Mountain Crossing at Neel's Gap. Ms. Janet is well known on the Appalachian Trail. She has for years opened her home in Erwin, Tennessee, to thru-hikers one and all. Her place is a must stop along the way. With a cooking ladle in one hand and a foot bath massager in the other, she is a source of comfort to all who enter her door. Nobody knows the Appalachian Trail community and culture better than Ms. Janet. So it was a pleasure to work for her as she took time away from her home to manage Winton's hostel as the early rush of thru-hikers started their trek northbound. She would meet up with some of these same hikers when she returned home, after they had hiked to Erwin over another 309.2 miles. While at Neel's Gap, she told me of her countless discussions about Bryson's book at gatherings of trail folks and how she has seen the book's positive influence on the hikers coming through. She sees an expanded market of hikers created in part by a desire to experience the book. She sees the growth in the number of hikers as a plus for all—the trail; the towns and businesses along the way that feed, accommodate, and resupply the hikers; and for the country as a whole.

Ms. Janet related how her daughter had been threatened with in-school detention for an unexcused absence because her family went white-water kayaking on the Nolichucky River.

I had a little talk with the superintendent of schools....
"You do not want me to make a big issue of this. We are

50 percent federally held land, we have a population that is growing older, and our young people are leaving because they say there is nothing to do here. So they are all getting into trouble, drinking, dealing drugs, sitting in the parking lot. I have not seen one move to try to get these kids out doing the things that people come from all over the world to do in our backyard. Don't tell me my child is in detention because she spent eight hours on one of our biggest money makers in the county ... the Nolichucky River."

We got past that little issue. What bothered me was that she is twelve years old, [and] there was not another twelve-year-old in her classroom who had been white-water rafting. I have worked at school; I was "the mom" with all my children and have quit jobs so I could be there, especially [for] school trips. And I got so disillusioned as I got older; the trips started becoming such poor quality—a thousand dollars to go to Dollywood for three days. I'm like, "We are sitting with the Nolichucky River, white-water rafting, Appalachian Trail, historical area.... I want to have a place, a destination, everybody takes their fourth-grade class to learn about flora and fauna on the trail, learn about some geology, learn about the rocks they are seeing, what formed them, a whole-language kind of thing that you can do and at the end they have hiked a mile and each has a walking stick they can take home. It's starting to teach stewardship of our backyard.

Asheville, North Carolina, is well known as a beautiful, natural playground. Ed Raiola, PhD, explained how the outdoor leadership class at Warren Wilson College runs one-day workshops in conjunction with the Asheville public school system. Children come to the wooded college campus for some outdoor activities and are amazed by the outdoors. Even some of the high schoolers have never been in the woods before, and yet they live in the heart of some of the most beautiful mountains, trails, and rivers in the country. We are often disconnected from our surroundings, which in Ed's view "limits our growth as individuals, as a country, as a culture."

222 Circles

Rituals and Consistencies

The light that burns the brightest burns half as long.
—Laurence Gonzales, *Deep Survival*

There once was a rabbit who came upon a group of animals. They were all seated on the ground looking into the air. In the air flying around the trees was a bird. The bird was putting on a show. The rabbit didn't seem to think this was very interesting, but he stayed and watched anyway.

An hour passed, and everyone was still watching the bird do his tricks. The rabbit started to get bored of this, so without thinking, he said, "I can do that."

And everyone turned around and looked at the rabbit. A fox that was there said, "What did you say?"

So the rabbit said again, "I could do what the bird is doing."

The fox didn't think he could, so he said, "If you think you can, why don't you try?"

So the rabbit climbed the tree and got out onto a branch and jumped off. He came crashing down and landed with a big thump. Everyone started to laugh. The rabbit got up and left and never turned to look back.

Moral: Think before you speak.
—"The Rabbit's Dilemma," Jason Hunt, Immaculate
Heart of Mary Parish School, seventh grade

Rituals are all around us. Rituals are part of our religious experience as in sacraments, our work environment as in sales meetings, our daily community lives as in a person's morning routine. They can be stories told by the ancients to make a point, to show a way, or to offer a moral principle. They are performed to reinforce basic inherent aspects of our lives and the structuring of our lives. In my travels among wilderness programs, I saw some rituals recurring, some that were more limited in use, and some that were very formalized, but all were intended to allow the students to hold the center. The following is not meant to be all inclusive but to illustrate how rituals are used to effect change and support behavior.

From my own camping experiences, I can attest that properly maintaining oneself in the woods is an interesting issue. Some just flat out forget about hygiene; they don't even try. The problem is that the new, lightweight polypro clothes do a great job of wicking away sweat so one feels cooler, not as sweaty, and thus not clammy, but they also do an equally great job of picking up and retaining body odors. If you don't clean the clothes often and thoroughly, over time they will—well, I guess there is no other way to say this—they will smell like a dirty you. And no amount of washing will remove the you that you really don't want people to know. There were times when we thought of renting a hotel room near the house so Jason could stop off, shower, and change into the clean clothes we would leave there for him before coming home. But that thought came only after we wrapped him a long-time-no-see-and-welcome home hug.

String of Pearls

During staff training at the Wilderness School, I noticed that Chelsea Ambrozaitis was wearing a string of pearls. Now, I am fully aware that a lady isn't a lady until she wears her pearls, but then again we were out in the woods, carrying heavy packs, climbing up and slipping down mountains (all right, the one slipping was me), fording streams, and sweating in the hot sun. I really didn't expect to see pearls on the trail. But that was the point.

It seems that during the prior year's staff training, Shannon had asked everyone to wear something they normally would not wear in the woods. Chelsea chose a string of pearls, not cultured but plastic, and thus began what would become her signature in the woods. I have nothing against pearls. The image was everywhere as I was growing up in the 1950s, including June Cleaver on the *Leave It to Beaver* TV show, doing the dishes wearing her pearl necklace. And of course every year at Christmas time, there is Donna Reed in *It's a Wonderful Life* wearing her string of pearls. A lady is just not fully dressed without her pearls.

Chelsea's explanation about the pearls' being a subtle reminder to care for oneself was reinforced later by Nancy Dyer based on her years of leading crews in the woods. Even though one is in the woods with the dirt, mud, sweat, wood smoke, and various ointments accumulating on clothes and skin, one can still be clean and can command and show some respect. This is a point well made earlier by one of our Anasazi scholarship recipients when she wrote about feeling "beautiful in my skin" even after being dirty for weeks and wearing the "most unattractive clothing."

Chelsea and Nancy believed it was very important to maintain a sense of self, to be clean in the woods. They both made an effort daily to maintain an image for their respective crews to duplicate. It was a skill they taught.

Many sexually abused women begin to believe that their bodies are the reason for their abuse. In seeing their bodies as the problem, they begin to see their bodies as being dirty and unfit. They live in the turmoil of being wrapped in this dirty form that they can't leave behind. So the first part of their treatment is to change that image. They have to be taught that their bodies are not the problem. They have to be taught that their bodies are clean and should be respected. They have to be taught what it means to respect their bodies. They need the sense of wearing a string of pearls.

I ran into Chelsea at the September 2010 Wilderness School Alumni Reunion. I immediately noticed that she was without her pearls, which for her was like being out of uniform. She told me that one of the girls on her last crew was so taken by them that she asked if she could have them, and Chelsea gave them to her. But she wasn't without her pearls for long. Another crew member, knowing that Chelsea would be at the reunion, brought her a gift—a new string of pearls. Chelsea was getting her message across.

Much like a basketball player who goes through a set of moves in preparing for a free throw or a baseball player doing the same things each time he enters the batter's box, Chelsea created a ritual for her work in the field. Rituals, according to Father Tom Kreidler, "are those reoccurring events that have a learning element or a continuing element for the culture.... [Each] allows something to be captured that sets the structure within which different experiences can happen."

In the book *Deep Survival,* Laurence Gonzales writes that in a time of crisis, many of those in trouble will often turn to prayer even though they do not pray regularly. It is an ancient ritual that brings focus and clarity to the present. It allows them to fully direct their abilities, to cut through the distractions, and to face the present situation. "Turning fear into focus is the first act of a survivor," Gonzales writes. In reality, at the moment of truth, your equipment, the training you have had, as well as your bank of experience can fail you. It is your ability to focus, to maximize your attention on the present situation that defines your survival strategy's success.

With the ritual of prayer, as Peter Leschak describes in *The Ghosts of the Fireground*, "whether a deity is actually listening or not, there is value in formally announcing your needs, desires, worries, sins, and goals in a focused, prayerful attitude. Only when you are aware can you take action."

Prayer is meditation, a clearing of the mind, a settling of the muddy waters that swirl around in our minds. Prayer is ritual, and ritual leads to structure. Structure leads to confidence, and confidence leads to action.

Rituals are consistencies that within themselves develop a confidence of performance. Rituals provide a natural order of life. Sally Carrighar in *Home to the Wilderness* notes that "the animals of the forest interact with each other easily because they know and could depend that all would act consistently. Only man is the uncertainty factor."

A twenty-day expedition becomes a ritual in itself. It provides structures that allow the students and staff to interact, to challenge, and to grow. It provides the cloak of safety that Gordo found so liberating. It provides the support that makes Sal want to learn more. Within this overarching ritual, multiple smaller and valuable rituals happen. They happen in a seamless flow like the interplay of animals in the woods.

In his book *Roadshow,* Neil Peart, world famous drummer of Rush—and some say the most famous drummer today—continues a ritual he has used for the thirty-plus years that he has been on the road. Each night at the end of the concert, he immediately leaves the stage, gets into his motor coach, and goes to sleep while his crew drives through the night. At a predetermined spot around sunrise, the bus pulls over, he and a buddy get out fully dressed in their riding leathers, they drop the gate on the trailer the coach is pulling, and they retrieve their BMW motorcycles. When he was much younger, he used a bicycle, but it is still the same ritual. They turn on the GPS and head off to the next gig's venue via back roads and sometimes even dry creek beds. It is his chance to get away and to focus.

During Peart's rides, subplots or rituals play out. While he mocks the various church message board signs he finds along the way, he added a new ritual on this anniversary tour. The inside leaves of his book's cover show various National Park visitor stamps. He specifically drove to each park that was within range of his concert route, sometimes doubling back, and collected the stamps—just the stamps. In one park, the ranger actually offered a park map along with directions to that park's reason for being, its scenic wonder that the park protects, but Peart had no time to visit. He just had time to get the stamp. I wonder if the ranger was a bit stupefied that someone would come all that way just for the stamp. Acquiring each stamp became his outlet, his release for this tour and its demands.

Circle-ups

Call it what they might, every outdoor program has the circle, the huddle. Whether one places his arms on the shoulders of his neighbors or crosses his arms in front of his body and then grabs the hands of his neighbors, they all come to a point of equals. I remember Danielle telling stories of late-night, all-night huddles to work through issues within the group. They happen as needed.

When Anna co-led her first 20 day expedition the crew was challenged to count all the circles called. The crew counted 222 circles. That seems to be a large number, but the number itself is not that important. Circles happen for many different reasons; wake up and stretch circle, breaking camp circle, circle before meals, and circle before getting into a van, circle before paddling or rock climbing (safety briefing), circle at the 10 minute clothing check when hiking, circle to resolve issues, evening meeting circle and on and on. The circles, the coming together as a group/community, facilitates the group development process that is key to the experience of a wilderness program.

In the circle process, they learn a skill they can use back home. During the Alumni Reunion, I met Joan J., who told me about Dylan, her son, and the success he has had since his twenty-day expedition. The program helped develop his conflict-resolution skills.

> What he wanted was what he wanted. When he thought he was right, he was right; [he] wouldn't listen to anyone else. ...they would do a circle; it gave him a way to work through the issue. ... So it's kind of funny. After his twenty days at the Wilderness School, we're out with his sister and my husband. We're all out doing something, and there was some conflict in the group, and his idea was, "Okay, do I have to have a circle now?" ... so he brought that circle up into our family and learned some really great, I think, coping techniques.
>
> [It's] probably been the best thing in the world for my son, a totally different person [with] so much more

self-confidence. He's a kid that really kind of struggled, didn't have a lot of friends, has ADHD and other issues. And he found himself here—a sense of purpose.

The Process

Most of the time, every activity includes a circle before it and one after. This, in itself, is another ritual. It is all about the process: 1) explain the activity, 2) do the activity, 3) debrief afterward. The activity is explained so the participants know how to do it and what to expect. The debrief is not so much for the staff to gain any insight as it is to show the students that they actually know what they are doing. The process is always guided by the need to be consistent. Because of that consistency, the crew members realize that they are safe, that they are cared for, and that they are in a good place. Consistency and the striving to be consistent release both the staff and the students to be themselves.

Belaying Ninjas

The rituals are the consistencies. It is the staff's job to make the process fun and the skills easy to learn. For example, Micah teaches the crews how to be belaying ninjas. Just getting them to learn the skills has them laughing and quickly taking on the role. "Ninjas" assume the basic athletic position of feet shoulder-width apart, with one foot slightly in front of the other. Their elbows are bent; hands are raised in front but to the side of the face, with one hand in front of the other. And of course what would this position be without assuming it with a ninja shout? No sooner had Micah explained it than they were jumping to practice it. Along with this ritual comes another. Because this position is used to support another student as he, for example, climbs the slanted telephone pole, the position of the hands is critical to support the student should he lose his balance, stumble, or fall and to ensure that he does not injure the ninjas as well. So it is important to hold up cupped palms with fingers together as opposed to fingers separated or presenting the side of the hand; to remind the crew, the staff says, "Spoons, not forks or knives." In a very short time, the ritual is learned.

Putting Red Fred in the Shed

While it is one thing to walk on and follow a well-worn path or trail in the woods, it is totally different when you walk off trail and through the underbrush, bushwhacking. Then it is time for a map and a compass; knowing how to use them is knowledge that can save one's life. Compasses have a spinning needle that basically always tracks to magnetic north. The pointed tip half of the needle is often painted, usually red—thus Red Fred.

Next, the compass has a rotating bezel with the directional markings of degrees and the relating major points of direction: north, south, east, and west. Inside the bezel's housing and underneath the spinning needle is the face of the compass, where there is the red outline of an arrow, or the shed. Thus, in determining direction, it becomes necessary to rotate the bezel so that the needle lines up inside the needle outline; Red Fred lines up in the shed. By holding the compass flat in your hand or on a flat surface and placing Red Fred in the shed, the direction you wish to travel can be read as it is directly in front. While Red Fred in his shed may be pointing to the left, to the right, or even back at you, it is always pointing to magnetic north.

Directional or Popcorn Style

There are rituals for everything. When in group, the leader may ask for the crew's participation either popcorn style or directional. *Directional* means the discussion moves in one direction, with everyone taking a turn. *Popcorn style* means random participation is desired; people jump in as they wish, just like popcorn popping out of a pan.

Passing the Pulse

When concluding a special circle, the leader may ask for a moment of prayer. To end the circle, the leader squeezes (pulses) the hand of one of the people to his side. That person then continues the process, and eventually the pulse makes its way back to the leader.

First Foot In

There are more rituals than what I will cover here. The key is that children pick up on them quickly, often reminding others to wait their turn. For example, when in circle and holding hands, how does one request to speak next? Somebody must have been listening to the Hokey Pokey song because the solution is to raise one foot and extend it into the center of the circle. The person whose foot is first in speaks next—simple, easy, and effective.

During a staff training class on trauma, Mike Smith, one of the DCF trainers conducting the class, proudly proclaimed how quickly and easily he had caught on to the process. We had formed a food circle, which was his first circle ever, and after seeing two or three of the staff kick a foot in, he quickly picked up on it, which he boasted about as he put a foot in and made his comment. Even though Mike and I graduated many years apart, you just have to admire a fellow Stonehill College grad for being such a speedy learner.

Earning a Bead

A student who does a job well can earn a wooden bead. Over the length of the expedition, he can earn many beads that can be made into a bracelet, belt, or necklace. The beads are different colors, sizes, and shapes so students can better remember why they were earned. The one bead they all strive to earn is the graduation bead.

211

Five Alternatives

The crews love this one and pick up on it very quickly. When someone is caught saying a swear word, anyone in the crew can call him or her on it by yelling, "Five alternatives." The individual, whether a staff member or a student, must then rapidly say five clean words, even if they are irrelevant to the original discussion. Students can call another student, staff can call a student, and students can call a staff member on it. As mentioned earlier, children don't miss much; they see and hear everything, so the opportunity to catch a staff member gets their attention.

Ten-Minute Check

The ten-minute check is designed to allow for a clothing adjustment once hiking begins, whether in the morning, after lunch, or after any long break.

Being properly clothed is important to enjoying a day of hiking. When waking up to a chilly morning, one will want to dress warmly. However, once you start hiking, two things invariably happen—the day's temperature warms and the body's natural ability to produce heat gets going. Too much warm clothing may lead to sweaty clothes, discomfort, and problems. So it is a good idea to take five after hiking for ten minutes and check your clothing—too much, not enough, or even not the right stuff.

While I was visiting a camp in Virginia, I picked up eight ticks. The day had been hot, and I was wearing shorts, which made me an easy target. However, when I jumped ahead to Connecticut, the state that named Lyme disease, I made sure I would not be a victim. It was a staff training hike at the Wilderness School, and we were hiking to Bear Mountain. I dressed in full-length trousers with the cuffs wrapped tight, a long-sleeved shirt, and a floppy hat. I created my own steam bath. I ignored the ten-minute check, and I paid for it. I was overdressed and eventually began to overheat. I was sweating profusely when Micah suggested that I loosen up my clothing a bit. We took a break and I opened my collar, rolled up my sleeves, unzipped my leggings, and felt better, much better, the rest of the hike.

Games

While I could handle the circles, the briefings, and the debriefings, I had a hard time handling the games, the part in the middle.

"Okay, now who wants to play a game?"

"What games should we play?"

"Who's got a game we can play?"

It wasn't just at the programs I visited; they did them at the conferences I attended. Think about it. Here we have adults out in a field, flailing their arms and yelling, "Splat!" at one another. I mean, this is professional?

As a sales rep, I didn't play games; I sold product. We might role-play a possible selling scenario for a new product's introduction. But taking time to play Splat, On the Farm, or M&Ms—when did they do the magic, the real healing stuff? It was happening, but I didn't see it.

It didn't make sense during the conferences or staff training, but when I saw it with the students it became clear. Games opened them to learning. While talk therapy can work for adults, games work for youth, big time. After a while, I couldn't wait for the next game. I saw the crews getting really involved, really concentrating on participating. Some games are fun, while some are serious. The fun games relieve tension or get the group up and running, while the serious games begin the process of opening up.

To play Splat, one person moves to the center of the circle and proceeds to spin around, stop, and point to a person on the circle. The person selected stoops down, whereupon the people on either side of the stooping person turn and face each other over the bent-down player and begin—in rapid fashion and without stopping for a breath—to yell "Splat!" and to flail their arms at each other. Whoever runs out of breath first or stops first loses. It's fun, it's silly, it gets the blood flowing, and everyone laughs.

M&Ms can lead to more serious discussions. The leader assigns a topic to each color in the bag of the M&Ms. Then one at a time, each person in the circle gets to select a candy and discuss the topic represented. Through a careful selection of topics, the group can grow and come together.

I enjoyed participating when I saw how well it was working. But then again, I just may be a kid at heart.

Crew Journal

Each crew receives a pasted-up booklet that the staff literally pulls together for that specific crew. It is the silent staff member or resource that any crew member can use when seeking answers for such topics as a) the major do's and don'ts, b) the daily job chart of tasks that are assigned and completed by the crew members themselves, c) outlines of the jobs and the circles, d) the daily schedule as well as the overall expedition schedule, e) tips on hygiene, f) motivational stories, g) space for members' comments and thoughts, and h) whatever else the staff thinks the crew could use as a reference. For example, one page is all about VOMP, an acronym for a handy life skill in resolving conflicts: Vent one's feelings, Own one's share of the problem, Moccasin—put oneself in the other person's shoes, and Plan how to avoid it in the future.

"I" Statements

The Wilderness School taught me about "I" statements. They are a way for everyone—students as well as staff—to *vent* their anger, frustration, and displeasure caused by another without blaming the other person. Instead of a confrontational "you," the "I" statement would be "I feel hurt, and I just wanted you to know that." The person shares the feeling as a way of overcoming and moving on. The person accepts responsibility for the feeling and, as such, what might have been an argument between the parties becomes "an important part of the healing power of relationships," as Marianne Williamson writes in *A Return to Love*. It is a skill that carries over into everyday life.

So I thought it interesting when Dr. T and Mr. H told me of a twist on it. I visited them at Cedar Fire Farms (Kamp Kessa), their equine wilderness human development operation in Frankfort, Kentucky. Working with a very similar population as that at the Wilderness School, they use saddle horses as the agent of change. Each student takes care of and works with one specific horse while in the program.

The staff knows that change is happening when they hear the students use the "my horse" statement, as in "My horse wants to kick your horse's butt." The students transfer their feelings to the horse, giving them a means of expression without the threat of personal retribution. This is not taught directly; the students move to it on their own.

A Family Ritual

After Jason died, I felt emptiness whenever I visited the Gates of Heaven Cemetery where his body rests. I would go, pray to God and Jason, stand around, maybe brush away a leaf or two, but it just felt like something was missing. I longed to sit down and talk with Jason, maybe even share a beer. That is when it hit me—next time, I would bring a beer and share it with Jason.

Now whenever I go, whether by myself or with others, there is a bottle of beer to share with Jason. I open the bottle, take a sip, pass it around, and then eventually pour the remaining contents over the ground. I get the feeling that I (we) are doing something. It seems to give me peace and brings a little bit of closeness with him again. It seems to give me a deeper purpose for the visit than just standing there, hands in the pockets or clasped in prayer, head down, eyeing the ground.

The Ultimate Challenges

Contributing Adult, Supportive Parent

I think every family is really challenging. Parents are overwhelmed, or confused, or afraid, or too proud. They don't know how to ask for help, or they don't know what is the most appropriate thing for their child 'cause they heard of this one thing from someone but are not aware of all these other options. People are fearful of not having enough money or [whether] this [is] really safe. I think it is really hard to send your child away for five, ten, twenty, ninety days and say, "Okay, these people are going to take care of them and everything will be okay when they come back." I think if you are in crisis or in panic, you fear for the safety but [wonder,] "Is this really going to help?" And people just do not know. Like "We have tried so many things, I do not know where to start."

—Amy Pine, outdoor educator, DCF Wilderness School and
Carolina Trails, Asheville, NC, Interview, April 2010

I was a friend of Jason's.... Your son was one of the few people in the world who knew what it meant to really live life. I am a better person having known him. You and your wife were given a gift, a happy son.

—Galen W. Holland, Warren Wilson College,
e-mail, October 17, 2001

Parenting isn't easy under the best of circumstances. At times it feels like it follows the second law of thermodynamics—it tends to entropy; it tends to decay; it is a steady, predestined decline. Even for the best of parents, it's a battle. Success is not based on schooling or money. There is an old saying that says the happiest of people don't necessarily have the best of everything. They just make the most of everything they have.

There are typical scenarios at both ends of the spectrum: upper-income, highly educated parents who are, for example, medical doctors and alternate picking up their children. It plays out the same for either one: arriving in a BMW or Mercedes–Benz and yelling for the child to quickly get in as they talk on the cell phone. They live life in the fast lane, and missing is a warm hello, a hug, a kiss.

On the other end of the spectrum is the low-income scenario: a parent dead or missing and the other alive and present but strung out on drugs. The child must fend for himself or gets support from a grandmother or other adult relative. Which one is worse? Neither is a winning proposition. Both fulfill the old adage that on any day, a dysfunctional family is any family with more than one member.

Dan A. made us stay at his tarp so he could read his foster mom's letter to us. It was during a visit to the Aviators at the end of their thirty-six-hour solo phase of the expedition. Solo is a part of the trek during which the crew members are separated so that they cannot see or easily interact with one another. Each is given a tarp, emergency whistle, and food to be in the woods "on their own" for thirty-six hours. It is also a way for the crew to rest and regenerate before their final expedition, where they are in charge with the field instructors trailing behind unless needed.

I had hiked in with the ATC's course director, Nicky Wood, who has a way of making the complicated stuff seem easy. It's her knack because she has suffered from ADD for a long time. She has found ways to break down the details into manageable bits. For example, in school she broke down a Japanese artist's name into images she could remember and pronounce. In doing it on her own, she amazed her teacher.

From her experiences in the field, she realized that she needed a visual to simplify the manual on what to do when situations arose. So she drew a flowchart that asked the questions and gave the options quickly. That day, she was excited about hiking in her new "barefoot" shoes, the kind that had individual slots for each toe. It gave her such a new sensation of feeling the ground that she believed the shoes would be beneficial for children with ADD/ADHD. But her main mission was checking in and getting everyone prepped for the final expedition. She brought out mail, which she distributed as she sat with each student to review where they were in the program and what was left to accomplish.

Three times, she suggested that we leave so Dan could read his foster mom's letter in private, but he wouldn't have any of that. Before he had read the letter himself, he already knew it would be good. He wanted us to see and hear the positive reinforcement that she was for him. Dan wanted us to know Kathleen Kores.

> I have talked to your staff and they say you are a leader among your team. I always knew you could lead by example among the team. I want you to feel proud of all your efforts each day of the twenty-day expedition.... I hope you are getting the most you can from each day. There are so many new experiences [at] wilderness camp that will give you insight into yourself and show you all your strengths. It was wonderful to hear how you are taking charge and helping out and as they say be accountable for your part of the team by leading by example form of leadership. So I can only assume that you are having some fun moments, some great moments, and some tough moments. And every time you have lots of joy or soldier through them, you grow in strength and self-awareness. All of this is good and will help you greatly in your third year of high school.

As humans, we can never get enough true support—support that nourishes, not drowns; support that allows growth and expansion versus control; support that allows us to explore outside the box. Getting that mix right is hard; a parent's skills are tested constantly.

"Anyone can become angry—that is easy. But to be angry with the right person, to the right degree, at the right time, for the right purpose, and in the right way—this is not easy." Aristotle's quote is about getting angry but could really be said about any trait: supportive, loving, caring. Does the term "helicopter parent" create any images? Sometimes the best of intentions lead to unintended consequences.

When parents fail, the question becomes about how severe the failure is and who can help. Children are born with great needs, the greatest of which is the need for love, happiness, and belonging. The failure to know love, the failure to experience happiness, the failure to be accepted, and the failure to be safe leaves deep scars. Those scars take time to heal and demand a degree of sophistication by the child to accept the fact that parents as humans can fail and to move on. It's a demand on one's emotional intellect to accept such failure from parents.

I met Quartz in a hostel van the day I got off the Appalachian Trail. As we talked, she told me she was a psychiatric nurse working in a State of Tennessee psychiatric hospital servicing a full range of adults. She worked specifically with a program that taught selected patients to live off site in family group homes. It was a three-year process to move them from hospital to independent living that included taking the patients on camping trips in the woods to teach them responsibility. They used the woods to assess the individuals' skills because, in the hospital environment, long-term institutionalization fosters too much dependency on the staff. In the woods, the patients learn to stand on their own. That is how she met David (name changed).

His adoptive parents rejected him and asked the state to take him back as it was beyond their abilities or desires to handle him. They didn't love him or help him. He didn't fit their standards, and so he was re-institutionalized. The staff was told he could read only at a very elementary level, and he was more into acting out than reading.

But the staff thought he had some potential, so they invited him to go camping. He accepted and was given a list of specific items to bring. Additionally, he was allowed to bring one other item of his choosing. So it was a bit surprising when the staff saw that he was bringing books. When asked why, he answered, "To read!" Quartz wrote in a follow-up e-mail,

> When we realized the potential he had, we continued to rehabilitate him for discharge from the hospital with living and job skills. However, since he was so much younger (twenty years old) than the other men in the group, we located an apartment for him so that he could eventually advance to a higher functioning level. The older, more chronically ill patients could not tolerate being out of the hospital on their own.

Being the Right Parent

I was traveling when Rosemarie told how our neighborhood was shocked by the report of a missing boy, a foster child who lived just two blocks away. His foster mom had taken him to a local park and, while in the playground area, the boy "disappeared." People from all over the community, people who didn't know the parents or the boy, responded to the missing child reports by volunteering to search and aid as best they could. It was a park I knew well as it was also the headquarters for the township park district with which the Foundation had partnered previously. I had a hard time accepting that a child could just disappear in that area. At the same time, I felt for the park staff as I knew they would not rest and would be torn emotionally to have something like this happen on their watch, in their park, literally just outside of their office windows.

Eventually, it was revealed that the child was already dead. The foster parents and the foster dad's girlfriend went out of town for the weekend and left the child locked in a closet at home, where he died. It was all a hoax, a ruse. How could they be so cruel? How could they break such a critical and basic trust? It cast a shadow on the good done daily by the foster parents that care, foster parents like Kathy and Butch Lavigne.

I was especially pleased to visit with Wilderness School graduate Sal P. and his foster parents, Kathy and Butch. It was almost a year after my time spent at the DCF Wilderness School that I was back in Connecticut for my mom's ninety-fifth birthday, and as the book was developing I thought it might be good to follow up where I could.

I opened this book with the Wilderness School graduation day scene of Sal and Little G reuniting. I wrote about how they were wrapped in a bear hug of loving brothers. Don't tell them, but the secret is that they are not blood brothers; they are foster brothers. Even if you did tell them, it wouldn't mean anything. They are true brothers because of the love and efforts of Butch and Kathryn Lavigne, their foster parents. Actually, Butch and Kathryn have adopted four of their many foster youth, including Little G, and are currently foster parents to Sal and his older brother, Anthony. The Lavignes decided fourteen years ago to open their home to foster children, and they have found their niche and, as Kathy says, "my calling." It was not a hard decision as they have always had an open house.

Since she was ten years old, Kathy has taken care of others. It started with an elderly neighbor she visited daily to feed, dress, and assist until the lady died. As part of a family of seven, "a big Italian family," there were always things to do, and when her mom opened a day care, there was just that much more work to do. Currently, eleven people call their house home: Kathy and Butch; Kathy's parents; Tommy, her disabled uncle; their four children; as well as Sal and his brother. Over the years, they have been foster parents to hundreds of children, many of whom still call and visit them, even sleeping over at times. But I will let Kathy tell you that story when she writes her own book. It will be amazing and heartwarming for sure.

Sal and his brother came to their house after having problems at their previous foster home. The problem was that they were not allowed to do anything, literally. With such restrictions, the brothers quickly became bored, and as is so often the case with boys with nothing else to do, they fought. Sal came first and then Anthony. The brothers weren't sure what to expect when they arrived, but Kathy and Butch want and expect the children to be active. So when they first asked, "Can we go outside?" and Kathy responded, "Yeah," they couldn't believe it. They had to ask again but in an amazed, excited, and incredulous tone—"We can?"

Once they were there, Butch quickly realized that the boys' father was an old neighborhood buddy. While the biological mom and dad want to and do visit, they are not fully capable of fulfilling their parental obligations. Kathy and Butch fill that void.

Their ethics or overarching policy is that they treat foster children just as they would their own. If Kathy is giving one child too much attention, the others pull her back. They do not use the term "foster kid"; they do not like labels. Everyone gets treated the same. Butch and Kathy see their roles as teaching the children that they need to give to others and to put others ahead of themselves. Their goal for their children is that they graduate from high school and go to college. To keep them on track, Kathy attends every school conference with the social worker, sometimes being the only foster parent to attend. When a child is invited to a party, like Anthony was for prom night, Kathy will call the host parent and make sure the details match her standards.

Kathy explains,

> A lot of these kids, they have never seen a normal life. They don't know what it is. So many of the kids that have come through here are looking for it. We ground them and stuff. Some kids are like, 'Wow!' They enjoy that. They think we love them because we're grounding them.

Unable to have children of their own, they started as foster parents and then decided to adopt the four that they had, all the while continuing to be foster parents. They have never looked back. Kathy believes that this is the life that they were called to live as her heart breaks for a child without a home.

There have been some heartbreaks, like the young girl they were to have temporarily until space at a court-mandated residential home became available. In the short time she was with them, they bonded. But the judge would not change his ruling. Unable to stay in the first home where she ever felt comfortable, her situation deteriorated. She ran away from the court-directed residential facility and murdered someone. Now she is in jail for life.

There's also the time she had four teenage girls, all in the seventeen to eighteen age bracket, where they begin to push knowing that they will soon age out and be on their own. They were being abusive. Kathy called the social worker and had to have all four girls removed the same day.

Sal has grown because of their care. He enjoys playing the saxophone in the school band and has broken more family records in his stay with them than any other child. He revels in having broken the record for most records broken and smiles as he recounts how he has earned records for things like the longest stay, the first to break a bone (skateboarding), and the first to be allergic to himself. You get the feeling that he looks for other records to own.

Sal is fourteen years old, and his school marks range from 88 to 96. He has been the City of Bristol's wrestling champ for his weight group for two years in a row. His secret, as he says, is, "I'm large and fast." It probably also has something to do with his years of tae kwon do. His appearance is deceiving. He looks like he carries baby fat and is not that lean, trim image of a wrestler. But he has the strength to pull a 190-pound instructor over a thirteen-foot-high wall single-handedly, "like a toad." Sal just reached over, grabbed Matt's harness belt, and pulled. Matt said he "never felt lighter."

Regarding his appetite for food, Kathy says he eats everything. He and crewmate German were named by their crew "Chef Sal" and "Chef German" for their bean and rice dinners on the trail. Sal went to the first Wilderness School culinary class follow-up weekend. Sal loves to learn everything he can.

He also loves hugs. He will ask Kathy for hugs often and calls her "Mom 2" affectionately. When he first came, he would cry at times because he wasn't with his parents. It was hard for him to be separated; he needed their love and caring support. While he doesn't want to be adopted and wants to maintain a relationship with his biological parents, he happily realizes that he has love and support from Kathy and Butch.

When I asked Sal for his take on his twenty-day wilderness experience, he had two words: "Life changing!" He saw his crew start out as individuals and, over the twenty days, become a family. Notice that he used terms that tie directly to his life experience. He became good buddies with Anthony K. Jr. during the course, and they go together when the Wilderness School offers follow-up weekend programs, which he eagerly awaits.

He is active at school and at church, including participating in the bell choir. Sal loves helping others and getting involved; when his crew did the high elements, he stepped up and kept returning the zip line rope back to its starting point as each crew member finished. Sal has this openness and desire to learn that is infectious; you can see it in his eyes. I remember late one evening turning the corner of the men's cabin to find Sal with two of the logistics staff, Kevin Johnson and Micah Jankowski, practicing some rope procedures. Kevin explains,

> Micah and I were going over belay transfers from one of the trees, and Sal was pretty excited to observe and then start inquiring about what it was we were doing. Micah was explaining a number of scenarios to Sal revolving around escaping a belay, transferring loads from a belay to a lower haul system with an assisted locking belay device. What I thought was so interesting was that Sal was eating up every word and technique that we were talking about. Every time he did not understand a specific technique, he let us know and Micah did a wonderful job covering topics in a way that maintained his interest. Micah's slow, comprehensive delivery of each step was both engaging and exciting.

This was the night of day nineteen; Sal would be going home the next day, so the course was basically over. Sal has spent nineteen days and eighteen nights in the woods and ran a mini marathon that very morning, and yet he, alone, was still observing, still questioning, and still learning. As Micah wrote,

> It was awesome that Sal was so psyched about learning, and I think it was really good for him to see that he could do any of the things that we were doing if he spent some time practicing the skills.

The support Sal has received allows him the confidence to look, to question, and to learn. His foster parents are so involved in trying to create the best supportive atmosphere that Butch actually converted to Catholicism. He had been a Lutheran for fifty years and then, "one day," decided to become Catholic like Kathryn. Actually, the thought didn't just pop into his head. He had been thinking that the family didn't feel right, thinking that the children needed something more than Sunday school when they went, and had been thinking how best to keep them focused and involved. He realized that playing soccer wasn't helping when they really should be in church praying and reading the Bible. So he called Kathy late one night while he was on the road working and told her he was going to convert. She didn't think she had heard him the first time, so he repeated himself. When she realized he was serious, she was blown away. In the process of converting, they brought Sal and Anthony back to the Catholic Church, where they had been baptized but had fallen away. In a very emotional moment, Butch and the children made their First Communion together. The entire family is active in the church, and as a family they attend church regularly.

In such an environment, Sal learned how to treat other folks. When some of the crew thought it might be fun to put some red efts (salamanders) into Devon's sleeping bag as a follow-up to slipping one down his jacket, Sal at first thought it might be fun. But the more he thought about it and remembered Devon's reaction to the jacket incident, he realized it might cause Devon severe pain. Sal told the staff, and they stopped it. Later when the group met in circle to discuss the situation, Devon told them clearly of his fears. He explained to them that had he gotten into a sleeping bag loaded with red efts, he would have been traumatized in ways the boys could not understand or even imagine. He told them how hard it was to make friends and that to have something like this happen to him could have sent him over the edge. It was a major learning experience for all the ATC crew, and they learned it without inflicting harm or injury on anyone. All of this was brought to a safe conclusion because Sal had the confidence to stand up for another.

Dinners are another family event which gets funny looks from the teens who visit. The visitors can't figure out what is going on as they "have never had dinner as a family before," explains Kathy. They have never had a family sit-down meal. They have never had the structure to sit down, share, and talk with one another.

By any standard, Sal not only has the potential to do great things with his life, he has the support system that is letting his inner genius explore, learn, and expand. Whether he achieves his goals of going to Penn State and making the NFL remains to be seen. Sal has, in Kathy's words, "the mind-set to do what he wants to do." He knows it takes hard work, and he is not afraid to do it. Like hiking up the mountain, he relishes the challenge of what lays ahead.

Sal has a "big sister," Jamie. They are both fourteen, and Jamie is one of the adopted children and has lived with the Lavignes since she was six months old. She is quite the athlete as she recently qualified for the state finals in the four-hundred-meter dash by beating not only the field but also the meet's record for the event by four seconds, posting a *really* good time of 59.08 seconds. She has learned that hard work has its rewards. Unfortunately, the Connecticut State High School Athletic Board does not allow freshmen to participate in the finals; she had to sit it out. She is focused on going to state next year.

It was just another roadblock thrown in her way. She had to face some tough decisions early on. When her biological mother decided that she wanted to reconnect with her, Jamie had to make one of those decisions. She elected not to see her mother. Jamie is comfortable where she is in her life and does not want to disturb it. She might feel differently someday, but not now. She has no regrets.

Jamie's foster brother, David, younger by seventeen days, has been with the Lavignes since he was three weeks old and has found his own way of incorporating in his life their lessons of helping others. When he was fourteen, David joined Police Explorer Post #111, affiliated with the Bristol Police Department. As such, he gets to learn up close what it means to be a police officer. He plans to make it his career once he's finished with school and the service. In the meantime, every night he puts on his uniform and walks his neighborhood, checking in on the kids in the woods and looking for anything out of the ordinary. He brings a new meaning to the word *cop*, which originally stood for "citizen on patrol." You don't find too many fourteen-year-olds who are that dedicated.

Just before I was to start my hike of the Appalachian Trail, a friend and major customer of mine, Joe Dillhoff III, passed away. The Dillhoff family has owned and operated the OKI Bering Company, a major master distributor to the welding industry, for more than the thirty years I called on them. So it was that I got to meet and work with Joe III as he entered and grew in the business. Finally, he became president while his father, Joe II, who prefers to be called Big Joe, was chairman of the board. It was a pleasure working with both Big Joe and "Little Joe," although I never really figured out who was taller. Joe III traveled extensively nationally as well as internationally, visiting his branches, his customers, as well as his customers' customers. It was always interesting to hear of his latest trip and the shopping deals he found along the way. In fact, we had traveled on a Lear jet that one of my factories owned. To paraphrase the pilot, that was as close as I will ever come to flying in a jet fighter. On that trip Joe and I hunted pheasants in Nebraska. Additionally we traveled to play golf, and I always enjoyed listening to him tell others of our trips with so much zest that I sometimes wondered if I was on the same trip. But he was never too busy to stop, invite me to his office and ask about what was happening in my rep business or my family.

So it wasn't unusual when I poked my head in his office one day, and I got to meet Joe IV, working. Joe was "starting" Joey in the business, teaching him the ropes by having him clean the office—nothing fancy for the president's son but a chance for them to be together. It was a chance for Joe IV to learn something about work and starting at the bottom. Joe and I chatted for a while, and I could tell he really enjoyed having Joey there. So as I was leaving I jokingly advised Joey to get a good agent, to which his dad in reply advised, with that sly smile of his, that I had best leave before he found a new use for the locking pliers he had in stock, the very tools I sold him.

When Jason died, the Dillhoffs were very supportive. They took the time to come to the memorial Mass. It was great of them to do so as it showed that their support went beyond the business relationship. Afterward, Big Joe would stop me when I was in their offices to follow up. When Joe Jr. died, I tried to think of something I could do to show my gratitude for all the good years of knowing the family. That is when I thought of carrying Joe's picture on my Appalachian Trail hike all the way from Springer to Katahdin, where I planned to leave it. So with the help of his sister, Suzie, whom I have known and worked with the longest, I obtained a photo of Joe and tucked it in my pack.

When I realized the hike was not to be, that I needed to focus on the book and that I wouldn't take Joe on one last trip, I felt down, like I had failed. In writing this chapter, I was reminded of the Dillhoffs, who are very busy people, major players in their industry, and yet true-hearted folks one would want for family.

"Ranger Rick" Goes to the Wilderness School
One Child Referred—One Life Changed

The things that happen in a child's life mold them. It doesn't matter how much counseling they go through or how many outdoor programs they attend or even how many hugs they get after, they are changed and the people who work with those children need to understand that. I was lucky enough to have a counselor that knew that and taught me how to cope. She didn't try to change the way I felt about things; she taught me how to express those feelings in a more productive way.

—Ricky Harris, DCF Wilderness School grad and outdoor educator. Interview, July 2010

Growing up is never easy; it gets even harder when you never have a childhood. When you are the age of a child, it's natural to play with the neighborhood children. It's another thing to have to stop playing before you even start so you can be home to take care of your baby sister and prepare the daily meals. At an age when most parents would not let their children in the kitchen unsupervised, let alone allow them to operate an appliance like a stove, Ricky was there every day.

Ricky's family moved three times before he was fourteen years old. First, he lived in his grandmother's Danbury, Connecticut, Section 8 housing, with two bedrooms and one bath for five people: grandmother, aunt, mom, dad, and himself. When he was two years old, his sister was born. But his dad went to jail that year, and it would be a long time before Ricky ever saw him again; drugs made him unfit to be a parent.

At age four, the family left Grandmother's home, moved up the hill to another project building, and were joined by mom's boyfriend following his parent's divorce. They stayed a couple of years before moving to a duplex in Section 8 housing with, again, two bedrooms and a bath. It was there that Ricky moved to the basement—not a finished basement, but a place he could have as his own and not have to share with his younger sister. For Ricky, it was better.

During his junior year in high school, his family moved to a house that his mom and stepfather bought together. They had saved what they could to buy the house, and Ricky gained a stepsister and stepbrother when they moved in a year later.

Through all of this, his mom did what she could to stay close to Ricky and his sister, including being their school bus driver. She was with them for summer vacations, snow days, holidays, whatever. They never had a babysitter, but they did get up early for school. When your mom is the bus driver, you get up at 4:00 a.m. so you can go with her to get the bus, and then you ride the entire route to school. He knew all the students on the bus and memorized their stops, but he never really got to play with them.

In second grade, Ricky got a house key and would get off the bus at his normal stop so he could get home earlier and do homework, meet his sister at the bus stop later, and have dinner started before his mom got finished with the school bus routes. By age ten, he was doing his own laundry. Every night, they were in bed by seven o'clock, or eight o'clock, if they were lucky. Even in the summer when the neighborhood was filled with the sounds of children playing outdoors, they were in bed early. By fourth grade, he didn't have to get up at 4:00 a.m. to ride the bus with his mom. But he did have to get himself ready, eat, get dressed, and make it to the bus stop to meet his mom and the school bus. By sixth grade, he was walking to school, and his mom retired from bus driving when he went to seventh grade.

His grades were good until sixth grade. Because his father had left when he was two years old, Ricky didn't know him. But he did get to know his mom's boyfriend, who stayed with them through the moves in the housing projects. That man became his father figure.

At first, his mother had decided that his father was not going to be a part of his life due to the drugs and jail. But four years later, he reappeared, sober and with a new girlfriend. Ricky had a father again and started visiting him and his new stepmom at their house. They went on vacations together and did all the things a child growing up with divorced parents does. But then Dad cheated on the stepmom, they split, and he picked up with another woman. In response, the stepmom used Ricky, his stepbrother, and his stepsister against their dad when he got behind in his child support. Eventually, Dad left the state to avoid arrest, and Ricky was without a dad once again.

But he did have his mom's boyfriend, who had been helping him and becoming a father figure for Ricky since he was about two, when his father had gone to jail. But one night when Ricky was about ten years old, he walked into his mom's bedroom and found out the secret she had been hiding, something the children never saw. The boyfriend, Ricky's father figure, was abusing his mother. There he was, sitting on top of her chest with a pair of scissors to her throat, abusing his mom mentally, physically, and emotionally. What and how much can a ten-year-old take? Six months later, the boyfriend was killed over drugs, and sixth grade became a nightmare.

Unable to mourn because "boys don't cry" and forced to attend school the next day, anger became a way out. He didn't fight at school because he had been raised to believe that school was the most important thing in his life. So, while at school, while inside the building's walls, he held it together; but once he got outside, it all changed. His grades suffered because once outside those walls, he left it all behind. He didn't think about school until the next day when he walked back into the building. Anger that had accumulated over his early years of growing up took over; he began fighting, and he could not hold it back any longer.

As I write this, I am reminded of Rufio's death scene from the movie *Hook* that I mentioned earlier. His dying wish to Peter Pan to have "had a father like you" speaks volumes. To know what you are missing in your life, find it, and then lose it again cuts deeper than Captain Hook's sword ever could. While the sword is swift, the wound of a lost father or the father that never was bleeds for a lifetime.

Ricky's one escape was watching TV. He loved animals and the outdoor shows that cable provided, especially *Animal Planet* and *Discovery Channel*. He could and did watch them for hours. After a while, his family and friends began to call him "Ranger Rick" after the magazine of the same name. But his anger was still too much to bear. His mother took him to Danbury's Youth Services Bureau and its Good Friend Mentoring Program. Ricky writes,

> So the anger came mostly from these two men. There is always the sibling rivalry and not having money, but really it came from these two people. The counseling

didn't get rid of the anger; it allowed me to handle it better.

Fortunately for Ricky, in the course of treatment, the counselor picked up on Ricky's interest in the outdoors. She was "on her game" and suggested he attend the State of Connecticut DCF Wilderness School. Thus, Ranger Rick went on the first of what would become many twenty-day expeditions over a ten-year period of helping others discover within themselves the strength and ability to cope. But it wasn't an easy twenty-day expedition. In fact, it was tough; one student attempted to run away, and one girl, Rayella, caused a major series of problems, which I discussed in the earlier chapter "Leading from the Heart." But he thought he was ready for the challenge. First, it was different; there would be no baggage as it got him away from the bad memories and experiences. Second, he was already in a transition phase of his life being fourteen, trying to decide what he wanted to do and where he wanted to go with his life. Third, he never had a childhood, never had that innocence of youth that others had. He felt it would be a good experience, and so he visited the school on a graduation day, was interviewed by the staff, and was accepted into the program.

Any twenty-day trip is never easy, especially if you have never been away from home for any length of time. Then add the facts that you are living with nine other teenagers whom you have never met before; living outdoors in the wilderness; sleeping on the ground in a tent; hiking in the rain; living in the hot, humid, hazy New England summer; being eaten alive by bugs; carrying a thirty-pound pack that probably feels like fifty pounds; and hiking up and slipping down mountains. The challenges magnify themself exponentially.

One of the great benefits of the Wilderness School is their follow-up courses. At first, Ricky was reluctant to return following such a traumatic experience. At first he used his participation in football to beg off, but football ended and the call came inviting him to a ropes course on a weekend. He was available, and he accepted. After the weekend, he thought, *Nice. This is really fun. Amy and I did the Giant's Ladder together. It was way better than my twenty-day. No anxiety, just a fun day. It was cool.* [Author Note: Amy Pine, another student and future WS instructor]

After that weekend, paddling days, a five-day trip to the Adirondacks, and other "cool" activities followed. Then Ricky was awarded a scholarship to the North Carolina Outward Bound School (NCOBS) for a twenty-day expedition. At first, he didn't feel like he could leave his mom, but once again she stepped up and told him to go. She even drove him down to Asheville, North Carolina. NCOBS was great. It had a different population than the Wilderness School. At NCOBS, the students were more invested, their parents were spending a considerable amount of money for them to be there, and they wanted to be there. Now he was sixteen years old, meaning that he could understand more of what was going on, and he was beginning to see that he liked being in the woods and helping others through the group process. He was beginning to see a plan for himself.

Back in Danbury, he called the Wilderness School to inquire about a summer job. At seventeen years old, he was too young even for an intern position, and he needed to gain experience working in the woods with youth. Ever since he was fourteen, Ricky had been working in Brewster, New York, at Green Chimneys, a halfway house for mentally and physically challenged youth. He was working one on one with a different child every two weeks, which he continued do until a friend suggested that he try the Danbury YMCA's Great Hollow Wilderness School. It was there, under the guidance of Ali Sadiq, that he got his foundation for working with children in the woods. It was a good experience as he got to work with his younger brother, who was going through the program, as well as other teens he knew from growing up in Danbury. The familiar faces helped him transition from institutional-based work to field-operational work.

The next year, Ricky called the Wilderness School and said, "Dave, I'm coming." Dave replied, "Okay, you're coming." In 2010, he was still at the Wilderness School, still honing his educational skills and keeping crews safe. In each of the ten years since he started as a student, he has been back to CWS either to work or to visit with the staff and students. In that time period, he has contracted Lyme disease, and at one point he was stung by a bee and had to come off course for treatment. It happened at the same time that a student got hurt, and the decision was made that both Ricky and the student needed emergency care. Both were to hike out to meet the WS van, which would take them to the hospital. While Ricky was watching over the student, he instructed the student to watch over him, even showing the student how to administer an Epipen in case Ricky's conditions worsened.

Ricky has also seen childhood friends come through and graduate. Trevon had participated in multiple courses that Ricky led, and thus over time a friendship developed. Trevon was at the Wilderness School through a program with the Connecticut Juvenile Training System, where he had been for eighteen months. Ricky heard he was graduating, so he drove to the Wilderness School to be there. As he was walking down the path to find Trevon, their eyes met and there in the middle of the woods this tall kid with a big afro had tears in his eyes. Ricky said, "I don't want to see you out here in khaki and blue," referring to the CJTS uniform. Trevon replied, "No, It won't happen again." Ricky then told him, "I want to see you out here helping kids." The last Ricky heard Trevon was doing well.

Ricky said,

> A lot of people asked me why I do what I do because they know me as a city boy: [I] like to have my fingernails cut, like to have a haircut. That's just me. Why do you do what you do? I can't describe the why. I can't describe it. I know that when it happens, I know what it feels like and I love the way that it feels. I love watching a kid [grow and develop].

I included Ricky's experience of growing and developing here, in this section, because one person was always looking out for him. One person changed her life to accommodate his needs and his sister's needs—his mom. They lived in tight quarters, sharing space, but she was always there watching out for him. She drove a school bus so her hours matched his; her days off as well as her summer schedule allowed her to be there. When Ricky had a chance to go to the North Carolina Outward Bound School but was hesitant, she told him he needed to experience it. I asked Ricky how much credit he gives his mother for his success.

> That's a really good question and something that I have actually spent a lot of time thinking about. With my wedding right at the doorstep, I've had a chance to really look at where I am now. My mother has played a major role in my life, of course. The difficulty of a question like that is, when am I allowed to take credit for me? I would honestly not be here without my mother; you wouldn't be asking me these questions and I would not be sitting in an office with the opportunity to change lives without her support. She laid the foundation, and there is no denying that I wouldn't even want to try and deny it. I do have to be honest, though, and say that there are other people and events that had huge impacts on the person I am today. So to ask how "much" impact she has had is a very hard question to answer. I'm positive that if you asked me this question next year, I would give you a different answer, because my person and success will continue to grow. But if I have to answer the question I would give her a lot of credit. If I'm going to put a number on it, 40 percent of my success has come from her so far. The other 60 percent comes from me and the other events and people in my life, including my fiancée, who has also had a huge role in shaping me.

The Family Name

A family name has value, and so can a hiker's trail name. That is the name a hiker assumes or is given on the trail. Folks don't use their proper, given names but assume this other persona. One of the guys I started hiking the Appalachian Trail with had a trail name of JayB. Dave Tolbert told me he was from Athens, Georgia, and that his trail name had something to do with his family. But I never got to ask him what it meant or how it was spelled (JayBee, JayB, JB?). He was a friend of and the reason Jerry Horton was section hiking—to see Dave off. Since I left the trail almost as soon as I started, I never did find out his story. Once I tracked down and reconnected with Jerry, I got it.

It turns out that JayB is an acronym for his family that Charlotte, his wife, put together. If he couldn't be home, if he was going to be wet, tired, hungry, and sore, maybe he could have a reminder of and think of his family. *J* represents son Jonathan and grandsons Jack, Jonah, and Jacob. *A* represents daughter-in-law Amy, granddaughter Allyson, and son-in-law Ancona. Skipping to *B*, it represents daughter Beth and granddaughter Blakely. Saving the best for last, *Y* is for "yours truly"—his wife, Charlotte. It is catchy and does serve a purpose.

Matt Shove runs his own professional mountain guide service out of Manchester, Connecticut, when not handling logistics at the Wilderness School. In 2010, Matt actually returned to the Wilderness School after an eight-year absence. He sees a big difference in the approaches of the school and that of his guide service. Part of his responsibilities as a professional guide is to make sure that everything works, that everything goes according to plan, that his customers are well taken care of, and that they experience the least amount of discomfort. His customers are not paying to get lost in the woods, to have a canoe flip over, or to have to work through another member's temper tantrum, although it can happen. But in the woods with the young, those things do happen and become learning moments. As Matt sees it, "One has to learn to be uncomfortable on the trail. While it is possible to be comfortable, more than likely something will happen." There will be a hot burning sun, high humidity, cold winds, rain, mud, pesky flies, flipping canoes, and really tough climbs, many happening on the same day. What is more important is that one accepts the possible discomforts and learns to survive. For JayB, that is easy. He just breaks down his trail name and thinks of those he loves back home.

At the end of the movie *Hook*, Peter is asked what he will do since his adventures are over. He replies, "Oh, no. To live—to live will be an awfully big adventure."

The ultimate challenge is to live a good life as a responsible and contributing person and, if the opportunity presents itself, as a supportive and caring parent.

Mom,

It's a beautiful Wednesday afternoon. Warm, breezy, and lots of sunshine, I'm enjoying the beauty of the mountains from the garden. I'm preparing for the marathon this weekend and felt it would be a good time to tell you how much it means to me to have you as my mother. Thanks so very much.

I love you,

> —Jason William Hunt, Warren Wilson
> College, letter, December 10, 1997

A Culture of Joy and Belonging

Setting the Standards

The stitches we have dropped as a culture call out to be picked up and included and nourished and woven in as part of our humanity. Each stitch has its own special contribution to make to our individual and collective tapestries. One of the labors of our field is to befriend in our culture and ourselves those handicapped and underdeveloped parts of our nature that we have set aside. If we ignore such callings, consciously or unconsciously, collectively or individually, we do so at our deepest peril. May the spirit, truth, and healing power that therapeutic wilderness camping represents help us to find the wisdom to know the right, the courage to choose it, and the strength to make it endure.

—Anthony Howard, M.S. and Thecla Helmbrecht Howard, EdD,
Journal of Therapeutic Wilderness Camping, Vol. 5 No. 1, 2005

I know some of you have burned bridges back home; those bridges need to be mended. It takes a few minutes to burn a bridge but it takes years to build a bridge, so you guys have some work in front of you. You have done great things; you have proven to us that you are capable of doing anything you want to do. Go back home.... Show them who you are, show them you are a new man; show them you stand for something that is positive and different.

—Tex Teixeira, Director, Woodson Wilderness
Challenge Graduation Day, April 2010

Those individuals who have explored mountains and scaled cliffs have said they are not doing it for the summit, or the final destination. They are in it for the journey and the things they learn along the way. Where they are going receives less emphasis than how they got there and what will be required of them. Jason's journey has provided him with experiences and learnings that have allowed us to cross his path. His journey has also prepared him for where he is now.
—Danielle Hunt Palka, Celebration of Life, eulogy, October 20, 2001

Cultures stand and live by their ethics. Failure to create a positive ethical environment foreshadows the culture's demise. Ethics are the rules of the road for a particular culture. The ethics of a culture are a set of moral principles and values that provide for the common good and that are tested over time and practiced in daily life in the decisions about good and bad behavior. At first glance, there might seem to be a conflict in this industry over who should be the primary beneficiary of the ethics: staff or students, workers or customers. Staff comes to guide and guard but gains in their own personal development along with the students. They, like their students, have issues and needs that must be addressed in order for them to be safe and healthy.

Jason was really challenged when he led his first twenty-day expedition at the Wilderness School. He found himself in the woods for several hours removing a student who was threatening suicide. As Bonnie, his co-instructor, remembers, "Jason was challenged on a trip with the dynamics such as these and had a difficult time having confidence in his ability to manage situations such as this that can be extremely scary when you are starting out in the field."

The challenge caused him to doubt whether he had the abilities to reach the students. He thought his inability to reach them was a detriment to the program and weighed heavily on him. So it was a job for the logistics staff, his course director when they connected in the field, and Bonnie, his co-instructor, to give him the support he needed while in the field. As Bonnie told me during our interview,

I remember having conversations with Jason during

the trip about the importance of leaning on your co-instructor for support and trusting your instincts. He grew a lot in both of these areas while on trip, and I had felt that we had a strong bond by the end of trip. I felt very confident that Jason's openness and ability to be self-reflective would make him an incredible instructor and felt confident that I could rely on him while we were on course together.

But the true ethics are those that put the child's needs first. There would be no program without the child. Because so many of these children come from very "unstable" homes and experiences, the overarching principle becomes one of not harming the child but actually creating a culture of joy, a culture of belonging, a culture of safety.

One day while at base camp, Aaron stopped to give me a note. He had just talked to a former Wilderness School student who wanted to be sure the school was still operating. Although ten years removed, Heather was reconnecting. Now about to graduate as a veterinarian technician and, more important, about to have her first child, she was planning for his future. She wanted to be sure he could have the same experiences she had.

> One night we were at a campsite, and everyone got bit up by mosquitoes so bad we had welts on our faces. Really "roughing" it; going to the bathroom in a hole we dug, no showers for three weeks, and getting caught in the rain and lightning but still having to hike on with packs that felt like they weighed sixty pounds.... We became known as the Night Riders because we never seemed to be able to make it to camp before one o'clock in the morning, or later.

She had also had an experience one day when she and another girl lost control of their canoe and began spinning down the river through the rapids and eventually flipping. But she also remembered the support of her crew and the support of the staff and the instructors. Heather also remembers her exposure to the beauty of nature, "The Wilderness School is the first place I actually got to see the sun rise. It was beautiful."

Like Jerry's youth, she heard what she heard and she saw what she saw. At times, the experience was hard and painful, yet looking back, she realizes that in graduating, in meeting the challenges of the Wilderness School, she realized deep down that she could do anything. Through the chaos of the challenges, she gained more self-confidence and an appreciation for the little things "like indoor plumbing." It was more than a chance to get a break from her foster home.

> Little did I know that the Wilderness School was going to be a once-in-a-lifetime experience full of lessons I would never forget. I guess my DCF worker thought that I needed to grow up a bit and learn some things.

When Dave Czaja was interviewed for the directorship, he was asked what his primary goal would be for the school. He remarked that at the very minimum, no child should leave the school worse off than when he came. He said that the experience the child found must at least open his eyes to new opportunities, at least show him that there was a different way, at the very least give him a chance to stretch.

The Chinese have the word *Tao,* which means "the way" or "the path." Finding that way, finding that path and its underlying tie-in to the natural order of the universe is tough enough for an adult and even harder for an adolescent. In creating an ethics that is child first in focus, you automatically must consider the staff, albeit a very close second.

The highest goodness is like water. Water benefits all things and does not compete. It stays in the lowly places which others despise. Therefore it is near the eternal.

—Tao Te Ching

Steve Prysunka of Alaska Crossings wrote a very succinct list of the ethics and values that I have seen in practice at the Wilderness School and other programs that I have talked to and visited. He wrote,

We believe:

- Optimism and joy are learned behaviors
- In building children up, not breaking them down
- In real expeditions, in true wilderness, with a purpose and goal as part of the journey
- The wilderness is something to be lived in and not just survived
- In purposeful activities with a beginning and an end
- A consistent mentoring relationship is important to promoting positive change in young people
- Food should never be used to modify behavior
- A participant's basic needs must be met before emotional growth can take place
- Deprivation is not crucial to change
- Change should not come through the desire to cease physical discomfort
- Change must be based in comprehension
- Challenge and change are interrelated
- Each day is filled with teachable opportunities
- In taking manageable risks in order to grow and learn
- In allowing participants to learn experientially
- By teaching resiliency so that participants will be able to surround themselves with positive resources when they return home
- A child's family can be the most significant resource that

they have available to them; every effort is made to protect the sanctity of that resource

- The group is a tool to be used with caution
- By retaining qualified staff we will consistently deliver excellent service
- By paying our staff professional wages, we attract the best possible people and keep them
- In providing an extensive staff training program
- In using "real" language, not clinical or program jargon that makes no sense back home
- In a small guide-to-participant ratio
- In using the best equipment available to ensure a quality experience
- We can help to realign a participant's sense of self to a more positive and productive image
- We have an enduring belief in our participants; it's not in our nature to give up on anyone.
- We develop emotional skills in our participants that give them tools and metaphors to ultimately help them handle previously unmanageable situations

Such an outline of ethics helps to create an environment in which children can develop a sense of mastery, a sense of independence, a sense of generosity, a sense of belonging. It is in that focused environment that they are struggling, having a difficult time, when their frustration levels are high and their behaviors are coming out that they can be supported by caring staff members. They can go through that point of "I can't do this" and have different results. They can have a positive experience; have a positive exchange with another student; walk away from the critical point of frustration, and have something positive that lives with them for the rest of their life.

Much like a seed that can remain dormant for many years before finally germinating, such positive experiences may lay dormant deep in a child's psyche for years. But at the moment of need, that seed will awaken and expose the flowering of a path of change. A dormant thought waiting for the right time to kick in happens in everyday life. Ask any retailer how many years he has been in that particular location. Maybe the business is a first-generation one, or maybe it is second-generation or even older. Then ask how many times people come into his shop for the first time and ask how long he has been there. They don't see it until they have a need for the service or the product he provides. His shop could have been there for decades, he could use a bright attractive sign outside that is clearly visible to traffic and yet they don't see it until they need him. I have asked that question to more retailers over the years as I have called on them and I get the same smile and shaking of the head. It's human nature.

Socrates believed and taught that if people knew what is good, they would naturally do good. To him, the truly wise man would know what is right, do what is right, and "therefore be happy." He considered knowledge that has a bearing on human life to be the most important. This self-knowledge he considered necessary for success and inherently an essential good.

Aristotle proposed that a man is doing good and therefore content when he acts in accordance with his nature and realizes his full potential. He believed that a child at birth is only but a potential. To him it was important that the individual develop his own specific latent talents, which would ultimately result in happiness.

Thus, the unhappiness and frustration that people experience is really predicated on their inability to realize their full potential. Programs that bring optimism, joy, safety, caring, love, and support provide the opportunity for the student to reach deep within their being and to draw upon their innate powers while developing their talents to the fullest.

Nick K. spotted something specific in each of his Aviators crew members. At their graduation ceremony, Nick took the time to thank each one:

> I'd like to thank my three instructors for putting up with all the nonsense all these twenty days. Some haven't been as good as the day before (or) the day

after, but thank you nonetheless. They're probably the most patient people any of us ever met; I still don't know how. I like to thank everybody in my crew; everybody had some other type of thing that they brought. Whether it was:

JK – with all of his hilarious jokes every single day.

Johnny – complaining about one thing or another.

Brandon – always pushing people around saying, "Hey, my water bottle." Nobody would ever argue with him about it.

Andy – always stepping up to be the leader, always wanting to help people.

Dan – always writing something. No matter what it was Dan was always writing something.

JD – Whenever Amy, Bruno, and Kenny have tried something, whenever anybody needed some kind of help, everyone would pick on JD. Until it was time to go to bed, then everyone would get in their tarp, and see a spider, no matter how big … everybody would freak out except JD. And everybody would go, "JD, come debug my tent!" And he would come sprinting over and help. Then the next day everybody would be yelling at him until night came again; same thing every day. And Johnny would step in; stick up for him, because that's how Johnny is. So JD that's for you.

And Jon, I'll never forget climbing up those two mountains in one day. All of a sudden we all look back … and Jon sprints up the mountain! We couldn't believe it. All of a sudden he's got this burst of energy; he was so excited to go up the mountain. He always pushed through anything. Jon, I've noticed that.

The crew's culture was defined by the contributions each member made. Each member stepped up, and in the process the crew took on its own unique identity.

The Pathfinder

While I was at Woodson Wilderness Challenge, Ms. Janie told me how one young girl developed her talents in the background but sadly believed she had to dumb down in front of boys.

> One session … the girl knew how to navigate; she knew where we were. It was the final hike. I could see it in her eyes; she was oh so frustrated because this big and strong guy who had never navigated decided he was going to tell everybody where to go. He led; we're wandering around in the woods with no trail, and this was not supposed to be an off-trail experience. Finally, after following this guy they were all getting frustrated, sitting down, getting angry; we were there for a long time. The girl finally looks over at us. She goes and picks up the map and pointing with her finger says, "We are right here. When we were here, we made the wrong turn. Follow me; I'll show you." They marched back, and she handed them the map and said, "We go that way." And then the saddest thing happened. She dumbed herself down again for the rest of the hike. It hurt to see that she wasn't willing to continue, to go ahead and lead the hike. But, it was so awesome, and everybody at the next intersection looked her way. She would tell them but not volunteer. It was kind of neat that they asked her, recognized that they made an error in their judgment. They realized that she belonged.

Many of the great works of ancient history involve the journey, the rite of passage. It is a story of three parts: the calling forth, the journey, the return. It is told of a young person called by his society to leave family and home to go out on a journey in search of a goal. During the journey, the hero runs into many challenges that he must overcome if he is to successfully return and complete his mission. The mission is only complete when he contributes positively to his society, to his culture.

It is actually a call of initiation, and it is something that our culture does not handle well. Whereas the ancients looked to their young for inspiration, for new thoughts, and for a new fire of ambitions, modern society delays their entry into society as contributing members well into their twenties and even thirties. We put them in boxes called schools and separate them from contact with society at large. Thus is created a friction as well as a frustration by our youth for being ignored and for being marginalized (schooling). Men standing around on city street corners are not only a sign of unemployment but also a sign of lack of direction, lack of responsibility, and a failure of our system to utilize our assets. This failure of under-acceptance by society opens the doors for the growth of gangs offering their own form of family, society, structure, rituals, and culture.

Jon Rousseau said of this,

> Their time is spent in mind numbing confines when they already have the genius inside. They are fully equipped to deliver the cargo that they are carrying....
> It is a fatal flaw in our culture.

We come specifically gifted, not just generally gifted, and need to be accepted and nurtured by society, not delayed.

Culture and nature mirror each other. Aristotle said that nature does nothing in vain. Everything in nature has a purpose. Rocks, trees, plants, small animals, and insects all function together. They know their place and the role they play in nature. When they function together the right way, you have, for example, a garden. If the honeybee didn't pollinate, you would lose the garden. If the earthworm did not mix the topsoil with the subsoil and secrete nitrogen, you would lose the garden. It is the same with humans, but our reductionist way of life has forced us into age-based boxes.

Children learn better by doing, and yet we force them to behave, pay attention, and be quiet. It is not their nature. Jon Rousseau said, "We are all mythic by nature. We want to see more than the literal version of wow."

To be a culture of joy and belonging, it needs to ignite, and it needs to expose the person to new ideas, new passions, and new directions. It is then up to the person and the community at large to keep those fires burning.

In February 1998, Jason went on a seventeen-day expedition as part of his outdoor leadership studies at Warren Wilson College. The course was run by North Carolina Outward Bound School, just up Riceville Road from the college. In summing up the course, Jason wrote,

> What I have found is that this course has taught me new skills for becoming a more effective leader/teacher/follower. It has given me an opportunity to spend time outdoors. Most importantly, it has offered me the chance to look inside myself for answers to questions I have been asking myself over and over. What I will take from this course the most is the knowledge and awareness that my journey is a continuous challenge of checking and re-checking where I am and who I am. I have learned many new skills, but I have learned even more about myself as a person presently and the person I am striving to be.

The person Jason was striving to be and the person he was came through following his death in an e-mail from Jason Lord, a close friend from his days in Colorado.

> I wanted to let you all know something that you already know about Jason. He is a fantastic force. He was not only a friend to me, but felt like a younger brother. He and I met when he was in Ft. Collins (CO.). We gravitated to each other because of mutual

beliefs and respect for one another. Jason was an unexpected friend that I serendipitously came across at a time in my life when I needed a good friend. I don't have a lot of friends; the ones I do have the fortune of having are priceless to me. Your son was a positive force in my life and will continue to be so. I'm starting to get over the shock of his abrupt departure, and now the sadness is starting to set in. I'm realizing that he is gone from here, and my heart is heavy. I'll be missing the bright energy he always seemed to exude to people and the nature of how he was. I will miss the discussions about life and the status of where we were and where we were going with our lives and just hanging out.

I know he will always be with me and all of you in spirit; he is an indomitable presence. I know he wouldn't want me to cry for him, but I can't help but cry. I'm selfish in the fact that I miss him and his physical presence. I will always miss him. I can take solace in the fact that he knew I loved him as a brother and the same was true from him to me. I lost one brother when I was a young boy, and I cried because I was terribly sad. I'm crying again now because I have lost yet another brother.

A Telling

Eileen Speaks of Her Experience

I get knocked down, but I get up again
You're never gonna keep me down.

—"Tubthumping," Chumbawamba

I remember going mountain biking and climbing with Jason, but the one adventure that comes to mind is when a group of us from Turpin went camping in Kentucky. There was this cave that we heard had an opening on both sides that you can walk through easily. Well, a group of us started into this cave, and it wasn't hard hiking but there was water up to our calves. So when there was a pothole in the ground, it kind of was unsettling to think that the hole could have been much, much deeper. Some of the others turned back with fear, but Jason and I kept pushing on. As it turned out, both of our flashlights went out about three quarters of the way through, but we were determined to get through the cave, which in fact we did. If you don't take chances in life, then you don't know what's on the other side.

—Brian McCormick, Turpin High School friend, 2011

In 2002, the family gave a scholarship to the DCF Wilderness School in what defined the beginning of the Jason William Hunt Foundation. That scholarship went to a young girl named Eileen, whom we did not know. We were told she was recommended by a teacher at her school.

Presented here in their entirety are her graduation speech, which she gave in front of about one hundred people, her "Dear Funder" letter, and a follow-up letter written almost nine years later. You will see how well they tell the story of her growth and development. It is a beautiful telling.

Graduation Speech

Wilderness School, July 16, 2002

When I first started here in the Wilderness School, I wasn't confident about myself at all. When we would walk with those huge backpacks that weighed around 50 lbs. and walked 3–4 miles a day, I did not think I could do it. I wanted to go home the first night. I did not like it at all.

The second day, we climbed Bear Mountain, the biggest mountain in Connecticut. It was the hardest thing I ever did. I would tell myself that I couldn't do it, and I wanted to stop right there. We got up there, and then it felt great, although I was dirty, sweaty, and just felt really disgusted. But minus all that, I felt like a million bucks! I had made it and didn't really give up. I can definitely say that all of us have had many difficulties in the past. I remember this one time, I was climbing Mt. Everett, and there was this extremely steep part and I didn't want to get up because it was so hard. So Melissa and Kellie, along with the crew, said how I could do it and that I shouldn't give up. That helped me at least to get up the mountain. And then when we would be hiking and there would be those big step hills and I, along with others, would stop and say we couldn't do it, my group would say that we could do it, or as Vanessa always says, "You can do it if you put your mind to it," and that helped me and the others a lot. We got up the hill and to our campsite.

I just want to say thank you to Melissa and Kellie [for] always being there and helping us, listening to our problems and hearing us complain all the time. And thank you to Crew 3 for always motivating me and sticking with me through tough and easy times. I love you guys. Thank you.

Funder Letter

At the same time, she wrote what the school calls a Funder Letter:

July 2002
Dear Funder,

I just want to say thank you for funding the Wilderness School. I enjoyed the past 20 days. My name is Eileen. I'm 15 years old and wasn't really looking forward to going to the Wilderness School at first. I had two reasons or goals that I came here for: to work on my attitude toward myself and others and being less shy. The other one is I was coming here [to work] on being stronger emotionally, physically, and mentally. I can say that hiking, canoeing, and rock climbing have helped me in many ways. When a challenge comes toward my way, I can say to myself that I can do it.

I have really learned many things that I thought I couldn't do, like climbing mountains in a great amount of time, using muscles I never knew I had, and using my voice that I never really thought I had. If you weren't funding the Wilderness School, then my attitude wouldn't be so high.

Again I want to say thank you A LOT. I have enjoyed all the time here. Thank you.

Always,
Eileen

Follow-up Letter

In 2010, I was at the Wilderness School for five weeks from the end of May through June, and then I returned in September for the Alumni Day as a way to follow up with some of the students. It was there that I met Justin LaBaire, Eileen's husband. The staff was aware of the foundation's connection to Eileen and made sure that Justin and I met. I told Justin of my project and asked him to ask Eileen if she wanted to say anything about her experience now nine years later.

April 25, 2011

Dear John,

Hi, my name is Eileen LaBaire, but you might remember me as Eileen Garcia. I was a student at the DCF Wilderness School in the year 2002 and completed their 20 day program. So much time has passed since then, I have no idea where to begin! First I just want to apologize for not getting back to you sooner.... I've been busy with work and pretty much life! But I definitely would love to catch up. So here we go!

I live in Stamford, CT, with my husband Justin LaBaire, who you met last year. We've been married for about 10 months now and have enjoyed every minute of it. We actually met at the Wilderness School about 5 years ago. That place is truly like my second home. Justin works for the City of Stamford in the Youth Services Bureau, where he creates programs for youth at risk. Since the Wilderness School, I have always wanted to work with young people and keep them connected to the outdoors. The outdoors truly saved me and helped me see what's important in life. Now I work with Justin and spread the word of the outdoors and its magical powers! For the past 4 years I have been working with Justin facilitating ropes course activities as well as backpacking, rock climbing, mountain biking, and canoe trips. During the offseason I find other jobs to work and save money for our little excursions up to New Hampshire to hike and camp! During the downtime, I have been working as a preschool teacher and recently have been nannying for a couple of families. No matter what, I always wanted to stay connected with kids, no matter what the age is. I have been going to school on and off for the past few years. I am currently aiming to finish my associate in general studies and then do an online program for nutrition.

No matter where life has taken me, I have never forgotten what the WS did for me. When I was a student there, I connected deeply with my instructor Melissa Buffington. I formed such an amazing friendship with her over that summer.... I had gone back to every follow-up course afterward, and the one follow-up that truly touched my soul and never left me was the canoe trip in the Adirondacks. Of course, Melissa was leading that trip, and we had awesome weather and it was just breath-taking up there. We had done a lot of paddling that day so we set camp up, had evening meeting, and went to sleep. The next morning I woke up a little earlier than everyone else so I just hung out with Melissa while she drank her coffee. We sat there for about 10 minutes and then she brought up your son, Jason. She said that she was happy that I won the scholarship because [otherwise] we would have never met. She went on and talked about how he was an amazing climber and how he was just so easy to be around. She had described Jason as a really down-to-earth, kind, outgoing, and a truly genuine human being. She then said something I'll never forget. She said the reason why she thought I deserved this scholarship so much was because I always reminded her of him. I felt so honored when she said that. She then started to cry and I was already crying. It's one of those moments that you experience that you know in your heart that you will never forget. It's one that I will always remember.

So on that note, I just want to thank you for everything you and Jason's foundation have done for me. The following summer I went to North Carolina. I not only got to see such breath-taking views but reconnected with myself and knew from then on in that I had a responsibility. It was my responsibility to share the powers of the great outdoors with all the kids I would work with in the future. For 9 years I have lived by what I have learned from both programs, so much so that when I was 18 years old I made a promise to myself that if I were to ever meet a man to marry that it had to be someone that shared the same passions and had to have the same feelings of the outdoors that I do.... A year later I met Justin at the Wilderness School! Melissa made such an impression on me that after I did Outward Bound, I heard she was a coordinator for a program in New Jersey and being one of her followers, I decided to attend and completed a 7 week program called F.I.T, field instructor in training. I got paid and enjoyed every minute of it! Since then Melissa and I have kept in touch, giving each other updates along the way.

Your foundation and scholarship provided me with the amazing opportunity to attend the WS and opened the doors to all the awesome adventures I have ever been on. Thank you for helping me be the person I am today. You have something truly amazing and life changing going on. I hope you will continue to change many lives over the years like you did mine. Words cannot express what you have done for me and what you have given me. So, thank you John and all of the Hunt family with all my heart.

Sincerely yours,
Eileen Garcia LaBaire

PART THREE

Epilogue

You Raise Me Up

You raise me up so I can stand on mountains
You raise me up to walk on stormy seas
I am strong when I am on your shoulders
You raise me up to more than I can be
—Lyrics by Rolf Lovland and Brendan Graham

What I Have Learned

I worked with your son Jason in Montana at the Wilderness Treatment Center in the winter of 1998. He and I worked a trip together in Yellowstone N.P. along with my wife Kerry. I have fond memories of Jason and our brief time together, but I was shocked and saddened when I heard about his death from one of his friends who was working at the Outdoor Retailer show in SLC.

I was glad to have known your son and to have been given the opportunity to work with him. He had such great passion for the outdoors, and it was obvious that his work with youth would impact and influence others. For example, [one young man from that crew] has been clean and sober for six years and is now a drug and alcohol counselor in New York. I still receive updates from [him] now and again and we continue to be amazed at the grace God has provided us both.

—Steve Sutorius, Co-worker at Wilderness Treatment
Center, Montana, E-mail, March 29, 2004

Synchronicity, to paraphrase Carl Jung, means the concurrence of two or more events unrelated by cause but yet occurring to produce a meaningful relationship. Jung believed it was as important as any explanation based on causality. He was right. I can't explain otherwise how standing in the middle of a US Forest Service dirt road in Georgia means I am going to meet *Quartz* with not only her story of David taking his books to the woods but also that she remembered Danielle from a ladies getaway weekend two years earlier.

Most people who saw Jerry Horton's gloves would not think twice about them. Had I never sold work gloves, I might not have either.

But I represented a line, and so I noticed that the embroidery was well done and his name was large enough, as he said, "to find them in my son's tool box." Add that to the fact that I remember that he said he came from Athens or Rome, Georgia, and I was able to track him down months later to get his story.

To be in the right spot at the right time to meet the right person to hear that specific story was a truly great experience of this journey for me. It was everywhere I went.

When Danielle told us she was pregnant, I knew I had to help her during Charleston County Parks and Recreation's East Coast Canoe and Kayak Festival. This is an international event that is twenty-one years old. Danielle is in charge of the vendors, and I knew that meant considerable running around. So I was glad when Joshua Hall, her boss, told me to "sit her down and be her gofer." One of my jobs was a run to the airport to pick up a guest speaker from the University of Sea Kayaking. It wasn't until Wayne and I got to talking that I realized he had a story to tell of his twenty-five years' experience with outdoor programs for the University of California, Santa Barbara. He became another interview source for the book.

How does one explain why Dominic, a middle school student, would ask me to help him through the ropes course when other, younger, and better trained Wilderness School staff members were there? By virtue of just being there, good things happen.

Why now, as I am writing this book, would Brain McCormick contact the family to open a dialogue? His kind act of making the effort to contact us opened a door on Jason's early climbing experiences that we could not have included without his assistance. He really helped fill in the details of how Jason got into climbing.

Or how does one explain the synchronicity that occurred when I was invited to update my former customers of the Central States Locksmith Association of Kentucky? They have been very supportive of the foundation as sponsors of our charity events in the past. When I retired, they invited me to attend a meeting to explain the hike and its mission. Once back, they asked me to give them an update. I was the second speaker that night.

The first speaker was Dan Panzenbeck, sales manager for US Lock, a major supplier to the industry. There I was sitting in the back of US Lock's Louisville, Kentucky, warehouse listening to Dan when I realized that he was using the same buzz words as were used in outdoor experiential education. He was challenging these locksmiths to get out of their business practices' comfort zones in order to grow their businesses. I was about to explain to the group how the wilderness helped children grow by getting them out of their comfort zones. Dan's presentation provided a great segue.

Things change. Rudy Brooks has retired, and Aaron Wiebe left the Wilderness School's program coordinator position due to budgetary cuts, became a social worker for the State of Connecticut, and finally returned to the Wilderness School in January 2011 in the newly formed capacity of field program coordinator. Ricky Harris decided it was time to move on, which he did—cross country. He became the teen programs coordinator for the Border View Family YMCA of San Diego, California. Micah moved from logistics to field staff, which is a big move, but then again not so big. Micah never missed a chance to be with the crews, so even when he was doing his logistics, he would find a way to be involved with the field staff. Betta Hanson returned to the United States to obtain a master's in social work.

Jeremy Poore and Jason Michaels have both changed jobs but remain in Asheville. Woodson Wilderness Challenge is no more, but in its place is the proposed Pisgah Wilderness Challenge. Much of the staff remains in place in hopes that once financing is secured they will be able to carry on the work with teen boys referred by the North Carolina courts and social workers.

Along the way, I learned how truly amazing wilderness educators are in the work they do with youth. Whether it's cold, wet, hot, humid, a hard climb, a shallow river, or a late night getting to camp, they take it all in stride and work through it. The process always works because they always work the process. If three guys want to challenge one another to a stand-off (sit-down) in a cold running stream, let it happen. Somewhere in that challenge there is a lesson to be learned. For Jon, at least, it was that all three challengers won.

I even learned to handle a stand-up paddleboard. It was while I was with Danielle at ECCKF. I have always loved to canoe, so I thought it would be fun to use a paddleboard. It seems fairly simple—one stands on what is basically an oversized surfboard and moves by use of a long-handled paddle. Simple, yes, but at first I had no balance. I could not take a stroke without falling off. It was while I was sitting on the board paddling that I noticed a paddler heading right for me. He stopped, and we switched boards. It seems that just before my class started, one of the vendors wanted to demo that model, so I was initially on a board that was a bit too small for me. Being in Charleston, I decided to call the model I should be on the Yorktown, after the *USS Yorktown,* the aircraft carrier permanently berthed at Patriots Point in the Charleston harbor. It is big, long, wide (or beamy, as the sailors say), and thick. Riding that board was great; all my canoeing strokes came back and worked. The board moved as directed, and I stayed on top.

I learned about Brenda Partyka, who is a full-time social worker with the State of Connecticut and yet in her spare time is the Old Saybrook Youth and Family Services wilderness coordinator. She had her own twenty-day Wilderness School outdoor experience and now is paying it forward with the youth group of Old Saybrook. She relates her overcoming the fear of rock climbing and the success she had so that the members of her youth group can develop their own "I can" attitudes.

Time

I learned that the Greeks have two words for *time*: *chronos* and *kairos.* Chronos time is measured in seconds, minutes, hours, days, months, and years. It is the time on the clock that we can lose track of. It is the time that hurries by.

Kairos time cannot be measured. It is quality time that can be defined only by what happens in it. It is the most important type of time because it affects us, who we are, our lives, and our futures. As Father Lou Guntzelman writes,

It indicates that something is happening inside us for the betterment.… (It) occurs when we realize and feel within ourselves it's the appropriate time, "to grow up, to be more responsible."'

It is the time of stretch, of personal growth, and of development. It is the time of the Wilderness.

I learned that there is actually a third time—a time to walk away, a time to regroup. As I wrote earlier, the emotional trauma of not being able to help Jason caused me to leave the National Ski Patrol. It wasn't something I could just pick up from the previous season without seeing Jason's face in every injured skier.

Jason's death was a time of its own wilderness, its own sorrow. Time was normal, time was fast, and time was slow all at once. We had time to think and time to carry on but little interest in doing so. Everything seemed to take longer, but time passed before we were aware of how late it was. Friends suggested numerous books that dealt with death and especially the death of a child. There are two that I remember especially: *Sometimes Mountains Move* (1979) by Dr. C. Everett and Elizabeth Koop, and *Lament for a Son* (1987) by Nicholas Wolterstorff, PhD. It so happened that I read the books in the sequence they were published, unintentional as it was. Both families, like ours, lost a son to climbing. The fact that struck me the most was that their sons had already died by the time they were informed of the tragedies. One family even had to wait some fifty hours just for the son's body to be recovered from the mountain.

We—Rosemarie, Danielle, Amy, and I—had nine days with Jason before he finally passed. He was airlifted from Squamish, British Columbia, to Vancouver. The family assembled there, and for nine days in Vancouver General Hospital's intensive care ward, we spent what seemed to be an eternity of praying, waiting, and more praying while some really great, caring professionals did all they could to save him and support us. Since then, I have often asked myself why we were given the time to be with Jason and to share his final journey while others who were presumably better trained and prepared to understand and handle death—a famous pediatric surgeon and a divinity school professor—were not. I am certain that if the circumstances had allowed, each family would have been there for their respective son as well. But they weren't, and we were.

My only answer, my only justification is that our traumatic journey with Jason in 2001 planted the seed for my journey since. The Foundation, the Appalachian Trail venture, the many interviews, the different camps and schools visited, and the seminars attended were all continuations of those nine days, or rather, a chance to be with Jason longer. It was a chance to understand the person of Jason as well as what he found in the outdoors and his work with youth that gave him so much pleasure and growth so that maybe we could in some way help others like he had.

At the time of Jason's death, the outpouring of support told us, his family, that others understood the person he was, the man he was becoming, and the contribution he made to their lives. We looked for a way to continue such contributions and decided to create the foundation in his memory. To date, the foundation has helped boys and girls alike from across the country to experience wilderness programs in Connecticut, Maine, and Arizona. The many testimonials excerpted here speak directly to the profound impact that Jason's foundation and wilderness programs have been fortunate to facilitate.

Wilderness programs are expensive and thus cost-prohibitive for many. Proceeds from this book will be used exclusively to provide scholarships for others to experience a wilderness expedition and its opportunities for growth and development. Those interested may find more information, contact me, and make a donation at the foundation's website: www.jwhf.org.

Justice, dignity, equality—these are words which are often used loosely, with little appreciation of their meaning. I think that their meaning can be distilled into one goal: that every child in this country live as we would want our own children to live.

—Robert Kennedy

My Friend
Eulogy Poem by Jay Austin Seals

*I could feel the strength of your blood, when it was your hand that I
 shook.*

*And I could see the compassion of your soul, when I took a deeper
 look.*

*You said, 'Did you know that the stones we threw could melt away like
 the snow?*

*If it comes deep down that you are afraid, well I'm telling you you're
 not alone.'*

*I so admired your style, when the day after high school graduation you
 left your home.*

Bound for the glorious Rocky Mountains, on a bus, all on your own.

*I followed you for the first time right up that rock, to gaze out on a vast
 Colorado plain.*

And I knew then, what I know now, that I would never be the same.

The adventures, oh the adventures you had, they were so grand,

You were living and breathing a philosophy,

That in the meantime I have come to understand.

That for this moment and every moment I do believe,

That I shall always follow my dreams.

*To achieve the impossibilities, and to say my friends, it's much easier
 than it seems.*

It was about a year ago, to this very day,

*Together we charged up to the top of Angora Peak on a beautiful Tahoe
 day.*

It was there, you and I, we became like the wind.

And that is how I shall always remember you my friend.

For I know in my heart that this is not the end,

And I await with many smiles to the times we walk together

Again … my friend,

Jason William Hunt 1977–2001

A Celebration of Life
Eulogy by Danielle Marie Hunt Palka

On behalf of my father, mother, and sister, I want to thank you all for being here for this celebration of Jason's life. Many of you have traveled a ways to be here. To Marc, KT, and Storm, and the Cochrens; Jason has been as much a part of your family as he has been ours. I am glad to have you all here. I encourage everyone to please take the opportunity and introduce yourself to those around you. There are no strangers here, only family and friends we have not met yet.

Those individuals who have explored mountains and scaled cliffs have said they are not doing it for the summit, or the final destination. They are in it for the journey, and the things they learn along the way. Where they are going receives less emphasis than how they get there and what will be required of them. Jason's journey has provided him with experiences and learnings that have allowed us to cross his path. His journey has also prepared him for where he is now.

I would have to attribute the origination of my brother's interest in the out-of-doors to my father. Dad had been an active member of the Boy Scouts. When he married and began a family, my mother found herself camping—a Nova Scotia honeymoon no less, as was typical for the early 1970s—and thus began a family founded on togetherness, love, an appreciation of the natural world, and a touch of adventure. I remember family camping trips. … many times in Connecticut and to different state parks in Ohio. When Jason was old enough, he became a Boy Scout and Dad reenlisted.

By the time Jason was in high school, his need for adventure had found him involved in sailing, swimming, skateboarding, basketball, track, and football. He enjoyed them all immensely, but yet, there was just something not quite there. I really don't know when or how my brother began to rock climb.… I just remember it as something he always did. Near the end of high school his love of climbing had entangled itself completely into his being. Decisions about college— where to go, what to do—were miniscule and seemingly unimportant to him. He wanted Colorado, and the chance to go out west to the mountains. Confused and exasperated parents, a frustrated youth; my parents and Jason finally came to an agreement about college and Colorado. The mountains won, and college would follow.

On a cold and snowy day shortly after New Year's, Jason returned from Colorado. The young man who stepped out of the car was hardly the youth my family had remembered. Jason had matured and grown up. There was a steady calm about him, an awareness of self, like he had come into his own. He had discovered something in the mountains that he was certain was out there, but really had been within him the entire time.

Jason's journey developed him into a caring, thoughtful, warm, conscientious, loyal, passionate, and true-of-heart person. He loved life, and he lived to love. He loved his friends and the people he met along the way. Jason was a traveler … too many miles on his truck, but never too many people to visit or places to see.

In the last few months, Jason's journey brought him to Colorado, home in Cincinnati, Georgia, Connecticut, Asheville, Charleston, and Canada. He had visited with old friends he hadn't seen in a while, relatives, his family, and friends near and dear to his heart.

When Jason was climbing, he was fully engaged in body, mind, and soul. In order to climb, a person will be on belay. The term *belay* refers to the rope that connects the climber to another person on the ground who is their belayer. *Belay* is a French word, and it means "to hold fast." To be on belay signifies an amount of communication and trust between climber and belayer. Climbers know the risk they take when they climb. To climb with a friend, to have them keep you safe, and to know that you both have each other, requires the strongest sense of love and trust humanly possible. It is this partnership on the rock that Jason loved, and what he lived for.

Jason, we have been blessed because we have known you. I am honored to be your sister. We love you, Jason. And we will miss you. You are on belay. Climb on, Jason. Climb on.

Appendix

A crew is defined by the contributions of each member. In the process of stepping up, the crew's unique identity is revealed. At graduation, each member's special contribution was noted.

ATC Crew
Anthony – Support for all
Devon – Once awake, funny and engaged
German – Leader
Sal – Always smiling and learning
Shane – Bombproof backpack

Staff:
Greg Gates – Lead
Alison Hodgkin
Jo Welch
Nicky Wood – Course Director

Aviators Crew
Andy – Supports others
Brandon – Paddler
Dan – Writing
Johnnie – Hair
Jon – Tarp and knots master
Josh K. – Pushing others
Josh S. – Spiderman and debugger
Nick – Leader

Staff:
Amy Pine – Lead
Jeff Bruno
Kenny Riley
Betta Hanson – Course Director

Interviews
Trail names in italics

Mariette, OH
Enertia Trail Foods, Keegan *Little Dutch Boy* Haid

Appalachian Trail
Hikers of the Big Three (Appalachian Trail, Continental Divide Trail, Pacific Crest Trail): Hugh Hill (one circuit) and Mike *Hawkeye* Johnson (two circuits).

Folks I met on the Appalachian Trail: Jerry Horton, Riley Kurtz, *JayB, Sherlock, Quartz, Alpine, Cool Breeze, Skywatcher, Bag-o'-Tricks, Lumpy, Slingshot, Lefty, Gray Wanderer, Loon, Swan, Razor, Death by Cotton, Nimrod Heathen of the South Georgia Heathens.*

Asheville, NC
Warren Wilson College: Ed Raiola, PhD, Outdoor Leadership Department Chair; Jason Michaels, Outing Club Director; Morning Naughton, Associate Director of Admissions.

North Carolina Outward Bound School: Travis Herbert and Erin Karasik.

Amy Pine, Outdoor Field Educator at Trails Carolina and DCF Wilderness School (CT).

AEE SouthEast Regional Conference: Sandy L. Newes, PhD, Clear View Psychological Services; Jon Rousseau, MSW.

Stone Mountain School: Jeremy Poore, Program Director.

Charleston, SC
East Coast Canoe and Kayak Festival, Charleston County Park Recreation Commission; Danielle Hunt Palka, Outdoor Recreation Coordinator; Wayne Horodowich, President, University of Sea Kayaking; Katie Coley, University of South Carolina Outing Club Director.

Black Mountain, NC
Woodson Wilderness Challenge: Steve "Tex" Teixeira, Director; Robert Randolph, Chaplain (North Carolina Department of Juvenile Justice); Field Educators: Dave Cowart, Dave Nelson, Abe Reid, Janie Moore, Jenna Cruite, Jenny Knaus, Noel Swinburne; Specialists: Bill Silver, social worker (good luck in your retirement); Jason McDougald, classroom instructor; Becky Kluge, cook and former instructor.

Columbus, OH
AEE Midwest Best Practices Conference: Bobbie Beale, PsyD, Group Programs Director, Child & Adolescent Behavioral Health; Lee Gillis, PhD, Georgia College and State University; Steve Prysunka, Director, Wilderness Programming, Alaska Crossings; Sean Hoyer, LCSW, DCSW, Omni Youth Services; Denise Mitten, PhD, Ferris State University; Dene Berman, PhD; Jennifer Davis-Berman, PhD, University of Dayton; Ed Spaulding, Executive Director, Northland Adventure.
Erkis Consulting Group: Andy Erkis, PhD; Paula Leslie, MA, LCPC

Clifton, VA
Adventure Links: Chad Skowronski, Adam Procell, Ted Teagarden, Joshua Pearl.

Paris, VA
Adventure Links: Austin Birch, President; David Duke Cutshall, COO.

South Mountain, PA
Dennis Call, Director Vision Quest; Shane Sloat, Manager, LEAP, Cornell Companies

East Hartland, CT
DCF Wilderness School: Rudy Brooks, Director, State of Connecticut Bureau of Prevention; Dave Czaja, Wilderness School Director; Don Pelletier, Logistics Coordinator; Kim Thorne-Kaunelis, Outreach

Coordinator; Bonnie Sterpka, Enrollment Administrator; Aaron Wiebe, Program Coordinator; Emily Dombrowski, Enrollment Assistant; Ricky Harris, Lead Instructor.

Course Directors: Nicky Wood, Shannon Zich, Betta Hanson, Danielle Costa.

Field Educators: Alison Hodgkin, Anna Boysen, Chelsea Ambrozaitis, Greg Gates Jr., Jeff Bruno, Josephine Welsh, Kaleena Rivera (Intern), Kayla Kawalick, Kenneth Reilly, Nathan Bliss.

Logistics Staff: Kevin D. Johnson (American Mountain Guide Association Certified), Erin MacPherson, James Dombrowski, Lindsay MacKintosh, Matt Shove (American Mountain Guide Association Certified), Micah Jawkowski.

Food Staff: Jess Dang, Coordinator; Cat Raiti (Intern); Codie Kane.

DCF Trauma Tool Kit Trainers: Jane Goodell, Michael M. Smith.

Former WS Field Educators: Andrew Snelling, Bonnie Dyck, Marc Sacks.

WS Supporters and Alumni: Gene Merchand; Bill Dumond; Lena Lam; Roy Charette-CEO and Founder of TrainingPath;

Parents of WS Students: Joan J., Mark M., Anthony K. Sr. (author note: At the request of the State of Connecticut Department of Children and Families, students' last names are abbreviated to protect their identities.)

Danbury, CT
YMCA Great Hollow Wilderness School: Ali Sadiq, Director; outdoor staff: Kathleen Salmon, Clarence Gilmer, Alex Harrison, Sa'mel B.

Peoples Sate Park, CT
Tom Dyer, Director, DCF Wilderness School, retired; Nancy Dyer, Educational Consultant and former instructor, DCF Wilderness School

New Hartford, CT
Don Gagliardi, Coordinator, Pine Lake Challenge Course, Bristol, CT; Becce Reslock, Director, Wethersfield Youth Services Outdoor

Programs, retired; William "Sully" Sullivan, Adventure Program Manager, Riverfront Recapture; Liza Wilson Bocchichio, full-time mom and part-time outdoor instructor, former Wilderness School staff; Dave Bocchichio, Physical Ed and Leadership Program Educator, Synergy Alternative High School, East Hartford, CT.

Southington, CT
Lori Bauchiero concerned mother and special education activist.

Hamden, CT
Joseph Juliano, Educator and Director of Fine Arts Department, Hamden Public Schools, retired.

Great Barrington, MA
Eagleton School: Becky Mitchell, Marketing Manager; P.J. Haley, Garden Manager; Steve Robinson, Equine Manager.

Frankfort, KY
Sheltered Risks Inc.
Kamp Kessa: Thecla Helmbrecht Howard, Ed D; Anthony Howard, MS; Mark Vied; Daniel Drengacs; Nikomis Burns.

By Phone
Brian McCormick; Geoff Heath.

E-mails and Letters

Eileen G. LaBaire, July 16, 2002, and April 25, 2011
Galen W. Holland, October 17, 2001
Heather Bush, July 29, 2010
Jason William Hunt, December 10, 1997
Liza Wilson (Bocchichio), November 6, 2001
Marc Sacks, October 15, 2001

Steve Scheper, November 15, 2001
Steve Sutorious, March 29, 2004
Tyler Stracker, February 10, 2003
Marsha Wagner, October 2001

Literature

Ambrozaitis, Chelsea I. Conceptualizing Success in Therapeutic Wilderness Experiences, Honors Thesis, University of Connecticut, 2010.

Blehm, Eric. *The Last Season*. New York: Harper Perennial, 2006.

Bryson, Bill. *A Short History of Nearly Everything*. New York: Broadway Books, 2003.

Bryson, Bill. *A Walk in the Woods*. New York: Broadway Books, 1998.

Campbell, Joseph. *The Hero's Journey*. San Francisco: Harper and Row, 1990.

Carrighar, Sally. *Home to the Wilderness: A Personal Journey*. Boston: Houghton Mifflin Company, 1973.

Child, Lee. *Bad Luck and Trouble*. New York: Bantam Dell, 2007.

Fletcher, Joseph. *Situational Ethics*. Louisville, KY: Westminster John Know Press, 1966.

Freidman, Hal, and Patterson, James. *Against Medical Advice*. New York: Little, Brown and Company, 2008.

Goleman, Daniel. *Emotional Intelligence*. New York: Bantam Books, 1995.

Gonzales, Laurence. *Deep Survival*. New York: W. W. Norton & Co., 2003.

Guntzelman, Fr. Lou. "Silence frightens us but has so much to say," *Community Journal*, August 25, 2010.

Guntzelman, Fr. Lou. "How many kinds of time are there in our lives?" *Community Journal*, December 29, 2010.

Guntzelman, Fr. Lou. "All some people need is just a good listening to," *Community Journal*, February 2, 2011.

Hillman, James. *Healing Fiction*. Barrytown, NY: Station Hill Press, 1983.

Howard, Thecla Helmbrecht, and Howard, Anthony. Notes from the Margins, Author File Copy.

Howard, Thecla Helmbrecht, and Howard, Anthony. You Can't Raise a Horse in a Box, Author File Copy.

Hume, Cardinal Basil. *Basil in Blunderland.* Brewster, MA: Paraclete Press, 1999

Kersjes, Michael E. *A Smile as Big as the Moon.* New York: St. Martin's Press, 2002.

Kranz, Cindy. "Rethinking how boys are taught," *Cincinnati Enquirer,* May 23, 2010.

Leschak, Peter M. *Ghosts of the Fireground.* New York: HarperCollins, 2002.

Levine, Madeline. *The Price of Privilege.* New York: Harper Collins, 2006.

Louv, Richard. *Last Child in the Woods.* Chapel Hill, NC: Algonquin Books, 2005.

MacKaye, Benton. "An Appalachian Trail: A Project in Regional Planning," *The Appalachian Trail Reader.* David Emblidge, Editor. New York: Oxford University Press, 1996.

O'Donohue, John. *Anam Cara: A Book of Celtic Wisdom.* New York: HarperCollins, 1997.

O'Reilly, Bill. *Who's Looking Out for You?* New York: Broadway Books, 2003.

Otto, Rudolph. *The Idea of the Holy.* New York: Oxford University Press, 1970.

Parker, Brant. *The Wizard of Id,* Creators Syndicate, January 9, 2011.

Peart, Neil. *Roadshow.* Cambridge, MA: Rounder Books, 2006.

Porter, Winton. *Just Passin' Thru.* Birmingham, AL: Menasha Ridge Press, 2009.

Raymo, Chet. *Skeptics and True Believers.* New York: Walker and Company, 1998.

Raymo, Chet. *Honey in the Stone.* St. Paul, MN: Hungry Mind Press, 1987.

Rubin, Robert. *On the Beaten Path: An Appalachian Pilgrimage.* New York: Lyons Press, 2000.

Sacre Coeur Center. *Year of Grace.* Franklin, WI: Sheed & Ward, 1999.

Scott, Jim, and Borgman, Jim. *Zits,* King Features Syndicate, January 21, 2011.

Stutzman, Paul. *Hiking Through*. Austin, TX: Synergy Books, 2010.

Straus, Martha B., PhD. *No-Talk Kids Therapy*. New York: W. W. Norton & Co., 1999.

Sugerman, Deborah A.; Doherty, Kathryn L.; Garvey, Daniel E.; and Gass, Michael A. *Reflective Learning*, Dubuque, IA: Kendall/Hunt, 2000.

Tolstoy, Leo. *Anna Karenina*. New York: Penguin Books, 2000.

Unsoeld, Willi, PhD. *Spiritual Values in Wilderness*, paper presented at Association for Experiential Education Conference, Estes Park, CO, 1974.

Walker, Brian, and Walker, Greg. *Hi and Lois*, King Features Syndicate Inc., July 22, 2011.

Williamson, Marianne. *A Return to Love*. New York: Harper Collins, 1992.

Wolf, Fred Alan, PhD. *The Spiritual Universe*. Portsmouth, NH: Moment Point Press, 1999.

Audio, Music, and Movies

Hook, a Steven Spielberg Film, TriStar Pictures Industries, Inc. 1991.

Zac Brown Band featuring Jimmy Buffett, "Knee Deep," 2010.

"This Little Light of Mine" Written by unknown.

Lovland, Rolf, and Graham, Brendan. "You Raise Me Up," Universal-PolyGram International Publishing Inc., 2002.

Norbert, Gregory, "Hosea (Come Back to Me)," The Benedictine Foundation of the State of Vermont, 1972.

Portnoy, Gary, and Angelo, Judy Hart, "Where Everyone Knows Your Name," 1982

Shaver, Billy Joe, and Shaver, Eddy. "Live Forever." Copyright BMI.

Stand and Deliver, Warner Bros. Pictures, 1988.

Wolf, Fred Alan, PhD, *Dr. Quantum Presents Meet the Real Creator—You*, Session Two, Quantum Heaven Quantum Hell, Boulder, CO: Sounds True, 2005.

It's a Wonderful Life, Liberty Films, 1946.

Take the Lead, New Line Cinema, 2006.

Online and TV

American Pickers, "A Banner Pick," *History Channel*, Season 2, 2010.

"Aristotle," http://www.inspirationalstories.com/quotes/t/aristotle-on-nature/Aristotle, http://www.inspirationalstories.com/quotes/aristotle-all-art-all-education-can-be-merely/

Carlin, George. "Philosophy of Old Age," www.youtube.com.

Castle, "To Love and Die in L.A.," Season 3, Episode 22. ABC, 2011.

"Empathy," http://en.wikipedia.org/wiki/Empathy

Gatto, John Taylor. "Underground History of American Education."

Lips, Dan; Watkins, Shanea, PhD; and Fleming, John. "Does Spending More on Education Improve Academic Achievement?" *Heritage Foundation*, September 8, 2008.

Muir, John. www.thinkexist.com/quotes/John_Muir

"History of Psychology." http://en.wikipedia.org/wiki/history_of_psychology

St. Bernard of Clairvaux, Epistola CVI, sect. 2; Translation from Edward Churton, *The Early English Church* ([1840] 1841) p. 324.

The Mentalist, "Red Sky in the Morning," Season 2, Episode 23. Warner Bros., 2010.

Wolf, Fred Alan, PhD. "Something from Nothing." http://www.youtube.com/watch?v=6zMr7Z_f0jM

Leave It to Beaver, MCA Television, 1957–1963.